Water and the Environmental History of Modern India

Water and the Environmental History of Modern India

Velayutham Saravanan

Centre for Jawaharlal Nehru Studies
Jamia Millia Islamia
New Delhi

BLOOMSBURY ACADEMIC
LONDON • NEW YORK • OXFORD • NEW DELHI • SYDNEY

BLOOMSBURY ACADEMIC
Bloomsbury Publishing Plc
50 Bedford Square, London, WC1B 3DP, UK
1385 Broadway, New York, NY 10018, USA
29 Earlsfort Terrace, Dublin 2, Ireland

BLOOMSBURY, BLOOMSBURY ACADEMIC and the Diana logo
are trademarks of Bloomsbury Publishing Plc

First published in Great Britain 2020
Paperback edition published 2021

Copyright © Velayutham Saravanan, 2020

Velayutham Saravanan has asserted his right under the Copyright, Designs
and Patents Act, 1988, to be identified as Author of this work.

Cover design: Tjaša Krivec
Cover image: Dry river bed in central India.
River's name is Naranghi. (© Franck Metois/Getty Images)

All rights reserved. No part of this publication may be reproduced or transmitted
in any form or by any means, electronic or mechanical, including photocopying,
recording, or any information storage or retrieval system, without
prior permission in writing from the publishers.

Bloomsbury Publishing Plc does not have any control over, or responsibility for,
any third-party websites referred to or in this book. All internet addresses given
in this book were correct at the time of going to press. The author and publisher
regret any inconvenience caused if addresses have changed or sites have ceased
to exist, but can accept no responsibility for any such changes.

A catalogue record for this book is available from the British Library.

A catalog record for this book is available from the Library of Congress.

ISBN: HB: 978-1-3501-3082-1
        PB: 978-1-3502-4673-7
        ePDF: 978-1-3501-3083-8
        eBook: 978-1-3501-3084-5

Typeset by Integra Software Services Pvt. Ltd.

To find out more about our authors and books visit www.bloomsbury.com
and sign up for our newsletters.

Contents

List of Maps	vi
List of Tables	vii
List of Appendices	ix
Author Note	x
Preface	xi
Acknowledgements	xiv
Acronyms	xvi
Measurements	xix
1 Introduction	1
2 Hydrology, Commercialization and Ecology	33
3 Competing Demand for Water and Pollution	63
4 Water Supply Schemes and Conflict	99
5 Canal Irrigation, Technology and Conflict	129
6 Disasters of Linking Rivers	163
7 Conclusion	183
Glossary	188
Notes	190
Bibliography	224
Index	241

Maps

1 Bhavani and Noyyal River Basins 22
2 Water conflict in LBP Canal and Kalingarayan Channel 23

Tables

1.1	Domestic and industrial water requirements in different river basins in Tamil Nadu	26
2.1	Number and length of canals in Cauvery, Bhavani, Noyyal, Amaravathi and Aliyar Rivers in Coimbatore district: 1880	35
2.2	Month-wise average rainfall in Coimbatore district for sixty years: 1870–1930	38
2.3	Occupied area of different kinds of lands in Coimbatore district: 1821–81 (in acres)	39
2.4	Different sources of irrigation and irrigated lands in Coimbatore district: 1892–93	43
2.5	Credit facilities to sink new wells and repair old wells in Coimbatore district: 1909–29	44
2.6	Different sources of irrigation and irrigated lands in Coimbatore district: 1929–30	45
2.7	Cropping pattern in Coimbatore district: 1881	46
2.8	Area cultivated with the chief food and non-food crops in Coimbatore district: 1920/21–1950/51 (in acres)	47
2.9	Trends of land utilization in Coimbatore district: 1960/61–2003/04 (in hectares)	49
2.10	List of dams and their irrigated area in different river basins of Coimbatore district during the post-independence period: 1947–2007	51
2.11	Area under different sources of irrigation in Coimbatore district: 1960/61–2003/04 (in hectares)	52
2.12	Water supply scheme of corporation, municipalities and town *panchayats* of Coimbatore, Erode and Tirupur districts	55
2.13	Cropping pattern in Coimbatore district: 1960/61–2003/04	59
3.1	Trends of population growth in the Coimbatore city and agglomeration areas: 1871–2001	69
3.2	In-migration details of Coimbatore city: 1931–71	71
3.3	In-migration details of Coimbatore urban agglomeration: 1971–91	72

3.4	Occupational classification of Coimbatore city and agglomeration: 1961–91	73
3.5	Population growth in Tirupur city and agglomeration: 1891–2001	74
3.6	In-migration details of Tirupur: 1971	76
3.7	In-migration details of Tirupur agglomeration areas: 1971–91	76
3.8	Occupational classification of Tirupur city and agglomeration: 1961–91	77
3.9	Land use pattern in TLPA: 1984–2001	78
3.10	Industrial growth in Tirupur city: 1911–2001	81
3.11	Trends of Siruvani and Pillur domestic water supply in Coimbatore: 1931–2001	83
3.12	Different kinds of pollution load generated in Tirupur: 1980–2000	94
4.1	Statement of rainfall at Coimbatore: 1892/93–1908/09	101
4.2	Results of chemical and bacteriological examination in different wells of Coimbatore city: 1890	102
4.3	Expenditure on Coimbatore municipal water supply: 1888/89–1899/1900	103
4.4	Different sources of Coimbatore water supply proposals/schemes	103
4.5	Results of chemical and bacteriological examination of Noyyal River water: 1890	105
4.6	Results of chemical and bacteriological examination of Chitrachavadi channel water: 1906	106
4.7	Results of chemical and bacteriological examination of Kistnambadi tank water: 1906	107
4.8	Results of bacteriological and chemical examination of Siruvani water: 1923	109
4.9	Statement of rainfall at Tirupur station: 1909–29	113
4.10	Results of chemical examination of Koilveli springs	114
5.1	Details of illegal river pumping from the Kalingarayan channel as on 2 July 1953	143
5.2	Quantity of water released in the LBP canal: 1954–55 to 1970–71 (in M.cft)	149
5.3	Changing cropping pattern in the LBP canal: 1952/53–1962/63	150
5.4	Planned and existing cropping pattern in LBP in 1959–60 (in acres)	151
5.5	Number of pumpsets and oil-engines in the LBP area in 1955–56	154
6.1	Surplus water from Bhavani dam: 1956–96 (TMC)	179

Appendices

4.1 List of local bodies, sources of water supply and rate of charges in Madras Presidency: 1927   127

4.2 Property tax and water and drainage tax in different municipalities in Madras Presidency: 1926 (in per cent)   128

5.1 Cropping pattern in Bhavani, Erode, Gobichettipalayam and Dharapuram taluks of Coimbatore district in 1971 (irrigated crops only)   159

5.2 List of petitions from the lower-reach farmers and the nature of problems in LBP channel   160

Author Note

Velayutham Saravanan is engaged with economic and environmental history, and his area of study pertaining to South India encompasses the late eighteenth, nineteenth and twentieth centuries besides the contemporary period. With interdisciplinary research interests, he has made significant contributions to the fields of economic history and environmental history. He is the author of *Colonialism, Environment and Tribals in South India, 1792–1947* (2017) and *Environmental History and Tribals in Modern India* (2018). He has published more than seventy research articles both in national and international journals and presented more than fifty articles at national and international levels both of historical and contemporary periods.

Preface

Water is one of the basic requirements for the very survival of human beings, animals and other living organisms. It is not only essential for their survival but also important for the production process and regeneration. Though a renewable source, there is no guarantee or assurance of its continued abundance. Hence, throughout the ages, people all over the world took strenuous efforts to store the water in ponds, tanks and dams. In addition to manmade storage, the green cover itself remains as a reserve of water. Since the early nineteenth century, importance of protecting the green cover, particularly forests, has become the felt need to control floods, droughts, soil erosion, etc. However, conservation initiatives were introduced only from the last quarter of the nineteenth century. And it is to be noted that only from the last quarter of twentieth century, the importance of protecting the green cover gained prominence at the global level. Since then, it was emphasized that the green cover reserve should be at least one-third of the geographical area.

As indicated earlier, realization about the importance of protecting the green cover emerged during the early nineteenth century, though population density was not a threat with vast extent of natural resources was left unexploited. However, with population growth witnessing a remarkable increase since the mid-twentieth century, the demand for basic requirements, such as food, housing, education, health, transport, has increased manifold, resulting in the greener cover to be brought under greater utility. In the process of enhancing these facilities, more and more green cover was encroached upon at the expense of polluting natural resources, particularly water. Except a few cities, untreated sewage water is being discharged into the rivers, polluting not only the surface water but also the groundwater table. Similarly, while expanding irrigation facilities, preservation of traditional water bodies, such as tanks and ponds, as well their management has been abandoned. In the post-independent period, construction of about 4,621 dams is considered a feat, but the area under irrigation has not increased as it should have been. The new dams were constructed without considering their impact on the traditionally irrigated areas. For example, in Cauvery River basin, around twenty-one dams have been constructed in Karnataka region without considering the requirement of the erstwhile irrigated areas of Tiruchirappalli and Thanjavur districts in Tamil Nadu. The effort towards providing irrigation facilities to new areas has ultimately undermined the needs of traditional tanks and other riparian rights. In other words, the process of modernization was carried out in a manner that was detrimental to the traditional resource management. Coining catchy phrases and newer term(s) like 'watershed management' could not be a substitute to water conservation. Half-hearted attempts have not made any positive impact on water resource management, which remains a perennial question. As long as the government extends financial support, people are involved in a project. Once the government stops financial support, no one is seen engaged with that. Given the background, the present book attempts to analyse water-related issues spanning more than 200 years in a particular river basin as well as the factors responsible for the present crisis. Further, it details as to how it is being managed/mismanaged besides looking at the various facets of the challenges that it has thrown up in that particular region, that is, erstwhile Coimbatore district.

This book attempts to study the ecological crisis of water and environmental history due to competing demand for water and pollution in the Bhavani and Noyyal River basins of South India from the early nineteenth century to the early twenty-first century, in a historical perspective (1800–2017). Further, it tries to capture the bourgeoning demand from different sectors, viz. agriculture, industry and domestic, as well as how that was managed through the different sources of supply within the basin and from other basins.

While the main objective is to analyse the competing demand for water in the Bhavani and Noyyal River basins in the light of resources culled out from unexplored areas of environmental history of nineteenth and early twentieth centuries of the colonial period, the focus, however, is largely restricted to the erstwhile Coimbatore district of Madras Presidency for the colonial period and Tamil Nadu for the post-independence period.

The existing literature in this domain is by and large confined to the contemporary period. Again, what is available mostly deals about the macro-level, particularly relating to the recent decades. Further, none of the studies attempts to look at these issues in a historical framework and context. A historical perspective would help understand the issues and problems that will in turn aid in visualizing and framing appropriate policy measures.

Given this background, this book raises several important questions: (1) Did the policy-makers visualize the future demand while diverting water from distant places or other basins? (2) While diverting water from distant places, was efficient use ensured or rather effected in a manner that resulted in causing pollution and serious damage to the entire river basin? (3) While diverting water, have natural flows been taken care of to preserve the ecology, environment and the recharge mechanism to maintain the water table or not? (4) What were the factors that aggravated the competing demand for water and its consequences for the future?

In the context of the current discourse on the competing demand for water, this book would certainly be a contribution in carrying forward the debate. Also, it expands the horizon of environmental history. For, the debate on environmental history has so far neglected agriculture, industry and domestic water supply and their consequences on ecology, environment and livelihood. A comprehensive account of both the colonial and post-colonial periods either has been ignored or has not received due attention in the literature pertaining to environmental history. Therefore, an attempt has been made to arrive at an interdisciplinary understanding of the problem in its historical context.

Acknowledgements

It is my privilege to express gratitude to the several academicians who gave me an opportunity and constant encouragement to explore the water-related issues of both historical and contemporary periods. First and foremost, I must thank Professor Paul P. Appasamy, who gave me an opportunity to work in his project, that too in a crucial stage of my academic career. He further encouraged me to explore the water-related issues of the Noyyal and Bhavani River basins, historically. If Paul P. Appasamy had not given me this opportunity, I could not have brought out this manuscript; in fact, I would not have ventured into the water-related problems.

This opportunity helped me connect with other scholars, namely A. Vaidyanathan, Nirmal Sengupta, S.Janakarajan and K. Sivasubramaniyan, who enriched further understanding of mine on water-related issues through several discussions. I am grateful to A. Vaidyanathan, who tirelessly went through my papers and offered incisive comments, which further reinforced my understanding on water-related issues and sources. I am equally grateful to Mr. Rajan, a reputed journalist and his family for their support and encouragement. Indeed, discussions with Rajan has always enriched my understanding on the subject to a great extent.

In addition, several colleagues, viz. Jothi, Mariyasusai and Sivasubramaniyan, enlightened me further through their field experiences on my understanding of water-related issues and problems. It is my privilege to work with the Madras Institute of Development Studies as a Project Associate on ad-hoc basis, which provided me to work and to interact with a number of prominent scholars who really helped me to emerge as an interdisciplinary scholar. Major portion of this output came out when I was working on the project *Local Strategies for Water Supply and Conservation Management*, sponsored by the International Development Research Centre (IDRC), Canada, between May 1997 and August 1999, at the Madras Institute of Development Studies, Chennai.

I thank Professor K. Sivaramakrishnan and Mahesh Rangarajan, for their comments and encouragement. My sincere gratitude to Mr B. Damodaran, Lawyer, High Court, Chennai, and Dr (Mrs) Vijayalakshmi Damodaran, for their help in accessing the court records and clarifications related to the legal issues.

My sincere thanks to Tamil Nadu State Archives, Chennai, which provided me enormous support to access the records to recount the water-related problems in the Noyyal and Bhavani River basins. My sincere acknowledgement to Coimbatore Municipal Council and Public Works Department, for giving me permission to access the documents to analyse the water-related problems in the Noyyal and Bhavani River basins of Coimbatore district.

I acknowledge the third chapter published in *Journal of Social and Economic Development*, 2007. The earlier version of the fourth chapter published in *Rethinking the Mosaic: Investigations into Local Water Management*, 1999, along with Paul Appasamy. The fifth chapter published in *Environment and History*, 2001. The Sixth chapter published in *Man and Development*, 2004 and *Mainstream*, 2018. I thank the respective editors not only for their encouragement but also for the grant of permission to publish the materials. I humbly acknowledge all the anonymous referees for their invaluable inputs and suggestions, which has helped me to enrich the argument.

Last but not least, I want to thank my wife Ajitha Saravanan, daughter Soumya Saravanan, and sons Gautham Saravanan and Manish Saravanan for extending their immense support to complete the task.

Acronyms

ADB	Asian Development Bank
AIADMK	All India Anna Dravida Munnetra Kazhagam
AVIP	Attappady Valley Irrigation Project
BCM	billion cubic metre
BOD	biological oxygen demand
BOOT	Build, Own, Operate and Transfer
BOR	Board of Revenue
CE (I)	chief engineer (irrigation)
CETPs	common effluent treatment plants
COD	chemical oxygen demand
CPCB	Central Pollution Control Board
CPI	Communist Party of India
CWC	Central Water Commission
CWDT	Cauvery Water Disputes Tribunal
DMK	Dravida Munnetra Kazhagam
DVC	Damodar Valley Corporation
E&PH	Education and Public Health
GO	Government Order
HELA	Health and Local Administration
HP	horse power
IDRC	International Development Research Centre

IETPs	independent effluent treatment plants
IIT	Indian Institute of Technology
IPC	Indian Penal Code
IWS	Institute of Water Studies
KWA	Kerala Water Authority
L&M	local and municipal
LA	local administration
LBP	Lower Bhavani Project
LIC	Life Insurance Corporation
lpcd	litres per capita per day
LSG (LM)	Local-Self Government (Local and Municipal)
LSG (PH)	Local-Self Government (Public Health)
MCF	thousand cubic feet
MCM	million cubic meter
Mha	million hectare
MLA	Member of Legislative Assembly
MLD	millions of litres per day
MP	Member of Parliament
NDA	National Democratic Alliance
NEP	National Environmental Policy
NGO	non-governmental organization
NTADCL	New Tirupur Area Development Corporation Limited
NWDA	National Water Development Agency
PAP	Parambikulam-Aliyar Project
PH	public health

PW&L	Public Works & Labour
PWD	Public Works Department
PWD (B&R)	Public Works Department (Buildings and Roads)
PWD (I)	Public Works Department (Irrigation)
SIHMA	South Indian Hosiery Manufactures Association
SPV	special purpose vehicle
SSA	Sardar Sarovar Project
TADP	Tirupur Area Development Project
TDFOA	Tirupur Dyeing Factory Owners Association
TDS	total dissolvable solids
TEA	Textile Exporters Association
TETCO	Tirupur Effluent Treatment Company Pvt. Ltd.
TLPA	Tirupur Local Planning Area
TMC ft	thousand million cubic feet
TNEB	Tamil Nadu Electricity Board
TNSA	Tamil Nadu State Archives
TNSAR	Tamil Nadu State Administrative Report
TSS	toxic shock syndrome
TVA	Tennessee Valley Authority
TWAD	Tamil Nadu Water and Drainage Board
UA	urban agglomeration
UBP	Upper Bhavani Project

Measurements

1 acre	0.405 hectares
1 chain	22 yards.
1 cubic kilometre	1000000000 metres
1 foot	12 inches
1 gallon	4.546 litres
1 hectare	2.471 acres.
1 kilometre	0.6214 mile
1 mile	1.609 kilometres
1 yard	3 feet

1

Introduction

Industrial Revolution, which has made a wide range of ecological consequences in the developed countries since the late eighteenth century, has not left untouched the developing nations. This revolution has not only facilitated the process of transformation of natural resources but also played a pivotal role in their transportation to distant places. It further favoured the conversion of different types of natural resources into commodities, resulting in an ever-increasing demand over the period. In fact, such commodification of natural resources was not restricted to cultivated land and non-agricultural land but was extended to water bodies. According to Gadgil and Guha,

> The revolution in the mode of resource use brought about by industrialization enormously enlarged the possibilities of transforming resources from one form to another, and of transporting them over large distances. With these technological advances, a great range of objects became commodities, objects for which the demand could go on increasing indefinitely, almost limitlessly .... The advances in technology brought about by industrial mode, however, prompt an outflow of a much greater range of resources from both cultivated and non-cultivated lands, and from water bodies.[1]

In addition to this, Industrial Revolution has changed the nature of community rights and community ownership. Again, in the words of Gadgil and Guha, 'Non-cultivated lands and waters were no longer dedicated exclusively to providing for flows within a local region.'[2]

In India, we see European colonizers adopted three strategies in tune with the European industrial experience. The first one lowered the importance of resource gathering and food production for subsistence. In the second one, cooperation between settled agricultural communities and those engaged in gathering for food production gained least importance. The third one prioritized manufacturing and commerce, with the market acquiring prominence in accessing resources. These three strategies of European industrial mode of resource use led to ecological issues of greater magnitude in India.[3] While questioning the colonial strategy on ecology and hydrology, D'Souza aptly puts, 'elements such as revenue maximization, commercialization, commodification, or the urgency to extend the agrarian frontier served as strong push factors for transforming prevailing relationships between pre-colonial society and nature'.[4] Precisely, Europeans adopted the strategy to commercialize natural resources through market mechanism, which undermined the erstwhile social structure and the method of utilization of natural resources.

Until the last quarter of the twentieth century, the focus of India's economic history in general and agrarian history in particular was on issues related to arable land, like productivity, commercialization, irrigation sources, land revenue, wage rate, wage differences, de-industrialization, railways, trade and commerce, mode of production, etc. As such, due attention was not given to ecological and environmental aspects of economic history or agrarian history. In other words, literature on India's economic and agrarian history remains largely confined to issues other than the ecological and environmental aspects. No wonder, studies on economic history and agrarian history of south Asia have mainly dealt with the issues concerning the arable landscape.[5] Hence, non-arable land resources, such as forests, pastoral land, fishing and other common property resources, domestic water supply, water pollution, have failed or have not received adequate attention.[6] This was the situation until the last quarter of the twentieth century.

Till recently (the 1990s), literature on environmental history in south Asia has mostly neglected agrarian history, as the main focus was on the forests and pastoral regions besides the tribals.[7] A major difference between agrarian history and environmental history is while the former looked at clearing of forests as agrarian expansion, the latter considered it as deforestation.[8] However, the dynamic linkage between the two has not been established yet.[9] As rightly pointed out by Bhattacharya (1998), 'If the old agrarian history neglected the forests and pastures, environmental history now has banished the peasant fields and farms from the realm of historical concern. It was as if these histories were not connected, as if environment did not impinge on the agrarian world.'[10]

To be precise, literature on environmental history in India that emerged during the last quarter of the twentieth century had its focus on forestry, wildlife and the impact on livelihood options of tribal folk and other forest-dwelling communities.[11] Further, those studies which cover the pre-colonial and colonial era also touch upon the post-colonial period to some extent.[12] As such, several aspects of ecological and environmental history of the colonial period have been either left unexplored or gained little attention. As D'Souza rightly pointed out, 'the phenomenon of colonialism itself has been little explored or explained through its ecological footprint'.[13] Furthermore, urbanization, industrialization, water diversion and pollution, technological advancement and its impact on ecology and environment too have been left out. According to Champakalakshmi, 'The central concern in historical research in India has more often been with agrarian systems, peasant history, and the general pattern of socio-economic change rather than urbanization *per se*. Growth of urban centres is of marginal interest even to studies on trade patterns, and merchant and craft organizations and the role of the state in the promotion of such activities.'[14] She implies that not only urbanization but related issues like population, domestic water supply, drainage and the outcomes of industrial products and its consequences as well as the role of state have not been studied in depth. In other words, this urban dimension is conspicuously absent in environmental history. According to Wilhelm: 'the near absence of research on India's colonial river pollution history is one of the biggest lacunae within the historiography on south Asia's environmental history: the lack of studies on urban environments and, more specifically, pollution'.[15] She further adds: 'colonial urban environmental history has remained a largely untapped field, and existing studies moreover have mostly concentrated on the major Indian cities of Calcutta, Bombay, and Delhi'.[16] So far, studies on river pollution have largely focused on the post-colonial period.[17]

While emphasizing economic growth to eradicate poverty and unemployment, the post-independent governments have not given due attention to protect the environment.[18] Consequently, industrialization, population growth and urbanization have resulted in overuse and pollution of natural resources.[19] According to Wilhelm, 'immense amounts of human, industrial and agricultural wastes were dumped into water bodies, and most of the India's major streams turned into nothing short of sewers'.[20] She further adds, 'river pollution emerged from British policies on waste water disposal during the late nineteenth and early twentieth centuries'.[21] In her reasoning, 'the colonial government during the second half of the nineteenth century introduced the technology which today contributes the largest pollution load to the Ganges and other Indian rivers: municipal sewerage system'.[22]

Urbanization and its impact on population, industry and domestic water supply; diversion of water resources; sewage; pollution; etc. during the colonial period require more focused research. For, it is well known that urbanization and industrialization are integral to the process of economic transformation. While it goes without saying that water continues to play an important role in that process, how it is being abused, leading to environmental degradation, needs to be properly understood.

The pre-colonial canal irrigation system and its prosperity in different parts of the Indian subcontinent actually gave an idea to the British to develop major irrigation works. According to Narain: 'Some Irrigation canals existed in India prior to British rule, and as a matter of fact, the Grand Annicut in Madras and the remnants of old Mohamedan channels in Punjab suggested to the present rulers of the country the idea of the big works which, have contributed so largely to our prosperity.'[23] He further added that 'most of the existing inundation canals in the Multan, Muzaffargarh, and Dera Ghazi Khan districts, were contributed by the former Muhammedan and Sikh rulers'.[24] 'A canal known as the Hasli, was also constructed by the Sikh or Muhammedan rulers of the Punjab to carry water to Lahore from a Point on the Ravi River at a distance of 130 miles.'[25] 'In the fourteenth Century, Firoz Shah Tughlak constructed a canal, taking water from the right or western bank of the Jumna (Yamuna), a distance of about 150 miles, to irrigate his favourite hunting ground at Hissar.'[26] Around mid-seventeenth century the canal was further extended up to Delhi for irrigation and lakes to provide water supply to Delhi.[27] Interestingly, Western Yamuna Canal was originally built in fourteenth century to extend the irrigation facilities and water supply to Hissar Fort town, and later in around mid-seventeenth century, it was further extended to Delhi for water supply.[28]

Existing literature on India's environmental history on water is predominantly confined to the colonial period, with an emphasis on the impact of canal irrigation system and how the British era modernization has disturbed water courses and to some extent caused river pollution due to urban sewage disposals. Again, available literature was centred on the north Indian river basins particularly Yamuna and the Ganga. According to D'souza (2006), existing literature on water for the colonial period can be divided into the three clusters. The first cluster dealt about the impact of canal irrigation on environment, politics and economy. The second focused on the decline of the traditional sources, and the third's focus is on definitive patterns in colonial strategies towards hydraulic endowments, which require much exploration.[29] He further adds that the third cluster consists of several aspects like 'floods, drainage, wetlands, lakes, in-land navigation, traditional fisheries, urban water supply, water legislation, culture and water use, ideologies on river-improvement and Multi-Purpose River Valley development'.[30] Given the above context, the present manuscript attempts to capture most of the unexplored aspects of water to understand the colonial strategies towards the hydraulic endowments.

Islam has analysed the expansion of canal irrigation and its impact on the area under irrigation and increase in productivity, particularly cash crops in the Punjab province during the last six decades of colonial era. It was an analysis of the economic aspects of canal irrigation system of that province. Islam argues that in Punjab, the colonial administration has expanded irrigation infrastructure through repair and renovation of old canals, construction of new canals as well as improving the method of drawing water from wells between 1887 and 1947.[31] According to him, the area under irrigation has shot up from 7.4 million acres in 1987–96 to 17 million acres in 1937–46. The average area under canal irrigation has increased from 2.6 million acres to 12.0 million acres; the percentage of canal irrigated area has gone up from 36 per cent to 70 per cent and total sown area under canal irrigation leapfrogged from 12 per cent to 37 per cent for the same period. He observed that though the percentage of well-irrigated area and percentage of well-irrigated to total sown area have declined from 50 to 26 and 16 to 13 respectively, the area under well irrigation has increased from 3.7 million acres to 4.3 million acres during that period.[32] Another pertinent observation of this is that the waterlogged area has progressively increased from the third quarter of the twentieth century up to the end of colonial rule.[33] While analysing the economic aspect of canal irrigation system in the Punjab province, Islam, however, failed to address the consequences on ecology and environment except merely pointing out about the area under waterlogging from the last decade of the nineteenth century to the mid-twentieth century.

However, from Gilmartin we get a historical perspective of the changes in the Indus basin environment in terms of pastoralism, migration, agriculture expansion, commercialization of agriculture and changing relationship between society and the state from the pre-colonial era to that of the post-colonial period.[34] Precisely, his argument rests on the 'the relationship between changing natural environments and changing structure of community'.[35] During the mid-twentieth century, Indus basin became one of the largest integrated state-controlled irrigation system in the world. He explores how this irrigation system was managed during the pre-colonial period and under the colonial administration during the nineteenth century. With the expansion of the Indus basin irrigation system in Punjab, particularly during the late nineteenth and early twentieth centuries, interprovincial water conflicts too have emerged. And they got further aggravated in the post-partition era.[36]

In India's water history, Whitcombe has made a pioneering attempt to capture the impact of canal irrigation system and its consequences on ecology and environment in the northwestern provinces that were developed during the late nineteenth century. She argues that the canal irrigation system has destroyed the traditional irrigation system, cultivation practices, forest and other common property resources besides adversely affecting soil fertility due to heavy cropping/over-cropping, resulting in frequent floods, salinization and waterlogging and diseases, particularly malaria. She further added that the process of modernization, like expansion of railway network, has hindered the natural flows, which has led to frequent floods in the northwestern provinces.[37] Sengupta explores how the British administration has destroyed the traditional irrigation management/maintenance systems, like tank and canal irrigation, in Bihar particularly in Gaya district due to the shift in the revenue system from produce-rent to fixed-rent and then cash-rent. Consequently, the responsibility of maintenance and servicing of the traditional irrigation system lost its relevance, which resulted in the decline of the traditional irrigation system.[38] As against this, Mosse argues that the decline of tank irrigation system was not a colonial phenomenon alone, since even during the pre-colonial era, it had undergone various phases of optimal management or decline due to shifting structure of power and governance, and hence it could not be validated.[39]

As against Whitcombe's claim, Ian Stone argued: 'As far as irrigation alone was concerned, on a policy level it was simultaneously linked with famine prevention, revenue stability, the settling of unruly tribes, expansion of cultivation, extended cultivation of cash crops, enhanced taxable capacity, improved cultivation practices, and political stability.'[40] 'The canal irrigation was an innovation which met their requirements, and it did so because it slotted into the productive aspects of the peasant system in a way which made it generally more advantageous than even the most favourable well irrigation.'[41] He further claimed that 'the heavily irrigated northern districts – enjoyed a degree of broad based material prosperity matched by few areas in India.'[42] Precisely, for Stone, despite ecological consequences, the canal irrigation has yielded several positive developments in the region. Countering this, Baghel argues that though the justification for large river control of hydropower stems from flood control and irrigation, there are several well-established negative developments, like environmental impact, such as sedimentation, precipitation, waterlogging, salinity, sea-level change and the orbit of earth; social impact, such as human sacrifice and displacement of people; and economic impact, such as fisheries, submergence of land and the increased the risk of earthquakes, catastrophic floods and diseases.[43]

Whitcombe has studied the canal irrigation and its impact on ecology and environment during the late nineteenth century, whereas Haberman analysed the impact of water diversion at Tajewala Barrage in Yamuna River and its consequences on the flow of the river from the ecological and environmental point of view during the post-independent period. Though the Western Yamuna canal was developed during the fourteenth century, it got neglected in the subsequent period, only to be restored in the sixteenth century, while modifications were made around the mid-seventeenth century and it got extended up to Delhi.[44] In the subsequent decades, it again fell into disuse until the mid-eighteenth century.[45] This canal was reopened in 1825 by the British administration. The Eastern Yamuna Canal, developed during the mid-seventeenth century, fell into disrepair subsequently and was reopened in the 1830s.[46] Since the third decade of the nineteenth century, both canals irrigated a huge extent of land. About 140 miles below the Tajewala Barrage, two more barrages regulate the Yamuna River flow. One is at Wazirabad and another one is at Okhla, serving for Delhi's water supply, and the Agra canal extended for irrigation purposes. At Okhla barrage, almost all water is diverted either for irrigation or for domestic water supply.[47] 'Extraction of water from the Yamuna for irrigation, industrial, and domestic purposes leaves almost no water in the riverbed around Delhi for much of the year.'[48]

Further, Haberman points out that since 1970s, water quality has gradually declined in Yamuna River.[49] From Tajewala onwards, significant amount of toxic industrial wastes were dumped from cities on its banks, mainly Karnal, Panipat and Sonepat, before it reaches the national capital, Delhi, which alone contributes more than 70 per cent of the pollution load into in the river.[50] When it leaves Delhi, Yamuna flows mainly with domestic sewage and untreated industrial waste. He further observes that the deterioration of the Yamuna begins at Tajewala barrage since all water is diverted into the two canals except during the rainy season. Hence, there is no flow in the river except the toxic pollution.[51] Pollution of the Yamuna is primarily due to 'rapid urbanization, industrialization, heavy extraction, modern agricultural techniques, and some religious and social practices'.[52]

> The flow of the river is diminishing rapidly because of the increasing demand for water for domestic use by a growing population and also for irrigation with modern farming techniques. Pesticides seep into the river from the surrounding farmlands and frightening amounts of untreated sewage and toxic industrial effluents pour into it continually from Delhi, a city of more than fifteen million people, located hundred miles upstream.[53]

As such, he argued that water diversion to agriculture and domestic water supply through canals, resulting in a little flow in the river, which added to the industrial and agricultural toxic waste besides domestic sewage as well as cultural practices have turned the holy river into a drainage.

Asit K. Biswas and others have reiterated that the Ganga River 'was highly polluted with three-fourths of the pollution contributed by untreated municipal sewerages from large and medium towns'[54] and the rest from the industrial effluents. The other pollution-contributing factors are: 'run-off from agricultural fields carrying chemicals and fertilizers, run-off from areas used for dumping of solid wastes and open defecation, dumping of burnt/half-burnt dead bodies and animal carcasses, cattle wallowing, mass bathing, floral offerings, etcetera'.[55] Precisely, 'Untreated industrial, municipal, and domestic discharges in most Indian rivers are creating considerable environmental and health hazards.'[56]

Brian Stoddart analyses how the colonial policies on land and water tax in Andhra, particularly Krishna and Godavari delta regions and surrounding areas, shaped the political movements of the landowners/peasantry since the late nineteenth century and how it played out at the national level during the early twentieth century. Further, he captures how the farmers' agitation against the land tax and water tax grew in strength with the support of the traders, educationists, media, lawyers and political leaders of different shades since the late nineteenth century. As he argues, issues concerning water have become a centre of the Andhra politics in the post-independent period.[57]

Forcefully arguing against the very basic idea of development of Sardar Sarovar Project in the Narmada Valley, Baviskar details how it will affect the ecology in general and the livelihood option of the tribal people in particular. The tribals have managed natural resources only for their subsistence, and hence there was no threat to the ecology and environment. She argues: 'Their low-impact use of nature in earlier time was probably as much adventitious as it may have been deliberate; adivasis were limited by demography and technology from using resources destructively.'[58] Historically, they were against assimilation by outsiders and not only against the Narmada Valley project. 'The assimilation of adivasi struggles into an anti-development agenda neglects history – that people have always fought against outside oppression, on their own terms. Their history of resistance long precedes the advent of development.'[59] The post-colonial policies attempt to convert the natural resources into commodities at the cost of tribal communities. 'In the name of development, national elites, through the institutions of the state and the market, and often in collaboration with foreign capital, have appropriated natural resources – land, minerals, forests and water – for conversion into commodities.'[60] Consequently, the tribals were forced to protest against the development initiatives mainly to protect their livelihood options and to keep traditional lifestyle patterns unaffected.

Prakash and colleagues reiterate that the water-related issues are a major challenge for the economy, polity and society due to 'falling or stagnant agricultural growth, increasing migration from rural to urban areas, swift industrialization process, and unplanned and unregulated urbanization'.[61] According to them, there are three important challenges, viz. urbanization, increasing dependence on groundwater and the effects of climate change.[62] Further, they argued that how the water resource policies in south Asia have developed, motives behind the formulation and the politics of implementation, which 'is not devoid of gender, class/caste, urban and rural biases and their successful implementation[,] have a bearing on people living on the margin'.[63] They have emphasized that water policies must incorporate equity, sustainability, gender sensitivity and diversity in managing water resources.[64] Precisely, they argue that the existing water policies were designed to allocate water to different sectors based on the differential priorities. As such, they called for a 'pluralistic and integrated approach' in the formulation and implementation of water policies.[65]

While commenting on the national water policy of 2002 with reference to supply-side solution, such as dam building and extracting underground water, Ray warned that 'short sighted policies have catastrophic consequences for the country as a whole, and the environmental and social consequences for the poor, in particular, could be disastrous'.[66] He further pointed out the major lacunae in policy formulation, viz. not engaging the different stakeholders to resolve the water problems.[67]

Asthana explores alternative public policy options to the existing top-down approach, which is least concerned about the rights of the common people based on the experience of proposed Delhi water supply scheme through the public-private partnership during the post-economic reforms era. She argues that the different stakeholders, viz. non-governmental organizations, religious organizations, intellectual communities among others, have addressed the consequences of privatization of water supply and how it will affect the basic rights of the marginal communities as well as its impact on the cultural and religious practices of different stakeholders. Hence, it becomes imperative to involve different stakeholders from formulation to implementation to assess the risks and to arrive at alternative solutions to the water problem. She argues that private entrepreneurs will treat water as a mere commodity to make profit, undermining the rights to basic life need; curbing water democracy; making water out of bounds for the poor; and ignoring the value of local knowledge, skill and technology. Precisely, she debunks the top-down water policy and advocates a process which considers the views of the different stakeholders in evolving water policies in the Indian subcontinent, particularly during the era of globalization and economic reforms.[68]

Narain and Prakash have emphasized the need for an appropriate policy design/intervention to deal the water insecurity issue in the peri-urban areas, because such areas were supplying the land and water resources but receive only the polluted water, which affects the livelihood options in different cities of south Asian countries. In the peri-urban areas, land-use pattern has changed, affecting accessibility to water sources, which in turn has increased the stress due to multiplication of claimants. Due to urbanization, water bodies have been encroached and groundwater table is getting depleted in the peri-urban areas. With the option for percolation being limited in the urban areas, rain water is going waste, resulting in implications for climate change, further aggravating the vulnerabilities of peri-urban areas. Hence, an appropriate policy mechanism has to be designed to tackle this problem.[69]

Klingensmith recounts how the idea of large dams like Damodar Valley Corporation (DVC) proposed on the lines of Tennessee Valley Authority (TVA) but only selectively adopted, ignoring the complexity to achieve modernity and legitimacy, as it was largely influenced by politicians, particularly the middle-class elites. Tracing the history of TVA, Klingensmith points out that the project was developed to benefit the nation and its progress without any political intervention. Contrary to this, DVC was proposed to control soil erosion, floods, migration, generating power and overall economic development, but it has failed because Indians' understanding of TVA was imagined coupled with apolitical technocracy and lack of political vision, resulting in a lopsided model.[70]

Cullet and Kanoon point out that one or other form of water regulation had prevailed since the ancient times up to the pre-colonial period.[71] Since the late nineteenth century, the colonial government had enacted several water laws like those for the protection and maintenance of embankments and regulation of ferries and fisheries.[72] These acts gave importance to economically productive uses of water, viz. irrigation, and did not pay any attention to the environmental or social aspects.[73] Since the early twentieth century, the colonial government not only exercised control over water but also linked it with the property rights to access water.[74] After independence, the constitutional provisions paved the way for designing a framework for water laws in India.[75] Different states enacted several acts for different types of irrigation sources, like minor irrigation, canal, tank and embankments.[76] Since the last decade of the twentieth century, reforms were brought in irrigation laws with a focus on the agrarian sector to accommodate water users associations as well.[77]

According to Mollinga, interdisciplinary and trans-disciplinary approach is important for water resources management to deal with the complexity or multidimensionality involved in it, requiring decision-makers to look for integrated, adaptive and comprehensive models.[78] He further added that the existing literature clearly emphasizes to adopt a comprehensive approach to address the 'socio-material complexity of water systems dynamics, and their contested and negotiated transformation'.[79] In addition to the emerging interdisciplinary and trans-disciplinary research through the socio-technical approach, Mollinga has suggested boundary work, which consists of the following three components – boundary concepts, boundary objects and boundary settings.[80] The first one is helpful to arrive at a conceptual clarity to the complexity/multidimensionality of the issues and problems of water resources management studies. The second one is involved in suggesting appropriate strategies and methods to deal with water resource management, and the last one is institutional arrangement, in which the above two can be fruitfully developed and effectively implemented.[81]

Scholars concerned about the nature and dimensions of environmental history expect that it has to give new knowledge to deal with the current and future environmental problems. According to Sverker Sörlin (2011),

> the study of contemporary history was seen as contributing to our understanding of how to avoid future disasters, both from the new knowledge provided, but also from the individual voices of witnesses. Something similar could be argued for environmental history; it was a history which came with a mission and wished to offer insights from humanity's environmental past in order to avoid future ecological disasters or unsustainable environmental behaviour.[82]

Accordingly, the present study will throw light on the historical understanding of water diversion, pollution and the ever-increasing competing demand among the different stakeholders and their consequences on ecology and environment, in a historical perspective with an interdisciplinary approach. In other words, this historical analysis with an interdisciplinary approach will offer some light to handle the water problems in future.

It is needless to say that water is an essential requirement for life on this planet. McNeill states:

Historically, world water demand was driven chiefly by population growth. That is because most water use went for irrigation for food production, and some of the rest went for domestic use in cooking and cleaning. In the twentieth century that link weakened because industry took a growing share of the world's fresh water, and industrial production levels did not vary tightly with population.[83]

Due to population growth, agricultural expansion, urbanization and industrialization, the demand for water has increased manifold. The bourgeoning demand has been met through diversion of surface water by constructing dams and extracting the groundwater sources.

At the same time, agricultural expansion has resulted in the shrinking of common property resources, particularly forests and other green cover, which were vital in sustaining availability and flow of water. On the one hand, increasing population and urbanization have created more demand for water; on the other hand, expansion of cultivation to increase productivity has also exacerbated it equally. While demand was galloping, conservation of water resources witnessed a decline due to rapid expansion of cultivated area and commercialization of crops as well as denudation of forests. This crisis has to be analysed to ascertain how the decline of natural water–conserving resources, like forests, have cast a long and dark shadow over the changing land-use patterns, cropping patterns and technological advancement in the agrarian sector, which also proved to be a threat to biodiversity and the entire ecosystem. Hence, water management, water diversion, water-lifting technologies, water pollution, etc. due to population growth, urbanization, industrialization and domestic water supply have to be understood historically from the ecological and environmental point of view.

The vast amount of literature on water and irrigation has failed to look at the ecological and environmental consequences.[84] Essentially, historical understanding of the problem is important for those concerned with environmental sustainability. For, this has a direct correlation to both the quality and quantity of water. According to UNESCO (2009):

> Demographic processes such as population growth, age distribution, urbanisation and migration create some of the greatest pressures on water resources, both quantitative and qualitative. These demographic processes directly affect water availability and quality through increased water demands and consumption and through pollution resulting from water use. They affect water resources indirectly through changes in land use and water use patterns, with significant implications at local, regional and global levels.[85]

Urbanization, which was very high during the twentieth century, would only get exacerbated in the twenty-first century. For instance, in 1900, only about 13 per cent of the population lived in the urban areas and it has increased to 29.53 per cent in 1950 and further up to 46.67 per cent in 2000, and it is expected to reach 68.37 per cent in 2050.[86] Consequently, urban domestic water demand, which has increased during the late twentieth century, would certainly witness an exponential jump in future. It has to be met with the diversion of water sources from distance places. For instance, water supply for Coimbatore city initially was met from the tanks, later from the nearest river, then from the river basins, later from other river basins and finally from distant river basins from the early twentieth century onwards. Despite these diversions, water problem will persist and it appears to continue for the foreseeable future due to the ever-increasing urbanization. Though, growth rate of urbanization has declined, it will nevertheless continue to be on the rise. 'While the world's urban population grew rapidly during the 20th century (from 220 million to 2.8 billion), the next few decades will see an unprecedented scale of urban growth across developing countries.'[87] In other words, more and more water is required to meet the increasing urban domestic water supply. Consequently, there will be competing demand for water the world over among different stakeholders. On the one hand, we have to provide safe drinking water for the growing population, and on the other hand, we have to grow more food grains to feed them by expanding cultivation besides generating employment opportunities and ensuring various infrastructural facilities. Unfortunately, the available sources are not only getting exhausted but are insufficient to meet this.

With the rise in the demand on the scarce resources, conflicts become inevitable among the different users. 'Water scarcity occurs when so much water is withdrawn from lakes, rivers or groundwater to such an extent that supplies can no longer adequately satisfy all human and ecosystem requirements, resulting in more competition among potential users.'[88] Hence, competing demand for water is inevitable not only for the present but also for the future. Even now, intractable problems persist in sharing river waters among the states and between the countries. 'An increasing number of river basins lack sufficient water to meet all the demands placed on them, and competition among users can be intense.'[89] 'Competition for water exists at all levels and is forecast to increase in almost all countries.'[90] Competing demand for water among the different water-using sectors – agriculture, domestic and industry – has led to provocative claims and resultant conflicts among them, and also within each sector, more so in agriculture, where it is greatly evident in different parts of the world, especially in the developing countries.[91] The ever-increasing demand and the attendant conflicts, which found expression in different forms, are widely visible in recent years in several developing countries.[92] Within the agricultural sector, different kinds of conflicts persist. For instance, in Sri Lanka disputes over water allocation have led to violent clashes, damage to systems, threat of court cases and intervention by politicians with vested interests.[93] Further, conflicts also exist among the groundwater users.[94] The competing demands of the various sectors had aggravated this crisis in different parts of Indian subcontinent, particularly after independence. In 1990s, about 93 per cent of the gross water use in India was for irrigation. It is expected that the demand for water for domestic consumption, industrial purpose and power generation would increase double and sevenfold, respectively, in 2025.[95]

In addition, effluents of cities/towns, industries and agricultural sector continue to pollute both surface and groundwater, further aggravating the crisis in most of the countries. 'Demand for water is often highest when availability is lowest, and water shortages and conflicts have increased accordingly. This trend has been paralleled by degradation in the quality of surface water and groundwater from the combined effluents of cities, industries and agricultural activities.'[96] In fact, only a very few countries are effectively managing the water resources. 'Few countries know how much water is being used and for what purposes, the quantity and quality of water that is available and that can be withdrawn without serious environmental consequences and how much is being invested in water management and infrastructure.'[97] As such, most countries are facing water scarcity due to ineffective water management. With freshwater options almost completely exploited, they appear to have reached a dead end. Consequently, the potential for future diversion of river water and further extraction of groundwater has reached zero level. For, basins or sub-basins have invariably become closed ones and groundwater extraction has reached the maximum level due to too many dams which curtail the natural flow of the river water, the main source for water recharge mechanism. Without considering the ways to use the surplus water or maintaining the natural flows, water was diverted for various needs and then let off as effluent(s). This should be seen along with the decline of water-conserving resources.

Water was diverted through dams/reservoirs with the aim of controlling floods and to expand agricultural activities. While floods were controlled, absence of requisite flow of water in the river is leading to serious health hazards, particularly in the cities and towns located on river banks. For instance, in 1908, there was a flood in Musi River in Hyderabad, which resulted in huge causalities.

Subsequently, dams were constructed on Musi River and water was diverted for agricultural activities. Consequently, floods were controlled. But the river had turned into an outlet of sewage since natural flow of water was diverted. According to Cohen (2011), 'While the volume of river has been controlled and no further floods have occurred; pollutants from human activity have continued to be dumped into the river unabated. The river is unable to adequately carry off these toxins, leading to a sludgy sewer-like composition along the banks, with what water does make it beyond Hyderabad city being extremely polluted.'[98]

At the global level, estimates show that the water demand has increased as a whole in different sectors of the economy during the twentieth century.[99] It will witness a further surge, particularly in the domestic and industrial sectors in the future. In the developing countries, competing demand for water among different stakeholders turned intense, particularly during the last quarter of the twentieth century, primarily due to the pace of urbanization with in-migration and population growth and industrialization with attendant water pollution. With an enhanced economic activities and the pressing need to provide drinking water for the bourgeoning populace, urban demand for water far exceeded the supply.[100] The possibility of this demand coming down appears very remote as it is only bound to shoot up. In short, the ever-increasing demand for freshwater, on the one hand, and limited as well as polluted water supply, on the other hand, have worsened the situation in recent years in most of the developing countries. 'In many parts of the world water resources have become so depleted and so much contaminated that they are already unable to meet the ever-increasing demands made on them. This has become the main factor impeding economic development and population growth.'[101] Population growth has resulted in the decline of per capita availability of water at the global level. 'The rapid population growth between 1970 to 1994 has resulted in the potential water availability for the Earth's population decreasing from 12.9 down to 7.6 thousand cubic metres per year per person. The greatest reduction in population water supply took place in Africa (by 2.8 times), in Asia (by two times), and in south America (by 1.7 times).'[102] The availability of per capita water will witness a further decline in future due to population explosion. 'Current water withdrawal in the world as a whole is not great in total, amounting only to 8.4% of global water resources. By 2025 this figure is expected to increase to 12.2%.'[103] '[I]n the decades to come most of the Earth's population will face a critical situation with regard to water supply.'[104] Water pollution has further aggravated the crisis. 'The major sources of intensive pollution of waterways and water bodies are industrial and municipal wastewater as well as water returning from irrigated areas.'[105]

It is estimated that in 1995 the volume of waste water was 326 km^3/l year in Europe, 431 km^3/year in North America, 590 km^3/year in Asia and 55 km^3/year in Africa. Many countries discharge most of their waste water containing harmful substances into the hydrological system with no preliminary purification. Prime water resources are thus polluted and their subsequent use becomes unsuitable, especially as potable supplies. Every cubic metre of contaminated waste water discharged into water bodies and water courses spoils up to 8 to 10 cubic metres of pure water. This means that most parts of the world are already facing the threat of catastrophic qualitative depletion of water resources.[106]

Hence, sustainable water management is a challenge not only at the country level but at the global level as well.

Water scarcity in developing countries has paved the way for conflicts. It has intensified due to a wide range of demands besides factors like pollution and inefficiency of the bureaucracy. Inefficient water management system has been a prime cause for the emergence of numerous conflicts in sharing river waters in recent years. 'Conflicts over water have steadily increased in numbers due to the various reasons of population growth, rapid industrialization, consumerism, pollution, environmental degradation, inequities in the access to and use of water, poor governance and complications arising out of managing multiple uses across multiple users.'[107] Managing water conflicts is much more a serious and complicated issue when the river basin involves different political boundaries of a country or state with a different cultural setup. 'The sharing of rivers across political boundaries is an area of both contention and conflict, be it at the international, national, regional or local levels.'[108] Till recently, demand for water has led to numerous conflicts at basins as well as delta regions among the farmers and the states.[109] In India, most of the rivers originate in one state and flow through other state/states. Hence, managing water conflicts is increasingly difficult despite provisions in the federal constitutional structure. All major rivers and several small rivers originate in one state and flow through another state or states before reaching the sea.[110] Compounding the problem is the states claiming the riparian rights based on historical rights, which is outdated as it has become irrelevant in the modernization process to use the natural water resources. 'Riparian rights have allowed holders to use water flowing past their land as long as the supply reaching downstream users is undiminished in flow, quantity and quality.'[111] Riparian rights were established by the court as follows: 'Riparian owner has a right to use the water of the stream which flows past his land equally with other riparian owners and to have the water come to him undiminished in flow, quantity or quality and to go beyond his land without obstruction.'[112] While the upper riparian states claim 'absolute territorial "sovereignty" the downstream states claim absolute integrity of watercourse'.[113] 'On the one hand, the upper riparian states claim complete control over the water within their borders without any regard of its effect on the downstream states. On the other hand, downstream states claim that the quantity or quality of water that flows down the watercourse should not be affected by the upstream states.'[114] For example, 'Those in Tamil Nadu felt that the free flow of the Kaveri, which they were used to for millennia, had been curbed by this agreement; on the other hand, those in Mysore state felt that their right to make use of a river which took birth and flowed for a longer distance on their soil had been interfered with.'[115] Whereas the issue has been aggravated manifold due to the surging demand from different users like agricultural and industrial besides domestic consumption. According to Vaidyanathan (2007), 'in several parts of the country, utilization of both surface and groundwater has been reached or even exceeded the limit of sustainable use'.[116] The problem has now been further exacerbated owing to decline of water quality, caused by pollution.[117] At the international level, in the river basin, there are four types of water conflicts, viz. conflict through use, conflict through pollution, relative distribution conflict and absolute distribution conflict due to the following causes, respectively, water use, water quality, water distribution and, water distribution and availability.[118]

In India, the current domestic water use is about 25 BCM, and in Indian industry and energy generation, it is about 67 BCM and it will increase to 52 BCM and 228 BCM, respectively, by 2025.[119] In 1990, water use in irrigation was 460 BCM and it is expected to increase to 770 BCM in 2025.[120] According to the National Commission for Integrated Water Resources Development (1999), total water requirement for the country was 694 km^3 to 710 km^3 in 2010, and it is expected to rise to 973 km^3 to 1180 km^3 in 2050, depending on the low-demand and high-demand scenarios.[121] The proportion of water requirement for domestic, industries and power may increase from 4.3 km^3 in 2010 to 111 km^3 in 2050, 37 km^3 to 81 km^3 and 19 km^3 to 70 km^3, respectively, in the next fifty years. Invariably, demand for irrigation, domestic water supply as well as industrial water supply is expected to increase in different river basins of the country. Further, the commission indicates that the proposed net water use for all sectors in different basins is higher than the utilizable surface water in the subcontinent in 2050.[122] Studies have found that Brahmaputra, Barak and west-flowing rivers from Tadri to Kanyakumari would be only a few among the water-sufficient basins by the middle of the twenty-first century.[123] Except a very few, most of the rivers would be 'closed basins', which means supply from those river basins would be distributed among the existing users and it will not be able to accommodate new users. In other words, a large number of 'open basins' at present will turn out to be 'closed basins' in future. According to Sivasubramaniyan, 'In Tamil Nadu all available surface (river) flows are mostly utilised and there is no scope for expansion of canal irrigation system. For the past five decades, the canal irrigated area in Tamil Nadu remains stagnant which is around 8 lakh ha.'[124] He further added that 'groundwater utilisation in Tamil Nadu has also reached its limit. Most of the district aquifers are already marked in the dark region and there is no scope for further expansion of this source. So, by all counts expansion of irrigated agriculture in Tamil Nadu will be difficult.'[125]

Due to population growth, urbanization, industrialization, expansion of agriculture and domestic water supply, the demand for water has increased manifold during the post-independence period. For example, the total population of the country was around 36 crores in 1951 and it has increased to 121 crores in 2011. The urban population has also increased from 6 crores to 38 crores for the same period. In other words, population has increased nearly fourfold, and urban population too had witnessed a more-than-six-fold jump within six decades. The number of water-consuming industries also has bourgeoned. The area under cultivation has also seen rapid expansion with the net-sown area going up from 118.75 million hectares in 1950–51 to 139.17 million hectares in 2009–10. The net-irrigated area too has jumped to 20.85 million hectares in 1950–51 to 61.94 million hectares in 2009–10. The gross irrigated area also has increased from 22.56 million hectares in 1950–51 to 85.08 million hectares in 2009–10.[126] To meet the increasing water demand, several dams were constructed and massive exploitation of groundwater irrigation sources has been encouraged over the period. During the post-independence period, 4,621 dams were constructed. Consequently, the canal-irrigated area has increased from 8.295 million hectares in 1950–51 to 16.596 million hectares in 2008–09. However, the tank-irrigated area has halved from 3.613 million hectares to 1.979 million hectares during the same period. Due to urbanization several tanks have disappeared. 'Rapid urbanization has seen a number of tanks becoming history.'[127] Consequently, floods have become a frequent phenomena in several cities. For instance, Chennai city is facing frequent floods.[128] At the time of independence, tubewell irrigation technology did not exist. However, since 1960s it has increased progressively and provided irrigation to about 26.013 million hectares in 2008–09. Wells and other sources of irrigation also have provided irrigation to about 5.978 million hectares and 2.967 million hectares in 1950–51 and 12.563 million hectares and 6.045 million hectares in 2008–09, respectively. Vaidyanathan (2006) pointed out that 'surface sources, which accounted for over 70 per cent of irrigated area in 1950 now account for only 44 per cent. The relative importance of groundwater has nearly doubled over this period'.[129] In other words, more and more number of wells were dug up and deepened, particularly since the green revolution period. Consequently, '[o]ver the last three decades or so, India has seen a massive expansion of ground water irrigation. There has been a progressive decline in the water table in most areas, and this has led to the farmers deepening wells in a competitive manner'.[130] The other source of irrigation like micro-irrigation – drip and sprinkler – was encouraged. As on 2015, 77.75 lakh hectares (33.87 lakh hectares drip and 43.88 lakh hectares under sprinkler) was brought under the micro-irrigation system. Due to the increasing demand from the different sectors of the economy, water scarcity has increased tremendously during the last three decades or so. Despite diverting river waters and extraction of groundwater, water scarcity arises invariably in different regions of the country. According to Wood (2007), there were three factors that have heightened water scarcity: (1) growing population, (2) new agricultural technology, rapid industrialization and rising consumerism and (3) environmental degradation.[131]

Together with rising water demand, water pollution has further aggravated the competing demand for water not only due to industrial water pollution but also due to the discharge of household wastewater. The problem has now been further exacerbated owing to decline of water quality, caused by pollution.[132] According to the National Commission for Integrated Water Resources Development's (1999) estimates for seventeen categories of industries, water requirement was 15282.9 Mm^3 per year in 1997 and the total wastewater generation was 3878.3 Mm^3 per year.[133] Whereas, in the next fifty years (2050), the required water for these (17) industries will be 102,535.75 Mm^3 per year and the wastewater generation would be 66,408.38 Mm^3 per year.[134] Of course, this estimate has not taken into account small and village industries. If included, the demand would increase manifold. 'The situation is becoming even more serious and complex with industrial wastewater discharges, which also, for the most part, receive inadequate treatment in nearly all Asian developing countries.'[135] In the developing countries, very limited quantity of sewage water is being treated that too in few cities, and in almost all the towns and villages, it is left untreated, further polluting the freshwater bodies.

> [I]ncreasing water pollution is a major issue for nearly all Asian developing countries. Unless the present perceptions and attitudes change radically, it is likely to be a critical issue of the future. This is because at the domestic level,

nearly all water that enters the household is eventually discharged as wastewater. Even in many urban centers where wastewater is collected through sewer systems, it is often discharged into freshwater bodies, land, or oceans with only limited or even no, treatment. This means that the problem of increasing wastewater contamination is not being solved: it is being simply transferred from one location to another. The philosophy has been somewhat akin to 'out of sight, out of mind'.[136]

It means that the used water has to be treated before being discharged into the river basins. According to the Central Pollution Control Board (2015), the number of polluted rivers in India has gone up from 121 in 2009 to 275 in 2014 and the number of polluted river stretches has also doubled from 150 to 302, respectively, for the same period. Further, it pointed out that out of 445 rivers in the country, there are 302 polluted river stretches on 275 rivers.[137] Further, it added that the sewage generated from 650 cities and towns situated along the 302 polluted river stretches has also increased from 38,000 MLD to 62,000 MLD, whereas the treatment capacity of the plants was increased from 11,800 MLD to 24,000 MLD for the same period. The gap in the treatment capacity has only widened from 26,200 MLD to 38,000 MLD.[138] It clearly indicates that in cities/towns, most of the households discharge the wastewater into the river basins, which further deteriorated the quality of water not only the surface water but groundwater sources as well.

In addition to the increasing water demand and water pollution, dilution of efficient and rational water management has crept in due to popular vote bank politics. Further decline was owing to inappropriate policies since the last quarter of the twentieth century. For example, in Tamil Nadu electricity supply to the farmers is free of cost since the 1980s. This popular vote bank scheme has only accentuated the water crisis. According to the ADB:

> A major problem with agricultural water use has been that many Asian countries have been pursuing incorrect policies in terms of water and energy used for groundwater pumping. Farmers in some subregions at present do not pay for the actual volume of groundwater pumped for irrigation. In addition, energy costs for pumping are very heavily subsidized by many governments. Accordingly, farmers often pump more groundwater than is needed for optimizing crop production. This over-pumping is resulting in a steady decline of groundwater levels in many Asian aquifers. As the groundwater levels decline, more energy is needed to pump the same quantity of water. Because the energy costs for farmers are heavily subsidized, the financial losses of many public electricity boards are continuing to escalate. This has contributed to a vicious cycle of overuse of

groundwater, declining aquifer levels, increasing losses to the electricity boards, and increasing adverse environmental impacts (like land subsidence), none of which are sustainable on a long-term basis.[139]

For its part, the World Bank too has warned that the electricity subsidies 'have created disincentives for water conservation and incentives for inappropriate cropping patterns'.[140]

Consequently, competing demands for water have emerged among the agricultural, industrial and domestic sectors. In the agricultural sector, the 'green revolution', with its attendant technology and mechanization and hybrid seeds pressure, created more demands for water. Due to this, sustainability of this scarce resource has become increasingly difficult in recent years. A case in point is the history of water demand and sources of water supply and the resultant conflicts between farmers, municipalities, urban residents, industry and the state over water in the Bhavani and Noyyal River basins, particularly in the areas surrounding Coimbatore and Tirupur (Map 1) since the nineteenth century.[141]

Within the agricultural sector, technological transformation; changes in cropping pattern; the role of the bureaucracy, politicians and the judiciary; and changes in government policy, particularly in the Kalingarayan and Lower Bhavani Project canal (Map 2), have been explored in a historical perspective.[142] With the increasing demand, serious environmental problems have also emerged largely due to discharge of dyeing and bleaching effluents from the textile and garment manufacturing units, which affected not only the surface and groundwater but also productivity, public health and the biodiversity resources in general. In other words, this was not only a decline in the availability of water but deterioration in the quality of water as well. For example, in twenty-seven villages along the Kadaganar River, houses, cattle, crops and public health have been severely affected due to pollution from tanneries.[143] For effective water management the present policies have to consider the following elements: national strategy, cutting power subsidies, water pricing and enforcing the polluters to pay principle, valuing ecological services and regulating groundwater extraction.[144]

Pollution, overextraction of groundwater, water scarcity and the unanticipated impacts of human activities on complex water systems have created strains on both the environmental and the economic foundations of society.[145] Though the prevention of water pollution acts – Indian Penal Code Act (1860) and Indian Easement Act (1882) – were passed during the second half of the nineteenth century, they were mostly not implemented rigorously. Since 1970s several acts

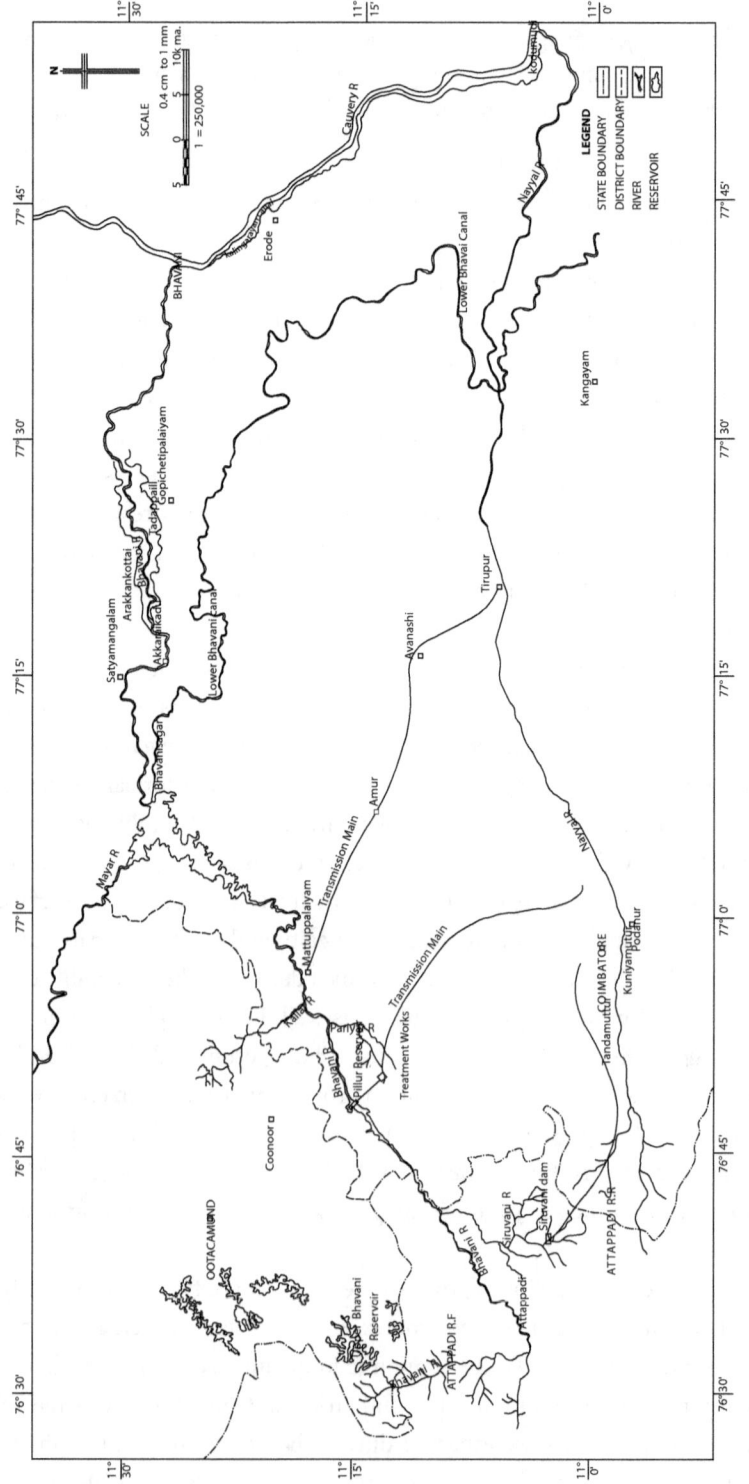

Map 1 Bhavani and Noyyal River Basins.

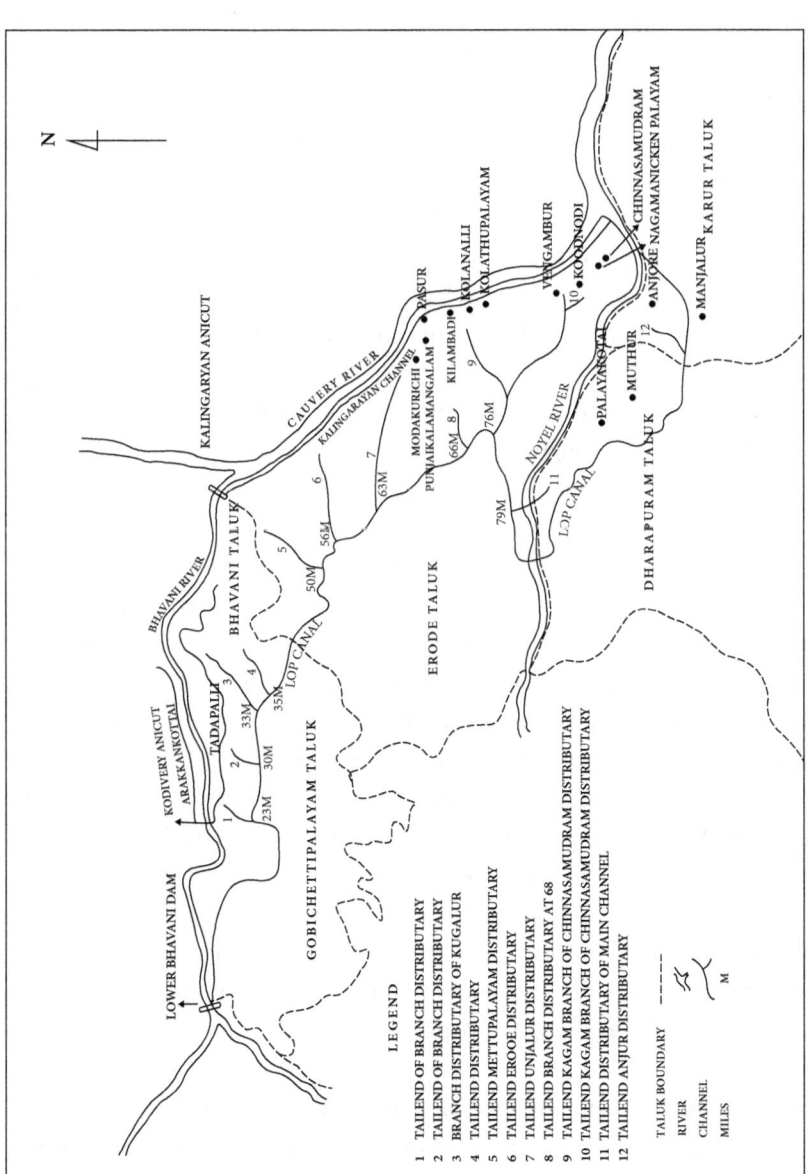

Map 2 Water conflict in LBP Canal and Kalingarayan Channel.

were introduced to curb pollution of water resources but their validity has been challenged in the courts often. Existing water laws are outdated and there is a crying need for new water laws to meet the new emerging challenges.[146]

In the early period, dams were conceived not only to enhance irrigation but also to exercise control over the floods. For example, Bhavani dam was constructed to control the frequent floods in Thanjavur. However, in the later period, more and more dams were constructed upstream, which completely disturbed the hydrology of the river basin. For example, until the 1970s, only a few dams were constructed in the Cauvery River, but now there are more than twenty dams which stretch up very close to the origin of the river and its tributaries both in Karnataka and Tamil Nadu. Even in the Bhavani River, prior to the Bhavani dam, there were only four diversions, of which three were meant for irrigation purposes and one for water supply scheme to Coimbatore city from the Siruvani, one of the tributaries of the river. After that, further water was diverted through the Siruvani-II and Pillur dam from Bhavani River. Lannerstad has rightly put it: 'Thus at the basin level, the allocation closure from the 1950s in a step-wise process has resulted in a hydrological closure. While the competition for water continues within the basin and water use moves upstream closer to the source, some downstream users risk being deprived of their water as return flows are reduced and stream flow decreases.'[147] 'When more and more water is appropriated in a basin in response to demands from an increase in population and economic activity, a "river basin closure" process arises. In a "closed" basin there is no usable water leaving the basin.'[148] Lannerstad and Molden observed that 'after basin closure, means must be found to align individual actions with the objectives of society. This will require a better understanding of what drives individual water use and of the hydrology of the basin, but many problems have built up over time and are difficult to resolve. These include the built-up dependency on electricity for pumping and the increasing pressure on agriculture from other sectors. Eventually, it may be that policies may have to gradually shift people away from agriculture to ease water scarcity'.[149]

At the global level, importance of water management and environmental implications came to be realized during the last quarter of the twentieth century. According to the Asian Development Bank:

> Environmental issues for water management became important during the 1970s, not only in Asia but also in the rest of the world. Increasingly, all development activities, including those on water, have to consider environmental implications seriously and comprehensively. These considerations received

considerable momentum during 1980s, and are now universally accepted as an integral requirement for efficient and rational water management.[150]

An increasing social and political concern arose in the 1970s about the impact of water development and management policies and practices on the environment. Since about 1995, the implications of environmental management policies on water development and management have received increasing attention. During the past 35 years, water and environment policies have affected each other in many significant ways, sometimes positively, but at other times adversely.[151]

The river basin water resources are already fully allocated in different river basins of the countries. 'At the practical level, water resources of many of the Asian rivers are already fully allocated and, in some cases, over-allocated, especially during the dry seasons and drought periods.'[152] For instance, according to the World Bank, in India only three river basins will have surplus water and the remaining basins will be insufficient to meet the increasing demand from agriculture, industry and domestic water supply by 2025. Given the scenario, there is a pressing need to assess the magnitude of water demand among the different sectors and its impact, the extent of pollution in terms of industrial effluents and drainage and its consequences and the various acts being enacted to meet the competing demands and to control pollution for protecting the environment and its sustainability.

In Tamil Nadu, demand for domestic water supply and industrial requirements will increase remarkably in future. According to the Institute of Water Studies (IWS), Government of Tamil Nadu's estimate shows that the demand for water in the agriculture sector is expected to decline while at the same time domestic and industrial water demand will shoot up in the next four decades in the sixteen major river basins of the state. Domestic water supply will increase from 1,088.21 MCM in 2004 to 1,793.67 MCM in 2044 and the industrial water demand will increase from 808.54 MCM to 2,196.63 MCM for the same period. In other words, the domestic demand will increase nearly twofold and industrial demand nearly threefold in the next four decades (Table 1.1).

In Tamil Nadu, nine major basins have been highly polluted by various industrial production processes. For example north Chennai – Petro Chemical Industries polluted Chennai River basin; Vellore – Ranipet-Tannery Industries polluted Palar River basin; Erode and Tirupur – Textile Industries polluted Noyyal River basin; Thoothukudi – Sterlite, Coral reeves polluted Kallar basin; Salem – Sago Factories polluted Vellar Basin; Dindigul – Tanneries polluted Vagai basin; Tirunelveli – Sun Paper Mills polluted Tamiraparani basin and

Table 1.1 Domestic and industrial water requirements in different river basins in Tamil Nadu (in MCM)

River basin	Agriculture water demand			Domestic water demand			Industrial water demand		
	2004	2019	2044	2004	2019	2044	2004	2019	2044
1. Chennai	2,864.70	2,582.00	2,393.00	253.32	320.62	432.79	155.25	258.60	431.15
2. Palar	2,532.00	2,532.00	2,532.00	127.82	160.64	215.33	66.86	102.50	161.90
3. Varahanadhi	1,604.00	1,364.00	1,204.00	47.13	59.22	79.38	34.42	50.17	91.70
4. Ponniyar	2,668.80	2,321.39	2,089.78	80.56	99.99	132.35	121.53	199.43	329.27
5. Paravanar	0.384	0.493	0.630	7.20	8.63	11.03	4.56	7.68	13.68
6. Vellar	2,229.26	1,946.25	1,759.47	73.55	87.41	110.52	58.04	96.21	157.97
7. Agniyar	2,344.00	2,344.00	2,344.00	31.48	37.29	46.98	30.77	51.27	85.45
8. Pambar & Kottakaraiyar	1,960.73	1,960.73	1,960.73	37.31	43.60	54.07	60.46	99.25	163.91
9. Vaigar	3,840.00	3,840.00	3,840.00	151.99	181.61	231.03	58.30	98.93	166.66
10. Gundar	1,758.00	1,556.00	1,421.00	53.58	64.21	81.94	69.98	114.98	189.98
11. Vaippar	1,302.65	1,386.15	1,386.15	66.02	98.00	152.01	37.11	45.36	103.10
12. Kallar	167.00	167.00	167.00	14.68	16.51	19.57	25.84	42.28	69.68
13. Tambaraparani	2,645.00	2,645.00	2,645.00	51.44	59.63	73.25	40.72	66.94	110.64
14. Nambiyar	566.00	566.00	566.00	12.91	16.31	21.98	3.29	5.49	9.15
15. Kodaiyar	728.33	728.33	728.33	31.33	34.57	57.28	2.31	3.48	5.45
16. P.A.P	1,558.00	1,558.00	1,558.00	47.89	57.74	74.16	39.10	64.54	106.94
Total	2,8768.85	2,7497.34	2,6595.09	1,088.21	1,345.98	1,793.67	808.54	1,307.11	2,196.63

Source: Government of Tamil Nadu *State of Environment Report of Tamil Nadu*, pp. 42–44 in www.environment.tn.nic.in/soe.pdf (accessed in May 2015).

Manavalakuruchi industrial activities polluted Kidaiyar basin and Sivakasi, Kovilpatti and Sattur industries polluted Vaippar basin.[153]

Water diversion is not a recent phenomenon, since it existed right from the early periods. The rivers and streams were diverted directly for irrigation purposes and for storage in the tanks for future needs. For example, in the river Cauvery, the Grand *Anicut* (kallanai) was constructed during the second century, Kodiveri dam was constructed in the twelfth century and in the Bhavani River, the Kalaingarayan *anicut* was built during the seventeenth century. A number of small diversions (*kalungu*) from minor rivers and streams also existed either for direct irrigation or for storage at tanks. Of course, there was hardly any diversion for purposes other than agriculture till the early twentieth century, when diversions to some extent were made for few cities and industries in different parts of Tamil Nadu. Until then, the water management was undertaken through the *kudimaramattu* system. The role of the government, however, was mainly confined to the collection of revenue from the irrigated land. The peasants were to lift water from well through the traditional methods. Emerging competing demands since the dawn of the twentieth century among the three sectors will be discussed in detail separately.

Agriculture

Until independence and even afterwards, there was not much remarkable development in the irrigation sector. Due to the green revolution, which ushered in the spread of agricultural technologies – high-yielding crops, electric and oil-engine pumpsets, mechanization – more water was required corresponding to the rapid expansion of agriculture. The government had constructed several dams, and all of them were being utilized to the maximum extent. Hence, the only available source is groundwater, which is also getting extensively depleted not only for the agricultural purpose but also for industrial and domestic needs. In the 1950s, of the total net irrigated area, about 23.48 per cent was under well irrigation and its proportion increased to 45.16 per cent in the 1990s. For example, in Coimbatore district, during the last thirty years, though the number of wells had doubled, the net area irrigated by them had increased only marginally. As a result, the average net-irrigated area per well has declined from 1.56 ha in 1960–61 to about 0.747 ha in 1989–90.[154] On the other hand, the number of abandoned wells in the district had increased from 4,033 in 1960 to 16,700 in 1990.[155] This was primarily due to the decline of water table and stream flow along with the drying up of traditional surface water bodies – tanks and springs – and pollution by industrial effluents on surface water bodies and groundwater as well.[156] For instance, during the early 1980s, more than 250 tanneries were there in the North Arcot district. Due to the discharges of effluents, an extent of 3,911.19 ha land was severely affected and 11,850.99 ha was moderately affected. Apart from lakes, tanks and river water, nearby wells and even far-off wells were contaminated. This led to a situation where both the yield and quality of produce also have declined.[157] Understanding the extent of water diversion for industrial and domestic water supply, and its implications on the agricultural sector; the extent of groundwater exploitation in agricultural sector; changing cropping patterns; government policies towards the tanks; the mechanism adopted to promote well irrigation (through credit facilities, subsidized power tariff and other regulations for restriction) and the role of legal and political system is an important area for research.

Industry

Until recently, environmental degradation was largely focused on the extent of deforestation, while other natural resources, like water, were not given the requisite attention that they deserve. Water pollution has emerged mainly due to effluent discharges of industrial units during the post-independence period. While water pollution has brought adverse consequences upon productivity and public health and endangered biodiversity resources, deforestation resulted in reduced rainfall, water availability and the sustainability of biodiversity in general. Again, industrial effluent discharges would set off an alarming chain of reactions besides producing direct and immediate consequences.

In Tamil Nadu, the major polluting industries are tanneries, textile-dyeing units, viscose, paper pulp, sugar, sago, oil refineries, fertilizer and chemical units – which are mostly located in the Bhavani, Kalingarayan channel, Noyyal, Amaravathi, Kodaganar and Palar Rivers.[158] The increasing number of industries in general and water-consuming industries in particular both in Coimbatore and Tirupur cities has created the demand for more water for industrial use, which has led to water scarcity as well as environmental problems in the Noyyal basin.[159] Though there is no comprehensive research on these areas, some studies have explored the consequences of industrial effluent discharges at the micro-level. For example, a study by Madras School of Economics (1998) found that there are 851 bleaching and dyeing units in Tirupur, discharging about a

60 million litres effluents per day. It revealed that about two-third of the landowning households were not cultivating their land either in part or in full due to non-availability or poor quality of irrigation; 90 per cent of the landholders attributed the sharp decline in productivity to water pollution and 43 per cent reported about the sharp decline in land value. A study by Jacob (1996) concluded that while groundwater was polluted in general, the open wells had a higher level of contamination than the borewells.[160] Given the scenario, there is a need to account the quantity of water diversion and the extent of pollution in terms of industrial effluent discharges and the rules and regulations and the laws enacted to curtail them to ascertain the overall impact.

Domestic Water Supply

Water has been diverted for domestic water supply due to urbanization and for rural water supply schemes. These diversions were executed since the early twentieth century, primarily for the major cities in Tamil Nadu. Over the period, a huge amount of water was diverted for the small cities and towns. According to the 2011 census, urban areas of the state accounted for a population 3.49 crores, constituting 44 per cent. In this context, the history of water demand and supply for both Coimbatore and Tirupur had been narrated historically by Saravanan (1999), and Saravanan and Appasamy (1999). The process of urbanization, quantity of water diversion, sources of water, rules and regulations and statutes which evolved in this process, the extent of water markets and its related issues demand serious attention and need to be researched upon.

A considerable amount of existing literature provides an analysis of the specific aspects like domestic water supply, industrial water supply and the consequences of industrial effluent discharges at the micro-level.[161] In our understanding, there are two major gaps in them. (1) Existing studies have confined themselves to either domestic water supply and industrial water supply or transformation in agricultural sector, with their focus on the micro-level. (2) Further, they have neglected the role of legal, judicial and political executive in the complex and competing demands for water – both in distribution as well as in pollution control. Hence, this study would attempt to address these major lacunae.

Understanding nature, in terms of rainfall, amount of water flowing into the sea and how effectively we can use that water in different river basins and the needs of the different regions without affecting hydrology of the river basins, is important for sustainable water resource management. Unfortunately, without a vision of the future requirements in the different regions of the basin and the quantity of water going into the sea, we have diverted water to meet the recurring demand. Consequently, natural flow of the river basin has been disturbed, affecting the recharge mechanism of the river basin, with droughts/famines becoming a frequent phenomenon in the different river basins of the country. For example, Vashistanathi that flows from Kalrayan hills of Salem district merges with the Bay of Bengal in Cuddalore district. In 2002, Kariyakoil Water Reservoir Project was constructed just below the Kalrayan hill range to irrigate a few thousand acres. The consequence is that catchment areas of Vashistanathi, like Eathapur, Peddanaicken Palayam and Attur, once with lush, green fertile lands having coconut and areca nut plantations and paddy fields have turned into a desert since water flow has come to naught downstream. This is the result of bringing new areas under irrigation at the cost of old irrigated area.

In this context, this book attempts to historically look at the ever-rising competing demand for water due to population, urbanization, industrialization, along with water pollution and technological advancement in the agrarian sector leading to diversion of water within a basin and between river basins, resulting in a water crisis in the Bhavani, Noyyal and Amaravathi River basins of Tamil Nadu from the early nineteenth to the early twenty-first centuries. The main objective of the study is to arrive at a comprehensive understanding of the varied and manifold implications of the competing demands for water and their consequences along with the role of government in regulating as well as satisfying the demands of various sectors in these basins with an interdisciplinary approach since the colonial period to the early twenty-first century. Further, it captures how the competing demands were met through several schemes both within a basin and outside over two centuries, and how this has further aggravated due to domestic and industrial pollution, causing a severe threat to the ecology and environment of the entire river basins, with the lens of interdisciplinary approach.

Synoptic view of chapters

This book consists of seven chapters. The second chapter captures the history of irrigation development and management in Coimbatore district of Madras Presidency during the pre-colonial, colonial and post-colonial period spanning over the late eighteenth to the early twenty-first century (1800–2017). While the first section deals with pre-colonial period, i.e. until 1800, the second section analyses irrigation management during the colonial period (1800–1947). The third section discusses the various facets of irrigation development during the post-independence period (1947–2017), and the last section ends with the concluding observations. In short, it presents a critical appraisal of irrigation development and management in Coimbatore district and how that has been neglected over the period. Also, it looks at the water conservation initiatives undertaken during the post-independence period, like watershed development programmes, water-harvesting technologies, drip and sprinkle irrigation and other measures like pollution control mechanism for efficient water management.

The third chapter attempts to analyse the emergence of competing demand for water resulting in diversion of basin waters to meet the requirements of the increasing population, urban domestic water supply and industrial needs and its consequential damages on the ecology and environment both in Bhavani and in Noyyal River basins of Tamil Nadu (1881–2017). It examines the impact on ecology, environment and public health besides the fauna and flora of these regions along with the emergence of a 'water market' in the basin areas. Further, it also analyses how the state has played the role of an active facilitator of the bourgeoning demand for water, thereby neglecting the ecology and environment of these river basins. On the one hand, it diverts water from the Bhavani River basin to the pollution-causing industries, despite the region facing acute water scarcity. On the other hand, the diverted water is again let into the river and water bodies due to an ineffective pollution control regime. The environmental degradation of Noyyal River basin should ring alarm bells. In short, this chapter examines the factors which have led to the proliferation of demand for water, bleeding the basins, and the consequence of environmental damages that not only created 'water market' but also poses a grave threat to the ecology, environment and people in the Bhavani and Noyyal River basins since the late nineteenth century to the early twenty-first century (1881–2017).

The fourth chapter is an analysis of the origins of water diversion for domestic and industrial water supply and pollution and emerging conflicts between the different sectors, viz. urban people, municipalities, farmers, Public Works Department and state, in the Bhavani and Noyyal River basins during the study period. It also elucidates the government policies on water diversion besides exploring the various facets of inter-basin water diversion, including their impact. This chapter also attempts to look at the origin and extension of water diversion for industries and the government policy in this regard. It also provides an account of water conflicts in the agricultural sector due to water diversion for industries since the late nineteenth cenntury.

The fifth chapter examines in a historical perspective (1930–70) canal irrigation, technology and water conflicts that have occurred due to technological transformation in water-lifting devices (viz. electric and oil-engine pumpsets) in the agricultural sector in the old Kalingarayan channel and new Lower Bhavani Project Canal of the Bhavani River basin in Tamil Nadu. It discusses the consequences of technological transformation leading to water conflicts between the head-reach and tail-end farmers during the colonial and post-colonial periods. It also analyses the role of the political executive in these conflicts. Further, it looks into the government policies and the role of the judiciary in resolving these conflicts.

The sixth chapter presents an analysis of the disasters of linking rivers and their adverse consequences on the environment and other serious issues. In most of the river basins, the prevailing widespread water scarcity has led to numerous conflicts among farmers in the basins as well as in the delta regions across the state. These conflicts are getting aggravated manifold due to the surging demand from different users. With the decline of water quality, caused by pollution, the problem has now reached an alarming level. It is argued that linking of rivers would further complicate the crisis by bringing in a host of new problems having a bearing on international relations, state autonomy, centre-state relations, ecology, environment and displacement. It contends that rather than managing the water resources within the basin by reviving the traditional tanks and ponds through appropriate strategies, inter-basin and intra-basin diversions will not be a lasting solution for water problems and sustainability of water resources. Instead, it would only fuel more conflicts between neighbouring countries and states; threaten state autonomy; and affect ecology, environment and marginalized communities. Given the macro-level picture, this chapter also analyses the issues and problems pertaining to diverting water from east-flowing rivers and the conflicts between Kerala and Tamil Nadu, particularly in the Western Ghats region, during the post-independence period. The last chapter ends with the conclusion.

2

Hydrology, Commercialization and Ecology

This chapter analyses the history of irrigation development as well as commercialization of agriculture and its impact on ecology in Coimbatore district of Madras Presidency during the pre-colonial, colonial and post-colonial periods, starting from the late eighteenth century to the early twenty-first century (1800–2017). Here some important questions are raised as to whether the colonial administration has maintained the traditional irrigation systems like tanks and canals or neglected them. Many studies have revealed that the colonial agenda was to extract more revenue from the canals and tanks, the traditional irrigation sources. Be that as it may, government policies towards irrigation in post-independent India and their impact in Coimbatore region of Tamil Nadu too require rigorous scrutiny. What kind of changes it had brought to the region's hydrology has to be necessarily assessed from the standpoint of environmental sustainability together with ecological balance. As such, the core question of the chapter is how hydrology has been dealt with by the colonial and post-colonial governments and its impact. The chapter consists of five sections. The first section deals with the pre-colonial period, i.e. until 1800. The second section analyses how the colonial government dealt with hydrology, undermining the traditional irrigation system, and encouraged irrigation modernization as a commercial enterprise (1800–1947). The third section sums up the development of various irrigation projects and their ecological impact during the post-independence period (1947–2017), and the last section ends with the concluding observations.

Pre-Colonial Irrigation System

In Coimbatore district, irrigation was largely dependent upon the monsoon and supported by channels, tanks and wells. The wetland was irrigated either by channels or by tanks, and garden land was irrigated mainly by wells.[1] Two rivers, viz. Bhavani and Amaravathi, were the main sources of irrigation in the district. The Bhavani in Satyamangalam and Erode taluks and the Amaravathi in Udumalpet, Dharapuram and Karur taluks are the most important sources of irrigation. In other words, irrigation sources were banking upon the monsoon despite it being scanty. While the rivers are sustained by the southwest monsoon, the rain-fed tanks and jungle streams are being fed by northeast monsoon.[2] Development of canals, tanks and wells were there but only to a limited extent in those days. Even the limited sources were not properly maintained due to the frequent wars between the rulers and natural calamities like floods. Several tanks and canals got breached due to floods and were left abandoned for years together. Let us see the different irrigation sources that existed during the pre-colonial period or at the time of colonial intervention in Coimbatore district.

Canal Irrigation

Coimbatore district is endowed with five major river basins, viz. Cauvery, Bhavani, Noyyal, Amaravathi and Aliyar, with the first irrigating Karur taluk; the second Bhavani and Erode taluks; the third Coimbatore and Palladam taluks; the fourth Udamalpet, Dharapuram and Karur taluks; and the last one Pollachi taluk. The district has forty-six canals, of which three are of Bhavani, three from Cauvery, twelve from Noyyal, twenty-two from Amaravathi and six from Aliyar. The three channels from Cauvery are Pugalur (12 miles), Vangal (9 miles) and Nerur (10 miles), all accounting for a total length of about 31 miles. Three canals from Bhavani River are Arakankottai (20 miles), Tadapalli (48 miles), and Kalingarayan (57 miles), with a combined length of about 125 miles. The Kodiveri dam across the Bhavani near Gobichettipalayam was constructed by Kongalvan in the year 1125 AD with two channels, viz. Arakankottai on the northern side and Thadapalli on the southern side. Kalingarayan canal was constructed during the thirteenth century, by the Kongu chieftain Kalingarayan. Actually, of the five canals in the Bhavani River, two from Nerinjipet *anicut* which have got breached before colonial intervention remained unrestored.[3] There are twelve canals in Noyyal River, with a total length of about 37 miles, and in Amaravathi River there are twenty-two canals, with a length of about 176 miles. In Aliyar River there are six channels, totalling for a length of about 39 miles (Table 2.1). Except five or six canals, all other channels irrigate less than 100 acres. Those irrigating less than that are from Noyyal, Amaravathi and Aliyar.

Table 2.1 Number and length of Canals in Cauvery, Bhavani, Noyyal, Amaravathi and Aliyar Rivers in Coimbatore district: 1880

Sl. No.	Name of the canal	Length M-C	Irrigated area in acres
Cauvery River			
1.	Pugalur Channel	12-0	1,952
2.	Vengal Channel	9-0	979
3.	Nerur Channel	10-0	1,630
Total	3	**31-0**	**4,561**
Bhavani River			
1.	Tadapalli Channel	48-0	13,650
2.	Arkankottai Channel	20-22	4,118
3.	Kalingarayan Channel	57-0	9,026
Total	3	**125-22**	**26,794**
Noyyal River			
1.	Puthukadu Channel	2-0	473
2.	Chitrachavadi Channel	7-0	1,902
3.	Kaniyamuthur Channel	8-0	521
4.	Coimbatore Channel	2-0	210
5.	Kuruchi Channel	2-0	51
6.	Vellalur Channel	4-0	286
7.	Singanallur Channel	2-0	412
8.	Oddarpalaiyam Channel	3-0	500
9.	Irugur Channel	2-0	284
10.	Sulur Channel	1-0	230
11.	Rasipalaiyam Channel	2-0	403
12.	Muthapur Channel	2-0	246
Total	12	**37-0**	
Amaravathi River			
1.	Kallapuram Channel	10-	1,129
2.	Karaumaralingam Channel	10-25	1,567
3.	Kannadiputhur Channel	7-10	532
4.	Sholamadevi Channel	4-10	490
5.	Kadathur Channel	8-9	975
6.	Kaniyur Channel	5-10	261

(Continued)

Sl. No.	Name of the canal	Length M-C	Irrigated area in acres
7.	Karatholuvu Channel	9-5	439
8.	Alangayam Channel	7-20	991
9.	Dalavypatnam Channel	7-13	792
10.	Dharapuram Channel	15-10	2,320
11.	Kolinjivadi Channel	8-45	758
12.	Nanjaitalaiyur Channel	3-56	237
13.	Chinnadarapuram Channel	13-26	1,798
14.	Sundakaypalaiyam Channel	5-6	106
15.	Nanjaikalakurichi Channel	6-26	300
16.	Pallapalayam Channel	17-49	3,308
17.	Tirumanallur Channel	8-25	782
18.	Balambapuram Channel	7-30	578
19.	Panchamadevi Channel	6-41	335
20.	Sanaparetti Channel	5-13	548
21.	Puliyur Channel	8-13	1,178
22.	Koyampalli Channel	3-30	814
Total	22	176-72	20,238
Aliyar River			
1.	Athur Channel	3-0	203
2.	Pallivelangal Channel	5-0	540
3.	Ariapuram Channel	8-0	971
4.	Karapatti Channel	7-0	551
5.	Perianai Channel	11-0	1,777
6.	Vadagalur Channel	5-0	592
	6	39	4,634

Note: M = Mile; C = Chain. One chain is equal to twenty-two yards. One yard is equal to three feet, and one foot is equal to twelve inches.

Source: F. A. Nicholson, *Manual of the Coimbatore District in the Presidency of Madras* (Madras: The Government Press, 1887), 538–40.

Tanks

During the pre-colonial period, there were more than 500 tanks in Coimbatore district. Most of them were rain-fed tanks, and even prior to the advent of the colonial era, they were not maintained properly. According to Buchanan (1807), 'In the Coleagala district (Kollegal taluk), there were between forty and fifty reservoirs, which about eighty years ago were put in good order by the *Dalawai of Mysore, Doda Déva Ráya Wodear.* From that time until the country has come into the Company's possession, after the fall of *Seringapatam,* they have been neglected'.[4] He further says, in Singanaluru (Singanallore), 'There are many large tanks; but these not having been yet repaired, there is at present very little rice cultivated'[5] Several tanks were to be repaired. Precisely, though a large number of tanks have existed in Coimbatore district, they remained neglected and unmaintained since the pre-colonial period.

Wells

In the Madras Presidency, most of the districts outside delta region are largely dependent upon tanks for irrigation, 'with the exception of Coimbatore where unusual facilities for well construction and markedly low rainfall operate against their extension'.[6] Prior to colonial intervention, there were only very few wells and their depth too was very low. About 18,000 wells were in existence in Coimbatore district at that time, supporting irrigation to a limited extent. Needless to say that irrigation management was very poor then as cultivation was solely dependent upon the scanty monsoon.

Irrigation Management during the Colonial Period (1800–1947)

Since the early nineteenth century, the colonial administration accorded priority to generate more revenue by developing irrigation infrastructure through building large dams. 'The interest of the British Government in increasing public investment in irrigation was to gain higher revenue'.[7] 'The colonial rulers in their pursuit of high returns/profits totally neglected minor irrigation works which were developed by the native rulers. Even the maintenance of these works, let alone establishing new ones etc, was not of any priority'.[8] The colonial government 'used all possible ways to extract maximum revenue in the name of irrigation development'.[9] The British government encountered a series of financial crises after constructing major irrigation works on Godavari, Krishna, Cauvery and Pennar Rivers during the second half of the nineteenth century. Consequently, it favoured private entities to develop new irrigation projects. In 1859, Madras Irrigation Canal Company (MICC) was approved by the East India Company.[10] Initially, the Madras Irrigation Canal Company came with two proposals, viz. Thungabhadra and Coimbatore projects. The Government of Madras approved the Thungabhadra project, while the other one was to be considered after the completion of the former.[11] Since the Thungabhadra project was a failure, the Coimbatore project was never attempted by the MICC. Finally, MICC projects were taken over by the Government of Madras in 1882. Consequently, during the second half of the nineteenth century, no major project was undertaken by the government. In the process, they neglected the tanks and the age-old irrigation management system like *kudimaramattu*. The *Kudimaramattu* system varied from basin to basin and also within the basin. Though it was recognized in all the taluks in Coimbatore district, the system has all but practically fallen into disuse.[12]

In Coimbatore district, rainfall was scanty and erratic. In sixty-two years of the nineteenth century, from 1803 to 1865, nine years had very bad rainfall, forty years unfavourable, only eleven years favourable and the remainder two years excessive.[13] A series of drought hit Coimbatore district in 1837–38, 1846–47, 1857–58, 1866–67 and 1877–78.[14] Rainfall was meagre, and for about sixty years from 1870 to 1930, the average rainfall variation among the months and the annual rainfall was about 32.8 inches (Table 2.2).

Due to the frequent droughts and other natural calamities, people used to migrate to other parts of the country. For instance, 391 persons migrated in 1884, and 134 ryots of Dharapuram migrated to Thungabhadra region.[15] As such, the

Table 2.2 Month-wise average rainfall in Coimbatore district for sixty years: 1870–1930

Months	Average rainfall (in inches)
January	0.59
February	0.48
March	0.72
April	2.08
May	3.68
June	2.81
July	3.25
August	3.17
September	3.52
October	6.79
November	4.45
December	1.33
Whole year	32.87

Source: A. R. Cox, *Statistical Appendix and Supplement to the Revised District Manual (1898) for Coimbatore District* (Madras: Government Press, 1933), 88–89.

farmers of different regions started demanding extension of irrigation facilities to Coimbatore district. For instance, 'the ryots of Periapalayam (Erode) suggested a short channel from near Tirupur to their tank ... the ryots of Palatoluvu (Erode) also suggest[ed] a channel from the Vadugapalaiyam anicut'.[16] Faced with severe drought, farmers asked for extending canal irrigation during the late nineteenth century. Let us see the development of various irrigation sources during the colonial period.

Occupied Area of Different Kinds of Lands

Until the mid-nineteenth century, only a limited extent of land was occupied in Coimbatore district. For example, in 1821, about 12.75 lakh acres of land was occupied and it has increased marginally to 14.11 lakhs in 1851. In other words, the occupation of land has not witnessed any significant growth during the first half of the nineteenth century. But the situation has changed dramatically since the second half of the nineteenth century. Though the Nilgiris was formed as a separate district in 1868, the occupied area has increased drastically in Coimbatore district. In 1875, the occupied area has gone up to 26.86 lakh acres. However, it reduced to 22.53 lakh acres in 1881 (Table 2.3). This decline may be attributed to the famine that occurred in 1875–77. The total cultivated area has not changed much till the mid-twentieth century (see Tables 2.7 and 2.8).

Since the early nineteenth century, the occupied lands of Coimbatore district were classified into three categories, viz. wetland, garden land and dry land. In 1821, the total occupied land was about 1,274,880 acres, of which, 56,232 acres, constituting 4.41 per cent, was classified as wetlands, 139,770 acres as garden lands (10.96 per cent) and the rest of 1,077,057 acres as dry land (84.48 per cent). In 1851,

Table 2.3 Occupied area of different kinds of lands in Coimbatore district: 1821–81 (in acres)

Year	Wetland	Per cent	Garden land	Per cent	Dry land	Per cent	Total
1821	56,232	4.41	139,770	10.96	1,077,057	84.48	1,274,880
1851	66,482	4.71	169,925	12.04	1,173,130	83.12	1,411,388
1875	89,708	3.89	–	–	2,217,327	96.11	2,686,268
1881	85,794	3.81	–	–	2,167,259	96.19	2,253,053

Source: F. A. Nicholson, *Manual of the Coimbatore District in the Presidency of Madras* (Madras: The Government Press, 1887), 287.

the occupied land of different categories more or less remained the same. Since 1864, garden land too was classified as dry land. The total occupied land in 1875 increased to 2,686,268 acres, of which about 3.89 per cent was classified as wetlands and the rest 96.11 per cent as dry lands (Table 2.3). Since the late nineteenth century, more and more land was occupied, and most of them belonged to the category of dry lands. In other words, while more and more area was brought under cultivation, the proportion of irrigated land has not increased. Consequently, the percentage of wetlands declined from 4.41 per cent in 1821 to 3.81 per cent in 1881. Here, it should be also pointed out that there was an expansion of area under irrigation because of considerable development of the existing canal irrigation system.

Canal Irrigation

Since the early nineteenth century, the colonial government has emphasized expansion of the old canal irrigation system and highlighted the importance of better water management. The three canals that were there in Coimbatore district at that time were Tadapalli, Arakankottai and Kalingarayan (62 miles long) from the Bhavani River. During the last quarter of the nineteenth century, three proposals were placed for the expansion of irrigation facilities. One was construction of a dam across the Bhavani near Satyamangalam to irrigate more than 50,000 acres in Palladam, Dharapuram and downstream of the Amaravathi River. The second was at Muttikkulam or Siruvani project to divert water through a tunnel to irrigate the upper part of the Noyyal River as well as to provide water supply to Coimbatore town. And the third one was extension of Kalingarayan canal to expand irrigation supply for an additional 13,000 acres.[17] While extending the existing canals, better water management was emphasized by regulating/limiting water distribution points, i.e. sluices. For instance, in the fifty-seven-mile-long Kalingarayan canal, the irrigation area was about 8,866 acres with 1,840 sluices, i.e. on an average, one sluice for 4.8 acres.[18] The Public Works Department (PWD) proposed to increase irrigation facilities to 46,752 acres during the last quarter of the nineteenth century.[19] Consequently, an attempt was made to regulate the number of sluices. The Nerinjippettai *anicut* built by the Mysore king got breached at the close of the eighteenth century, but the attempt to revive the project was abandoned in the 1880s.[20] However, the canal-irrigated area which got increased to 79,955 acres in 1892/93 had further gone up to 84,479 in 1929/30 despite Karur taluk being transferred to Tiruchirappalli district in 1910. Since the last quarter of the nineteenth century, creation of new irrigation sources together with the expansion of old irrigation facilities have gained momentum along with better water management.

Tank Irrigation

In Coimbatore district, there were two types of tank irrigation system, one was stream-fed and the other rain-fed.

Stream-Fed Tanks

The district was endowed with two series of stream-fed tanks, viz. the Appagudal series of Bhavani taluk, with their source from Bargur hills, and Dhali series of Udumalpet taluk, having Anaimalai hills for sustenance.[21] The later one turned dead due to the denudation of Bollampatti forests for the fuel-wood and timber supply to Coimbatore city and its neighbourhood during the late nineteenth century.[22] Consequently, these rain-fed tank wetland areas were transferred as dry lands during the settlement in the 1880s. For, the colonial administration was not interested in maintaining the stream-fed tanks. According to Nicholson (1887:381), 'They are all much silted; beyond strengthening the bunds, replacing the revetments where necessary, and repairing the sluices, little can be done; money spent is too often wasted'. Precisely, stream-fed tanks were neglected by the colonial administration.

Rain-Fed Tanks

A large number of rain-fed tanks have existed in Coimbatore district. According to Buchanan (1807), in Kollegal taluk forty or fifty tanks were in good order until 1720 but were ruined during the second half of the eighteenth century.[23] He further adds, 'I passed through the grounds of only one of these decayed reservoirs, and found them entirely waste'.[24] In the government's view 'it is almost useless to spend money on mere rain-fed tanks in the open country'.[25] In other words, 'It would be utter waste of money to provide storage for a flood that occurs once in a lifetime'.[26] This clearly indicates that the traditional tanks have been neglected by the colonial administration from the early nineteenth century onwards. Rationalizing this, Nicholson (1887:381) explains:

> The channels are in for repair, but require an immense amount of improvement; anicuts and retaining walls need attention, beds required clearing, sectioning, and reducing to a uniform level and fall; blasting is often required in beds; head works and sand sluices are to be built; escapes to be screw-shuttered and made water-tight; field sluices to be regulated and built; aqueducts, siphons or masonry kolvays (escapes) for the passage of surface streams to be constructed or improved; banks to be strengthened, new cuts to be made, and so forth.

In 1881–82, there were 161 tanks in Coimbatore district, of which, 70 were river-fed (37 major and 23 minor) and 91 rain-fed (16 major and 75 minor).[27] In the Bhavani taluk, a large ruined tank known as Swayamvara Eri, Kolatur tank, and four other tanks besides the one above Kolatur tank had been used for irrigation earlier but have been breached by flood and left unrepaired.[28] The Appagudal series of stream-fed tanks in Bhavani taluk were sustained by the various petty streams from the Bargur hills and the tanks get filled up usually during the northeast monsoon.[29] The Dhali series is fed by streams from the Anaimalais. In 1892/93, there were 156 tanks in Coimbatore district, irrigating over 12,099 acres, and the cultivated area has gone up to 19,798 acres despite the transfer of Karur taluk to Tiruchirappalli district in 1910.

Spring Channels

In Palladam taluk, spring channels were once important sources of irrigation but they lost their importance since the early nineteenth century. This can be 'directly attributable [sic] to the denudation of the Bolampatti forests'.[30] Consequently, the erstwhile wetlands in Palladam have become dry lands.

Wells

The number of wells in Coimbatore district has risen progressively since the early nineteenth century: from 22,000 in 1800, 28,719 in 1821, 35,107 in 1852 to 58,385 in 1882.[31] In the thirty years from 1857 to 1887, about 26,000 new wells have been dug at a cost of Rs. 65–70 lakhs.[32] Of the 65,461 wells in 1890s, 63,025 were in good condition and the remaining 2,436 were out of repair.[33] In addition to that, there were 2,912 wells in wetlands. These wells had one to three lifts depending upon the size and water supply.[34] Invariably, water lift was the single-bucket cattle lift (*yettam*), the *picotta* or basket used for shallow lifts from channels or pools.[35] In 1929/30, the number of wells swelled to 86,207. And, about one-fourth of the well irrigated area of Madras Presidency was in Coimbatore district during the early twentieth century.[36] Since then, the government has encouraged farmers to dig new wells and repair the old ones by providing credit facilities.

In 1892–93, land under irrigation was 372,444 acres or about 14 per cent of cultivated area. Of this, 272,354 acres, or 73.17 per cent, was dependent upon wells, 79,955 acres, or 21.47 per cent, from government canals and 12,099 acres, or 3.25 per cent, from tanks (Table 2.4).

Table 2.4 Different sources of irrigation and irrigated lands in Coimbatore district: 1892–93

Taluks	Government canals		Private canals		Tanks		Wells		Other sources	Total
	No	ACS	No	ACS	No	ACS	No.	ACS	ACS	ACS
Bhavani	–	19			22	1,203	4,084	14,830	657	16,709
Coimbatore	4	9,643			33	675	5,445	26,282	2,533	39,133
Dharapuram	6	8,201			2	244	10,299	47,319	712	56,476
Erode	1	11,251			18	478	11,138	33,195	388	45,312
Karur	12	18,240			3	880	8,564	24,117	178	43,415
Kollegal		1,853		588	18	4,496	69	69	42	7,048
Palladam	3	2,058			34	1,703	10,382	63,311	9	67,081
Pollachi	6	4,742		454	4	493	4,268	13,608	326	19,623
Satyamangalam	6	17,919			6	113	7,649	22,632	711	41,375
Udamalpet	13	6,029		1,249	16	1,814	3,553	27,171	9	36,272
Total	59	79,955		2,291	156	12,099	65,461	272,534	5,565	372,444

Source: F. A. Nicholson, *Manual of the Coimbatore District in the Presidency of Madras*, Vol. II (Madras: The Government Press, 1898), 185, 530.

Between 1909 and 1929, there were 1,378 applications to sink new wells and 816 applications for repairing existing wells and the sanctioned amount was Rs. 869,598 and Rs. 321,102, respectively (Table 2.5).

On 15 November 1910, Karur taluk was transferred to Tiruchirappalli district. The erstwhile Satayamangalam taluk was renamed as Gobichettipalayam taluk and new taluk Avinashi was formed.[37] Though the Kaniyampalaiyam *anicut* in Gobichettipalayam taluk was on the list of irrigation sources, its registered *ayacut* has been classified as dry.[38] In 1929–30, there was 466,380 acres of land being irrigated in Coimbatore district. Of this, 353,629 acres, or 75.8 per cent, was from wells, 83,980 acres, or 18 per cent, from government canals and 19,798 acres, or 4.2 per cent, from tanks (Table 2.6).

Besides carrying out extension of existing canals, the colonial administration encouraged private investments in wells. Consequently, the irrigated area has increased remarkably between the late nineteenth and early twentieth centuries. For example, the area under canal irrigation, which was about 61,715 acres (excluding Karur taluk) in 1892–93, increased to 83,980 acres in 1929–30. In other words, irrigation was extended to more than 22,000 acres through

Table 2.5 Credit facilities to sink new wells and repair old wells in Coimbatore district: 1909–29

Taluks	No. of applications for new wells		No. of applications for repairs	
	No. of wells	Amount	No. of wells	Amount
Bhavani	66	30,470	–	–
Coimbatore	182	169,350	–	–
Avanashi	88	51,035	408	149,547
Tirupur	220	150,641	131	63,110
Dharapuram	257	132,183	–	–
Erode	111	52,345	–	–
Gopichettipalayam	114	62,570	227	96,825
Kollegal	61	24,275	50	11,620
Pollachi	86	58,120	–	–
Udamalpet	193	138,609	–	–
Total	1,378	869,598	816	321,102

Source: A. R. Cox, *Statistical Appendix and Supplement to the Revised District Manual (1898) for Coimbatore District* (Madras: Government Press, 1933), 172.

Table 2.6 Different sources of irrigation and irrigated lands in Coimbatore district: 1929–30

Taluks	Government canals	Tanks	Wells		Other sources	Total
	ACS	ACS	No.	ACS	ACS	ACS
Bhavani	1	583	7,125	21,970	800	23,354
Coimbatore	5,738	7,598	5,061	24,910	109	38,355
Tirupur	2,120	1,081	12,407	69,239	–	72,440
Erode	23,501	1,003	15,928	55,000	586	79,590
Avinashi	2,658	945	8,500	33,879	218	37,700
Kollegal	1,958	3,564	305	674	74	6,270
Dharapuram	14,642	298	17,460	67,050	2,738	84,728
Pollachi	6,488	783	5,151	12,278	3,808	23,808
Gobichettipalayam	19,857	716	8,955	31,081	565	52,219
Udamalpet	7,516	3,227	5,315	37,098	62	47,916
Total	84,479	19,798	86,207	353,629	8,960	466,380

Source: A. R. Cox, *Statistical Appendix and Supplement to the Revised District Manual (1898) for Coimbatore District* (Madras: Government Press, 1933), 170.

the old canals. Similarly, the number of wells too rose remarkably during the same period. For instance, in 1892–93, there were only 56,897 irrigation wells in Coimbatore district (excluding Karur taluk), but it increased to 86,207 in 1929–30.

Cropping Pattern

Due to the limited irrigation sources, the farmers who remained at the mercy of monsoon predominantly cultivated food grains. The prominent food grains were: Cholam, Kambu, Ragi, pulses and other cotton products. Food grains, pulses, oilseeds and cotton accounted for 90 per cent of the crops (Tables 2.7 and 2.8). As extension of irrigation facilities was limited to a certain extent since the late nineteenth century, there was no major change in the cropping pattern during the early twentieth century. The same food grains, pulses, oilseeds and cotton continued to be the major crops. Of course, a few additional crops were cultivated but only to a limited extent. In other words, there was no major initiative to expand irrigation infrastructure in Coimbatore district during the entire colonial period.

Table 2.7 Cropping pattern in Coimbatore district: 1881

Crops	Area under each crop (in acres)	Per cent of total cropped area
Paddy	86,562	3.92
Cholam	562,984	25.49
Kambu	690,439	31.26
Ragi	197,731	8.95
Varagu	5,751	0.26
Thenei	29,154	1.32
Samei or Millet	66,923	3.03
Sugarcane	3,890	0.18
Cotton	230,355	10.43
Gingelly oilseed	26,367	1.19
Lamb oilseed	20,021	0.91
Horse gram	170,403	7.72
Tobacco	19,810	0.90
Chillies	9,252	0.42
Plantains	2,403	0.11
Turmeric	874	0.04
Coconut	3,439	0.16
Janappu or Sunn Hemp	299	0.01
Wheat	2,642	0.12
Total area cultivated	2,208,547	100.00

Source: F. A. Nicholson, *Manual of the Coimbatore District in the Presidency of Madras* (Madras: The Government Press, 1887), 585.

Irrigation during the post-independence period (1947–2017)

During the post-independence period, competing demand for water increased remarkably due to population growth, urbanization, agricultural expansion, industrialization and domestic water supply, with the last two factors aggravating industrial pollution and domestic wastewater – the prime causes for contamination of both surface and groundwater in Coimbatore district. While agricultural expansion has led to the expansion of canal irrigation, rapid increase in the number of wells and borewells have resulted in the decline of water table. Major changes that were witnessed in the irrigation system in the

Table 2.8 Area cultivated with the chief food and non-food crops in Coimbatore district: 1920/21–1950/51 (in acres)

Crops	1920–21		1925–26		1930–31		1935–36		1940–41		1945–46		1950–51	
	Area under each crop	Per cent of total cropped area	Area under each crop	Per cent of total cropped area	Area under each crop	Per cent of total cropped area	Area under each crop	Per cent of total cropped area	Area under each crop	Per cent of total cropped area	Area under each crop	Per cent of total cropped area	Area under each crop	Per cent of total cropped area
Paddy	9,520	0.51	108,400	5.07	99,600	4.84	101,010	4.91	99,600	4.96	128,320	6.23	141,330	7.55
Cholam	534,000	28.72	573,700	26.83	478,000	23.21	492,000	23.93	521,000	25.97	546,000	26.50	466,000	24.90
Kambu	512,200	27.55	427,000	19.97	427,000	20.73	387,100	18.83	335,200	16.71	297,400	14.43	263,000	14.05
Ragi	195,350	10.51	204,000	9.54	152,000	7.38	151,500	7.37	149,200	7.44	174,600	8.47	155,000	8.28
Varagu	7,850	0.42	7,800	0.36	7,828	0.38	9,600	0.47	5,000	0.25	6,810	0.33	9,390	0.50
Thenei	22,650	1.22	19,600	0.92	10,000	0.49	27,800	1.35	19,000	0.95	26,800	1.30	25,400	1.36
Samei or Millet	121,250	6.52	95,000	4.44	75,000	3.64	72,900	3.55	70,000	3.49	71,100	3.45	60,200	3.22
Bengal gram	6,050	0.33	4,600	0.22	4,000	0.19	5,260	0.26	3,930	0.20	2,920	0.14	3,370	0.18
Horse-gram	–	–	229,400	10.73	222,000	10.78	218,000	10.60	168,000	8.37	198,000	9.61	197,000	10.53
Gingelly	22,450	1.21	23,500	1.10	40,000	1.94	38,100	1.85	36,000	1.79	46,200	2.24	36,600	1.96
Groundnut	77,400	4.16	89,000	4.16	158,000	7.67	158,000	7.68	175,000	8.72	184,000	8.93	224,000	11.97
Castor	22,200	1.19	15,700	0.73	9,000	0.44	9,090	0.44	8,170	0.41	6,650	0.32	5,800	0.31
Sugarcane	9,700	0.52	9,800	0.46	8,000	0.39	7,340	0.36	7,140	0.36	10,800	0.52	15,190	0.81
Cotton	287,000	15.43	300,000	14.03	336,000	16.32	348,000	16.93	379,000	18.89	333,000	16.16	241,680	12.91
Tobacco	31,800	1.71	31,000	1.45	33,000	1.60	30,300	1.47	30,000	1.50	27,900	1.35	27,700	1.48
Total Cropped Area	1,859,420	100.00	2,138,500	100.00	2,059,428	100.00	2,056,000	100.00	2,006,240	100.00	2,060,500	100.00	1,871,660	100.00

Sources: B. S. Baliga, *Madras District Gazetteers: Coimbatore* (Madras: Government Press, 1960), 269–70; A. R. Cox, *Statistical Appendix and Supplement to the Revised District Manual (1898) for Coimbatore District* (Madras: Government Press, 1933), 81–85.

region were due to electrification and borewell technology, besides expansion of canals. Electrification and other technological advancement in the agricultural sector facilitated extraction of more and more water for irrigation. The popular vote bank politics like subsidized power encouraged the farmers to extract both surface and groundwater over the last four decades. Industrialization too has spurred the demand for water invariably in different parts of the district, particularly Coimbatore, Tirupur and Erode cities/towns. The ever-increasing demand for domestic water supply grew manifold due to the tremendous growth of population, urbanization – towns and villages during this period. For example, proportion of urban population in the district rose sharply from 32.93 lakhs in 1951[39] to 81.89 lakhs (present Coimbatore, Erode and Tirupur districts) in 2011. In 1951, 26.40 lakhs (80.17 per cent) lived in the rural areas with the rest 6.53 lakhs (19.83 per cent) in urban areas.[40] Interestingly, this trend has changed drastically during the subsequent decades. In 2011, about two-third of the population was in the urban areas. Increasing urbanization has led to phenomenal rise for domestic water supply. In addition to the growing demand from the agricultural and industrial sectors and domestic water supply, pollution caused by the industries and wastewater generated on the domestic front further aggravated the scarce resources of both surface and groundwater. To meet the increasing demand from the different sectors, water was diverted very close from the upstream basin and that was used/polluted, resulting not only in the decline of water table but also contamination of both surface and groundwater. Consequently, the option for quality of water has almost closed due to ineffective management. As such, the impending crisis became inevitable. Let us see the development of irrigation in the erstwhile Coimbatore district during the post-independence period.

Geographical boundaries

Geographical boundaries of Coimbatore district have changed during the post-independence period, particularly due to the reorganization of linguistic states in 1956 and following bifurcation of the districts within the state. In 1956, Kollegal and Palakkad taluks were transferred to Mysore and Kerala states, respectively. In 1979, Periyar district (Erode district) was formed and it comprised six taluks of Bhavani, Gobichettipalayam, Sathyamangalam, Erode, Perundurai and Dharapuram. In 2009, Tirupur district was formed after the bifurcation of Coimbatore district. For the analysis, the present districts of Coimbatore, Erode and Tirupur have been taken into account.

Land use pattern of Coimbatore district

Land utilization trend in Coimbatore district has changed during the post-independence period. Barren and uncultivable land, cultivable waste and permanent pastures have constantly witnessed a sharp decline during the last four and a half decades. In other words, the common property resources mentioned above started vanishing at an alarming rate during this period. At the same time, there was a quantum leap in turning cultivable land for non-agricultural purposes due to the ever-expanding process of urbanization and other development activities. Buildings, roads, canals and industrial plants occupied vast tracts of lands besides those put under non-agricultural use. Ironically, the area being categorized as other fallow lands increased, particularly during the post-green revolution period. The technology-driven green revolution has not only led to scarcity of water resources but also resulted in the increase of fallow lands since the early twenty-first century. Further, the area under the forest cover started declining during this period, which also saw the slow but steady elimination of common property resources in the district.

The net-cultivated area declined from 70,453 ha (45.03 per cent) in 1960–61 to 65,040 ha (41.37 per cent) in 1980–81 and then to 62,475 ha (39.95 per cent) in 2004/05. In other words, over the four and a half decades, the cultivated area shrunk over 11.32 per cent in the district. Other fallow land, which declined from 4.06 per cent in 1960–61 to 1.95 per cent in 1980–81, increased remarkably to 15.04 per cent during the early twenty-first century. The area under current fallow land which had increased till the 1980s reduced in the early twenty-first century (Table 2.9). Since the 1980s, the net-cultivated area registering a decline

Table 2.9 Trends of land utilization in Coimbatore district: 1960–2000 (in hectares)

Classification	1960–61	Per cent	1980–81	Per cent	2004–05	Per cent	Growth rate
Forests	394,077	25.20	388,597	24.70	387,365	24.78	−1.70
Barren & uncultivable land	43,073	2.75	19,316	1.23	17,218	1.10	−60.03
Land put to non-agri. use	62,827	4.02	136,918	8.70	182,324	11.66	190.20
Cultivable waste	50,401	3.22	6,496	0.41	3,362	0.22	−93.33

(continued)

Classification	1960–61	Per cent	1980–81	Per cent	2004–05	Per cent	Growth rate
Permanent pasture	21,308	1.36	8,620	0.55	1,324	0.08	−93.79
Misc. tree crops	6,497	0.42	13,847	0.88	5,773	0.37	−11.14
Current fallows	217,970	13.94	317,849	20.20	106,376	6.80	−51.20
Others fallows	63,437	4.06	30,665	1.95	235,053	15.04	270.53
Net area cultivated	704,153	45.03	650,840	41.37	624,475	39.95	−11.32
Total geographical area	1,563,743	100	1,573,148	100	1,563,270	100	−0.03

Source: *Season and Crops Reports* (relevant years).

and the corresponding rise of the fallow lands reveals the impact on irrigation as well as the area put under the non-agricultural use that was on the rise in the district.

Dams and Canal Irrigation

After independence, a large number of dams have been constructed in Coimbatore district. About twenty dams were built between 1947 and 2007, most of them very close to the upstream of the basin in the Western Ghats (Table 2.10). During the post-independence period, about seven lakh hectares of land was brought under irrigation in the district. In this scenario, no further option was available to divert the water, and there is no guarantee to ensure the natural water flow in the river basins. In other words, due to the dams and diversion in different rivers of Coimbatore district, the hydrology of the region was disturbed, resulting in grave damage to the ecology. Further dams have been developed at the upstream of the main rivers, tributaries and sub-basins. Canals accounting for a length of over 200 miles length were developed from the different reservoirs.

In addition to the old canal system, new canals for irrigation were put in place. About 2.5 lakh hectares was brought under the LBP canal. Even in the old canal system, additional area was brought under irrigation by lifting water

Table 2.10 List of dams and their irrigated area in different river basins of Coimbatore district during the post-independence period: 1947–2007

Sl. No.	Name of the dam	River	Year of construction
1.	Bhavani Sagar	Bhavani	1956
2.	Amaravathi	Amaravathi	1958
3.	Thunacadavu	Thunakadavu	1965
4.	Thirumurti	Palar	1967
5.	Pillur	Bhavani	1967
6.	Parambikulam	Parambikulam	1967
7.	Uppar	Uppar	1968
8.	Aliyar	Aliyar	1969
9.	Peruvaripallam	Thunakadavu	1971
10.	Sholaiyar	Chalakudi	1971
11.	Uppar Aliyar	Aliyar	1971
12.	Ponnaniyar	Ponnaniyar	1974
13.	Varathupallam	Varattupallam	1978
14.	Vattamalaikarai Odai	Vattamalaikarai	1978
15.	Gunderipallam	Gunderipallam	1978
16.	Lower Nirar	Nirar	1982
17.	Kadambarai	Kadambarai	1984
18.	Perumpallam		1989
19.	Athupalayam	Noyyal	1992
20.	Orathupalayam	Noyyal	1992
21.	Nallathangal	Nallathangal Odai	2007

Sources: Compiled from various sources.

through electric pumpsets.[41] Amaravathi dam was constructed in 1958, which irrigates about 60,000 acres of land in Tirupur and Karur taluks. There are ten canals in Amaravathi River, of which six are in Tirupur and the rest in Karur. Thirumurthi dam (Udumalpet) was constructed in 1962 primarily for irrigation purposes at the tail-end of Parambikulam-Aliyar system and the length of the canal is about fifty-seven kilometres. Uppar (Erode) dam was constructed in 1968, Sholaiyar dam (Pollachi) in 1971 and Varattu Pallam dam in 1978. In Pollachi, Lower Nirar Dam was constructed in Pollachi in 1982 and Kadamparai

Table 2.11 Area under different sources of irrigation in Coimbatore district: 1960/61–2003/04 (in hectares)

Year	Government canals	Tanks	Wells	Other sources	Total net area irrigated
1960/61	103,666	6,915	143,709	4,984	257,803
1980/81	135,327	5,899	198,183	768	334,191
2003/04	128,906	1,427	230,836	3,219	145,957

Source: *Season and Crops Report* (various years).

Dam in Pollachi in 1984. Athupalayam and Orathupalayam dams in Noyyal river were built in 1992. Orathupalayam dam has an *ayacut* of over 10,000 acres in Tirupur and Karur districts. Noyyal Athupalayam dam storage facility was meant to harness excess flood water flowing down the Noyyal and collect the draining from the Lower Bhavani Project (LBP) canal to irrigate more than 19,000 acres in Karur district.

Following the construction of over twenty dams, the length of canals increased. In 1960–61, the total length of canals the district was 999 km, and it increased to 1,438 km by 1980–81. However, it declined to 1,288 km in 2003–04. The net area irrigated by canals, which was about 103,666 hectares in 1960–61, jumped to 135,327 hectares in 1980–81 (Coimbatore 37,935 and Erode 97,392) but declined marginally to 128,906 hectares in 2004–05 (Coimbatore 46,173 and Erode 82,733). With the increase in the length of canals, the canal-irrigated area has more than doubled (Table 2.11).

Tanks

A number of tanks were not maintained during the nineteenth and twentieth centuries of the colonial era. In 1960–61, there were about 113 tanks in Coimbatore district, which irrigated about 6,915 hectares. In 1980, the number rose to 125, irrigating about 5,899 hectares. But, in 2003–04, though there were 129 tanks (Coimbatore 77 and Erode 52), the area under irrigation came down to about 1,427 hectares (Table 2.11). This declining trend is largely due to lack of maintenance and/or encroachment of both supply and distributive channels.

Wells

There was a proliferation of wells in the district during the post-independence period. In 1960–61, there were 108,897 wells, and they had gone up to 191,594 in 1980–81. For the two decades, their growth rate was about 76 per cent. The number jumped to 239, 539 in 2003–04.

The growth rate of wells in Coimbatore district was about 119.97 per cent between 1960–61 and 2003–04, which is responsible for the steep fall in groundwater table at an alarming rate. Well irrigation increased in the region, particularly after the green revolution. In 1960–61, about 143,709 ha area was under well irrigation and it shot up to 198,183 ha in 1980–81. It further increased to 230,836 ha in 2003–04.

Electric Pumpsets and oil-engines

Mechanization of agriculture witnessed a remarkable increase in the use of electric pumpsets in the district during the post-independence period. For example in 1980–81, the total number of pumpsets and oil-engines for agricultural purposes was about 115,772 and 33,354, respectively. It rose subsequently in the 1990s, and in 2003–04, there were 201,449 electric pumpsets and 18,387 oil-engines.

Borewells

The period also saw a rise in the number of borewells since the 1970s. In 2002–03, there were 30,679 borewells in Coimbatore district (Coimbatore 24,696 and Erode 5,983).

Urbanization and Domestic Water Supply

Urbanization as well as urban agglomeration and towns have expanded at a faster pace due to population growth. In 1951, about 20 per cent of the population lived in urban areas but it was about two-third of the population in 2011, witnessing an increase in the demand for domestic water supply. Coimbatore receives water from two sources, situated at Siruvani and Pilloor, located thirty-six kilometres and ninety-five kilometres from the city, respectively. The daily drawing of water from these sources account for 152 MLD, of which 87 MLD is from Siruvani and 65 MLD from Pilloor. From the Master Service Reservoir, water is distributed to the zonal service reservoirs and from them through distribution mains and the conveying mains. From the conveying main, wayside villages of seven rural village *panchayats*, five urban *panchayats* and ten village *panchayats* are supplied water. The designed capacity of the scheme is 101 MLD, with the current share of supply to Coimbatore Corporation being 87 MLD.

The Pilloor water scheme, commissioned in 1995 with a dam across the river Bhavani in the Western Ghats, was designed to extract 131.25 MLD, of which the share of Coimbatore Corporation stands at 65 MLD. Through the distribution lines, water is supplied to Coimbatore Corporation, town *panchayats*, and 523 rural habitations. Further, there are 436 open wells/borewells in operation to supplement the non-potable water requirement – 250 of them are under private operation and the rest by the Engineering Department, Coimbatore Corporation. Now, rain-water harvesting has been made mandatory for new developments irrespective of usage of the buildings. In addition to this, Siruthuli, an NGO, in association with the corporation, has developed more than 150 rain-water-harvesting structures, along road margins as well as in open spaces to infiltrate rain water into the ground.[42]

Water Supply Scheme to Municipalities and Town *Panchayats*

Water supply has been extended to several municipalities and town *panchayats*, in recent years under the Combined Water Supply Schemes (CWSS). This was implemented with the financial assistance from Minimum Needs Programme, National Bank for Agriculture and Rural Development, the National Rural Drinking Water Programme and Urban Infrastructure Development Scheme for Small and Medium Towns.[43] As on 1 April 2017, water supply scheme was extended to twelve municipalities, ninety-five town *panchayats*, in the present Coimbatore, Erode and Tirupur districts. In 2017, this benefited 5.83 lakh population in twelve municipalities at the rate of 75–139 litres per capita per day (LPCD). The total water supply to the twelve municipalities was about 6.45 million litres per capita per day. About 13.16 lakh people in ninety-five town *panchayats*, get drinking water, though varying from 70 to 200 CPCD. The total water supply to these ninety-five town *panchayats*, was about 14.5 million LPCD. The total water supply to the twelve municipalities and ninety-five town *panchayats*, is about 46.9 million litres per capita per day (Table 2.12). This water diversion has further aggravated the ecology of the basins.

Table 2.12 Water supply scheme of corporation, municipalities and town panchayats of Coimbatore, Erode and Tirupur districts

Sl. No.	Name of towns	Population	Present water supply level LPCD	Total water supply
I Coimbatore District				
		Corporations		
1	Coimbatore	1,050,721	128	134,492,288
		Municipalities		
1	Mettupalayam	69,213	125	8,651,625
2	Pollachi	90,180	104	9,378,720
3	Valparai	70,859	122	8,644,798
	Total	230,252		26,675,143
		Town panchayats		
1	Gudalur	38,859	137	5,323,683
2	Narasimhanaickenpalayam	17,858	213	3,803,754
3	Sarkarsamakulam	10,289	189	1,944,621
4	Edikarai	8,686	165	1,433,190
5	No. 4 Veerapandi	16,953	183	3,102,399
6	Karumathampatti	35,062	80	2,804,960
7	Karamadai	35,166	153	5,380,398
8	Anaimalai	17,208	74	1,273,392
9	Dhaliyur	11,500	94	1,081,000
10	Periyanaickenpalayam	25,930	123	3,189,390
11	Annur	20,079	181	3,634,299
12	Pallapalayam	11,910	181	2,155,710
13	Erugur	25,691	156	4,007,796
14	Vellalur	24,872	150	3,730,800
15	Kannampalayam	15,868	176	2,792,768
16	Madukarai	30,357	131	3,976,767
17	Othakalmandapam	12,207	100	1,220,700
18	Sulur	27,909	142	3,963,078
19	Thirumalaiyanpalayam	12,164	85	1,033,940
20	Ettimadai	9,352	202	1,889,104
21	Sirumugai	18,223	99	1,804,077
22	Zamin Uthukuli	14,859	132	1,961,388
23	Odaiyakulam	11,999	133	1,595,867

(continued)

Sl. No.	Name of towns	Population	Present water supply level LPCD	Total water supply
24	Vettaikaranpudur	17,392	137	2,382,704
25	Kottur	26,627	138	3,674,526
26	Perur	8,004	76	608,304
27	Chettipalayam	10,366	113	1,171,358
28	Thondamuthur	11,492	101	1,160,692
39	Vedapatti	11,658	121	1,410,618
30	Puluvapatti	12,853	110	1,413,830
31	Kinathukadavu	8,653	99	856,647
32	Sooleswaranpatti	20,104	90	1,809,360
33	Periyanagamam	7,098	105	745,290
34	Mupperipalayam	10,923	127	1,387,221
35	Samathur	5,672	92	521,824
36	Thenkarai	7,349	85	624,665
37	Alandurai	7,221	91	657,111
	Total	618,413		81,527,231

II Erode District

Corporations

1	Erode	157,101	110	17,281,110

Municipalities

1	Gobichettipalayam	59,523	139	8,273,697
2	Sathyamangalam	37,816	135	5,105,160
3	Bhavani	39,225	110	4,314,750
4	Punchai Puliyampatti	18,967	85	1,612,195
	Total	155,531		19,305,802

Town Panchayats

1	Kugalar	11,753	85	999,005
2	Bhavanisagar	7,710	169	1,302,990
3	Athani	8,430	95	800,850
4	Periyakodiveri	12,330	122	1,504,260
5	Ammapettai	9,677	103	996,731
6	Lakkampatti	11,716	72	843,552
7	Appakudal	10,610	104	1,103,440
8	Kodumudi	13,225	70	925,750
9	Nernugipettai	6,791	118	801,338

Sl. No.	Name of towns	Population	Present water supply level LPCD	Total water supply
10	Anthiyur	21,086	90	1,897,740
11	Chennasamudram	8,111	76	616,436
12	Nambiyur	16,379	92	1,506,868
13	Sivagiri	17,979	73	1,312,467
14	Chitthodu	8,550	105	897,750
15	Kollankovil	9,196	71	652,916
16	Nasiyanur	10,970	137	1,502,890
17	Karumandichellipalayam	23,868	117	2,792,556
18	Perundurai	24,930	94	2,343,420
19	Chennimalai	15,500	161	2,495,500
20	Salangapalayam	15,609	123	1,919,907
21	Olagadam	9,958	151	1,503,658
22	Ariyappampalayam	15,706	71	1,115,126
23	Vengampudur	7,443	70	521,010
24	Avalpundurai	11,789	70	825,230
25	Jambai	16,522	70	1,156,540
26	Kolappalur	9,607	134	1,287,338
27	Modakurichi	9,907	70	693,490
28	P. Mettupalayam	9,109	132	1,202,388
29	Pazur	3,670	70	256,900
30	Vellottamparappu	7,621	70	533,470
31	Archalur	12,034	70	842,380
32	Elathur	7,678	108	829,224
33	Kembanaickenpalayam	11,103	73	810,519
34	Vadugapatti	9,657	71	685,647
35	Kelampadi	6,422	70	449,540
36	Kasipalayam	9,093	141	1,282,113
37	Kanchikovil	11,294	106	1,197,164
38	Pethampalayam	7,152	168	1,201,536
39	Vaniputhur	12,044	125	1,505,500
40	Pallapalayam	7,263	138	1,002,294
41	Unjalur	2,482	70	173,740
42	Nallampatti	3,874	181	701,194
	Total	465,848		46,992,367

(continued)

Sl. No.	Name of towns	Population	Present water supply level LPCD	Total water supply
III Tirupur District				
	Corporations			
1	Tirupur	444,352	80	35,548,160
	Municipalities			
1	Dharapuram	56,007	75	4,200,525
2	Vellakoil	40,359	90	3,632,310
3	Udumalaipettai	61,133	123	7,519,359
4	Kangeyam	32,147	85	2,732,495
5	Palladam	7,263	85	617,355
	Total	196,909		18,702,044
	Town panchayats			
1	Avanashi	28,868	70	2,020,760
2	Chinnakkampalayam	11,546	70	808,220
3	Dhali	5,874	70	411,180
4	Kaniyur	6,180	70	432,600
5	Kannivadi	10,369	70	725,830
6	Kolathupalayam	17,819	70	1,247,330
7	Komaralingam	13,642	72	982,224
8	Kunnathur	8,774	125	1,096,750
9	Madathukulam	20,620	70	1,443,400
10	Mulanur	15,223	70	1,065,610
11	Muthur	13,212	70	924,840
12	Rudravathi (Kondadam)	6,807	70	476,490
13	Samalapuram	20,691	70	1,448,370
14	Sankaramanallur	10,283	70	719,810
15	Thirumuruganpoondi	31,528	70	2,206,960
16	Uthukuli	10,130	70	709,100
	Total	231,566		16,719,474
	Grand total of municipalities and town panchayats	4,410,613		469,156,164

Sources:
http://www.twadboard.gov.in/twad/coim_dist.aspx
http://www.twadboard.gov.in/twad/erode_dist.aspx
http://www.twadboard.gov.in/twad/tirupur_dist.aspx

Water Pollution

Since the 1970s, a large number of dyeing and bleaching industries have discharged effluents into the Noyyal River. The Orathupalayam dam, constructed in 1990, has become storage of industrial effluents. Adding to this, domestic wastewater of both Coimbatore and Tirupur has further polluted both surface and groundwater in Coimbatore district. An analysis of nine water bodies of the city by a local NGO indicates that most of the water bodies are contaminated. Discharge of industrial and domestic effluents, encroachment of tank and canal beds, reclamation and exploitation of groundwater are some of the important factors causing damage to these water bodies. A key factor responsible for polluting water bodies is the discharge of untreated effluents from small-scale industrial units lacking adequate individual treatment facilities. With major water bodies being polluted, an immediate effect is noticed on the health of the vulnerable communities residing on the banks of the canals and tanks.[44]

Cropping Patterns

The total cropped area increased from 3.27 lakh ha in 1960/61 to 5.83 lakh ha in 2003/04. In other words, the total cropped area almost doubled within four decades in Coimbatore district. But the cropping pattern too has changed drastically. In 1960–61, more than 63 per cent of the cropped area was under food grains but it decreased to 47 per cent in 1980–81. Invariably, the proportion of all food grains declined during this period and the area under food grains shrunk to 34.78 per cent in 2003–04 (Table 2.13). Interestingly, *cholam* and maize cultivation increased remarkably to 18.09 per cent and 5.55 per cent in 2003–04, while that of all other food grains declined. Significantly, while cultivation of water-intensive food grains decreased, raising pulses and oilseeds increased between 1960–61 and 2003–04.

Table 2.13 Cropping pattern in Coimbatore district: 1960/61–2003/04

Type of crops	1960–61	Per cent	1980–81	Per cent	2003–04	Per cent
Paddy	109,613	33.48	115,004	27.35	62,586	10.74
Wheat	33	0.01	267	0.06	9	0.00
Cholam	40,884	12.49	40,675	9.67	105,375	18.09
Kambu	20,708	6.32	14,747	3.51	2,066	0.35

(continued)

Type of crops	1960–61	Per cent	1980–81	Per cent	2003–04	Per cent
Ragi	27,982	8.55	14,777	3.51	8,603	1.48
Maize	77	0.02	11,472	2.73	32,334	5.55
Korra	4,736	1.45	675	0.16	1	0.00
Varagu	1,082	0.33	199	0.05	59	0.01
Thenei Samei or Millet	51	0.02	811	0.19	62	0.01
others	136	0.04	79	0.02	2	0.00
Pulses						
Bengal gram	30	0.01	463	0.11	4,927	0.85
Horse-gram	235	0.07	1,240	0.29	14,482	2.49
Red gram	105	0.03	980	0.23	3,510	0.60
Green gram	95	0.03	1,153	0.27	11,109	1.91
Black gram	68	0.02	1,238	0.29	3,910	0.67
Mochai					2,600	0.45
Cow Pea					13,149	2.26
Others	453	0.14	1,507	0.36	12,370	2.12
Oilseeds						
Gingelly	919	0.28	52,489	12.48	7,745	1.33
Mustard	1	0.00	16	0.00	72	0.01
Groundnut	19,141	5.85		0.00	48,719	8.36
Castor	228	0.07	384	0.09		0.00
Coconut	4,189	1.28	22,361	5.32	112,867	19.37
Others			452	0.11		
Condiments and spices						
Chillies	5,729	1.75	5,205	1.24	2,177	0.37
Garlic					18	0.00
Pepper			0		128	0.02
Coriander					1,944	0.33
Turmeric	2,633	0.80	12,353	2.94	7,648	1.31
Tamarind					1,229	0.21
Areca nut					1,711	0.29
Cardamom					813	0.14
Curry leaves					1,217	0.21
Others			1,450	0.34	14	0.00

Type of crops	1960–61	Per cent	1980–81	Per cent	2003–04	Per cent
Sugar						
Sugarcane	17,441	5.33	46,725	11.11	19,670	3.38
Palmyrahs					92	0.02
Fibres						
Cotton	53,545	16.35	19,461	4.63	9,696	1.66
Jute						
Bombay hemp	63	0.02				0.00
Sunnhemb					2	0.00
Drugs and narcotics						
Coffee	5	0.00			2,359	0.40
Tea	0				11,033	1.89
Tobacco	13,597	4.15	9,844	2.34	4,067	0.70
Cinchona						
Betel vines					96	0.02
Areca nuts					1,711	0.29
Cardamom					813	0.14
Fodder crops	553	0.17	9,096	2.16	87,859	15.08
Fruits and vegetables						
Plantains						
Mangoes					3,782	0.65
Banana					9,073	1.56
Onions	3084	0.94	5,425	1.29	2,650	0.45
others			19,691	4.68	23,189	3.98
Miscellaneous			2,174	0.52		
Total Cropped Area	327,416	100.00	420,517	100.00	582,560	100.00

Source: *Season and Crops Report* (for relevant years)

Conclusion

During the pre-colonial period, for water, the population was largely dependent upon tanks, canals, spring waters and wells. These water resources were managed by the village administration. At times, when the tanks and canals got breached by floods, they remained abandoned without any attempt to restore them owing to the frequent wars. However, the colonial administration placed heavy emphasis on large dams for irrigation rather than protecting the traditional water sources. All the same, the colonial administration, while expanding canal irrigation, adopted efficient water management practices. It also encouraged digging of new wells to expand the area under cultivation. The tanks and other spring-well sources were left unattended, considering them as non-remunerative. Consequently, there was no major change in the cropping patterns in Coimbatore district during the colonial period.

After independence, due to technological advancement like electric pumpsets and borewells, groundwater is being extracted from 1,000 feet and above. Consequently, wells of about 100 feet have become dysfunctional. Further, river water was diverted to bring more and more area under irrigation. In addition to the increasing demand in the agricultural sector, domestic and industrial demand has increased. To meet this, more and more water was diverted from the upstream sources, turning normal flow downstream almost non-existent. Further, the diverted water for domestic and industrial sectors is being discharged without any treatment. Consequently, both surface and groundwater has become polluted at an alarming rate and scale. Further, water diversion has disturbed not only the hydrology of the river basins, threatening sustainability, but the very ecological pattern of the region as well.

3

Competing Demand for Water and Pollution

Sustainable development is defined as meeting 'the [human] needs of the present without compromising the ability of future generations to meet their own needs'.[1] This implies that there is a limit and saturation point for environmental resources and the ability of the biosphere to absorb human activities. These limits are seen to have roots in technological inadequacies and inequitable social organization. Thus, sustainable development must entail a process of change in which the exploitation of resources, the direction of investments, the orientation of technological development and institutional changes have to be made consistent with future as well as the present needs.[2]

In recent years, sustainable resource use has been emphasized invariably in both the developed and developing countries alike. It is believed that sustainability can be guaranteed through market mechanism. Market enables the exchange of commodities (goods, services or resources) between producers/sellers and consumers/buyers within a specific geographic area during a given period of time. But the fact remains that market mechanism has proved to be a failure in ensuring sustainability of resources. It is because the cost/benefit of production of goods or their consumption is not included in the market price, neither in the supply price nor in the demand price. In other words, market is not taking into account the transaction cost while determining the cost or benefit of the goods. This spillover effects produce the externalities in the economic system and the entire process is known as market failure. For example, dyeing and bleaching industries use a large quantity of water and discharges almost the same amount into the Noyyal River and other public places. This effluent discharge affects the ecology and environment in these geographical regions. Neither the producers nor the consumers meet the cost of the damages suffered by the ecology and environment.

The earlier version of the paper was published in *Journal of Social and Economic Development*, 2007.

The basic theory of environmental policy describes pollution 'as a public "bad" that results from "waste discharges" associated with the production of private goods'.[3] To control pollution and protect the scarce resources, the theory suggests imposing taxes. Based on these ideas, the state too has imposed several restrictions through several laws and taxes. Yet, state intervention, which remained short of the expectations, proved to be ineffective. Failure of market, in turn, led to a greater threat to the ecology and environment of the basins, creating scarcity of water even as the competing demands from different sectors soared to new heights. To meet the ever-increasing as well as competing demand in the Noyyal River basin, water was diverted from the Bhavani River basin. But, instead of being a solution, it has only extended the problem to the entire Bhavani and Noyyal River basins.

Competing demand for water among the different stakeholders led to conflicts within the basin, between the basins of a state and between states and countries.[4] In the Bhavani Basin, there existed long-running feuds among farmers over sharing water.[5] Fierce disputes emerged between the states of Kerala and Tamil Nadu in sharing water resources.[6] Because, diversion of east-flowing rivers towards the west 'will severely affect human communities dependent upon Bhavani all the way down to Lower Bhavani dam and in a less drastic way further downstream in the Cauvery basin'.[7,8] Recently, Tirupur Exporters Association planned to divert the water from the confluence of Cauvery River, which was opposed by the Erode people, who were facing acute shortage of drinking water.

Drinking water problem emerged in Coimbatore towards the end of the nineteenth century.[9] Consequently, water supply schemes were initiated to meet the demand during the first quarter of the twentieth century.[10] Tirupur, on the other hand, grew rapidly only in the second half of the twentieth century, consuming water not only for domestic purpose but also for the mushrooming bleaching and dyeing industrial units. According to a bulletin of South Indian Hosiery Manufactures Association (SIHMA), 750 dyeing and bleaching units were there in 1998. The ever-growing water demand in the two cities was due to increasing population as a result of in-migration, in search of employment opportunities and other business activities besides the residential and institutional developments.

During the twentieth century, both the cities witnessed a rapid growth of different kinds of industries and other infrastructural facilities. As a result, population has increased due to the continuing in-migration from the villages of the district and neighbouring districts as well as other states. No wonder, the bourgeoning water demand has created a 'water market' for industries in Tirupur and for drinking and household purposes in the suburban areas of Coimbatore. With the increasing demand, water from the neighbouring Bhavani Basin was diverted to both Coimbatore and Tirupur, since local sources were inadequate to meet the exigency. The latest proposal is a joint sector scheme to divert water from the confluence point of both the Bhavani and the Cauvery Rivers to meet both the industrial and the drinking water needs of Tirupur, which has become the hosiery capital of the country.

On the one hand, growth of population density and industrial as well as infrastructural development have led to the rising demand for water from domestic, industrial and agricultural sectors and, on the other hand, water sources, both ground and surface water, are being polluted, aggravating the crisis further. Historically, increasing water demand in one place has been met through diversion of the water from other places. But, at present, diversion from new sources is no more an option due to the non-availability of surplus water.

In the Bhavani and Noyyal River basins, frequent conflicts and disputes have surfaced between farmers, municipalities, urban residents and industry since the late nineteenth century.[11] Not surprisingly, persisting disputes over demand for water coupled with pollution have made the crisis a major focal point. Until the early 1970s, the government, considering water diversion as source of revenue, was not compelled to act either on the concerns raised by the farmers or from the environmental point of view.[12] Despite enacting several statutes and framing rules aimed at pollution control and environmental protection, half-hearted implementation and institutional handicaps have defeated the purpose.[13] It is a sad commentary that institutions entrusted with the task of pollution control have not implemented the acts to rein in the small-scale industries.[14]

In addition to this, the technologies introduced during the green revolution turned the agricultural sector more and more water-intensive. At the same time, basin waters were transferred to the urban areas to meet the growing needs of drinking water supply and industrial requirements. Then, the used water both by the people and by the industries continues to be discharged untreated, affecting groundwater as well as surface water.[15] Blomqvist rightly pointed out that 'Bleaching and dyeing units do not bear the total costs of their activities but instead externalize them to other water users such as households and farmers'.[16] Due to this, water was diverted from distant places since the early twentieth century. For example, Siruvani River water was diverted to Coimbatore city to meet the demand.[17] In recent years, inter-basin transfers have also become a difficult task.[18] Because, 'taking water from one basin may harm the environment, and the pipes or canals may have to cut through forests, agricultural land, or habitations-causing environmental or land acquisition problems'.[19]

On the one hand, Tirupur[20] earns about Rs. 5,000 crores of foreign exchange through the knitwear export,[21] and on the other hand, it is using water resources in abundance only to pollute them and thereby gradually leading to decline in productivity, deterioration of ground as well as surface water and worsening health conditions.[22] However, export value has increased from Rs. 9.69 crores in 1984 to Rs. 5,000 crores in 2002–03. In 1984, 104 lakh of pieces worth of Rs. 969 lakhs were exported and it increased to 3,784 lakh of pieces worth of Rs. 301,700 lakhs in 1999.[23] And, in proportion hosiery and readymade garment exports of Tirupur not only have increased remarkably but have become a major component of exports from the country. The quantity of hosiery garment export, which was just 21.01 per cent in 1984, rose to 50.91 per cent in 1998. The value of exports too shot up from 10.86 per cent to 39.15 per cent during the same period.[24] In 1999, 3,784 lakh pieces of cloth worth USD 7,543 lakhs were exported and the quantity has jumped to 4,255 lakh pieces and USD 8,147 respectively in 2000.[25] Recently, the central government's Export Import Policy for 2003–04 has further encouraged this through supportive schemes for export clusters, resulting in the expansion and steady growth of the knitwear industry in Tirupur.[26]

Although the knitwear industry provides employment for a large number of people and earns huge foreign exchange, its consequences on environment and health not only affected those engaged in the industry and allied activities but the entire region immensely.[27] Reports of hospitals substantiate 'widespread incidence of skin diseases and pulmonological disorders'.[28] Till recently, pollution control measures were rather inactive. Even now, only small quantities of industrial effluents are treated through the Common Effluent Treatment Plants (CETPs).[29] According to the Pollution Control Board's estimation, about 80.70 million litres of effluents was discharged into the Noyyal River daily from dyeing and bleaching units in Tirupur and its vicinity, with another 30 lakh litres of untreated municipal wastewater too finding its way into the river.[30] Even after treatment, the total dissolvable solids (TDS) levels are more than double the permissible level of 2,100 ppm.[31] In addition to this, a large quantity of firewood is used to process the fabric. Studies reveal that around 3,600 truckloads of firewood per month arrive from different parts of the state within a minimum distance of 300 km.[32] Given the bird eye's view of the macro issues pertaining to the competing demand for water, let us see the picture in the Bhavani and Noyyal River basins.

There are several studies pertaining to the Bhavani and Noyyal River basins, focusing on labour markets, changing labour relations, cheapening of labour, feminization of labour and child labour since the last decade of the twentieth century.[33] Till the 1990s, the primary concern of such studies was labour issues, with environmental problems being ignored. In this context, the chapter attempts to analyse the competing demand for water that has risen owing to factors like urbanization, industrialization and environmental damage in the Bhavani and Noyyal River basins of Tamil Nadu since the late nineteenth century to the early twenty-first century, in a historical perspective. In other words, this chapter focuses on the major factors that have influenced water demand in Coimbatore and Tirupur, viz. (1) population growth and (2) the growth of industries and other institutional establishments along with the ecological and environmental consequences in these river basins. This chapter consists of seven sections. The second section focuses on demographic factors, such as population growth, migration trends and the occupational patterns of Coimbatore and Tirupur cities and the urban agglomeration[34] in the twentieth century. The third section discusses industrial development and the growth of water-consuming industries in both the cities. The fourth section is an analysis of the local water supply options for the two cities in meeting the growing demand. The fifth section recounts the industrial water demand. The sixth section deals with the ineffective pollution control measures and environmental damages, and the last section ends with some concluding observations.

Demographic Process in Coimbatore and Tirupur

Population growth in these cities is not only because of the high fertility rate of the region but also due to (1) the change/extension of the geographical areas and (2) increasing in-migration in search of employment and other economic opportunities/activities. This section examines the modes of extension of the geographical areas, population growth, trends of in-migration, out-migration, economic transformation, etc. of Coimbatore and Tirupur towns from the late nineteenth century to the early twenty-first century.

Coimbatore

Coimbatore is known as the 'Manchester of South India' due to the concentration of textile mills and industries. Located in the southwestern part of Tamil Nadu, it lies between 10°50' North Latitude and 76°56' and 77°01' East Longitude. The process of urbanization and industrialization has led to the growth of its extended periphery, which has become a part of the urban area over the period. Till the early twentieth century, the city did not extend much. For example, the geographical limit of Coimbatore city was only 25.9 sq kilometres (10 sq. miles) consisting of ten revenue villages in the 1870s. In fact, it became a municipal town only in 1866. It has expanded considerably in the subsequent decades, particularly since the 1940s. After independence extension of the geographical area has proliferated vastly.

The total geographical area of Coimbatore city, which was 69.56 sq kilometres in 1961, has reached an extent of about 105.6 sq kilometres in 1991. The concept of urban agglomeration was introduced in 1971. The urban agglomeration area, which was 156.31 sq kilometres in 1961, has increased to 289.96 sq kilometres in 1971 and to 317.23 sq kilometres in 1991. Expansion of the city limits over the period brought more population and industries within the urban limits and consequent rise in the demand for water.

Population Growth

During the 1870s population in Coimbatore city was very low, i.e. 35,310, and the demand for drinking water was met through the wells. The Coimbatore city administration did not feel the need for diverting water from distant places or water sources.[35] In the 1880s, when water problem was discussed for the first time by the government, the city's population was 38,967. Since then, different water sources were considered for supplying water.[36] Unfortunately, the schemes did not materialize either due to the high cost or bad quality of water sources.[37] Also, till 1931, population growth in the city was at a very moderate rate.

For example, between 1871 and 1921 the decadal population growth rate was less than 20 per cent. Since the 1930s, it increased quite remarkably spurred by in-migration and establishment of other business activities. In 1931, population in Coimbatore city was close to one lakh at 95,198 and it rose up to 565,293 in 1971 (see Table 3.1). The decadal population growth rate was very high, exceeding more than 50 per cent between 1941 and 1971. During this period, several *panchayats* viz. Singanallur, Vilankurichi, Telungupalayam, Komarapalayam, Sanganur, Ganapathy, Peelamedu, were merged with the city. Even as population has increased, there was a decline in the growth rate from 1971 onwards. For example, the decadal population growth rate, which was 54.12 per cent for

Table 3.1 Trends of population growth in the Coimbatore city and agglomeration areas: 1871–2001

Year	Town			Urban Agglomeration		
	Area (sq. km)	Population	Decadal growth rate (%)	Area (sq. km)	Population	Decadal growth rate (%)
1871	–	35,310		–	–	–
1881	–	38,967	10.36	–	–	–
1891	–	46,383	19.03	–	–	–
1901	–	53,080	14.44	–	53,080	–
1911	–	47,007	–11.44	–	47,007	–11.44
1921	–	75,491	60.59	–	65,788	39.95
1931	–	95,198	44.70	–	108,023	43.09
1941	–	151,875	59.54	–	189,612	75.53
1951	–	231,554	52.46	–	287,334	51.54
1961	69.56	366,799	58.41	156.31	448,201	55.99
1971	103.09	565,293	54.12	298.95	736,203	64.26
1981	105.60	704,514	24.63	290.73	920,355	25.01
1991	105.60	816,321	15.45	317.23	1,100,746	19.60
2001	–	923,085	13.08	–	1,446,034	31.37

Notes: The following towns were merged with Coimbatore city at different periods of time: Singanallur (M) part, with a population of 21,527 in 1941, 33,799 in 1951 and 66,318 in 1961, was merged with Coimbatore municipality. Vilankurichi (P) part, with a population of 5,190; Telungupalayam (P), with 27,101; Komarapalayam, with 14,224; Coimbatore non-municipality, with 2,256; Sanganur, with 26,099; Ganapathy (P), with 21,849; and Singanallur (M), with 112,206, were merged with Coimbatore town in 1971. Vapplipalayam (P), with a population of 23,207 in 1961, and Peelamedu (p), with a population of 8,297 in 1941, 13,947 in 1951 and 18,437 in 1961, have merged with Singanallur (M) in 1971, and with the merger of Singanallur (M) with Coimbatore (M) in 1981, they have also merged with Coimbatore.
Sources: Census of India (various years).

1961–71, decreased to 24.63 per cent in 1971–81 and again fell to 15.45 per cent in 1981–91. Population growth rate was very low at 13.08 per cent in 1991–2001.

Until the emergence of industrialization, the neighbouring villages remained isolated from the city. Since the 1930s, the adjoining villages too were absorbed into the urbanization of Coimbatore. For example, in 1921 the population of Coimbatore urban agglomeration area was 75,491, whereas in Coimbatore city, it was 65,788. Population in both the city and its agglomeration area witnessed a rapid increase between 1941 and 1971 (Table 3.1). And, this happened due to two reasons: inclusion of more areas into the urban agglomeration area and the rise in in-migration rate over the period. Again, this was stimulated by the growth of industrial employment and other infrastructural facilities, viz. educational institutions, business centres, recreational facilities and increasing floating population. Population growth in the agglomeration declined during 1981–91 but increased in the subsequent decade. Extension of the city's geographical area as well as the urban agglomeration led to the increase in demand for water in Coimbatore city and its peripheral regions.

In-Migration

Till the early twentieth century, the population growth of Coimbatore city was largely due to the natural increase of the respective population. Extension of geographical areas and the number of in-migrants had hardly played any role in it. But this trend has changed after the emergence and growth of industrialization, particularly since the 1930s. Due to industrialization, a large number of people within Coimbatore district and from other neighbouring districts and neighbourhood state, Kerala, migrated to Coimbatore.[38] This played a crucial role in the population growth of the city.

Industrialization in these cities also resulted in large-scale in-migration. However, it is difficult to estimate the actual number of in-migrants in 1931, since the number of births in Coimbatore city had not been enumerated in the census. However, the available data helps to ascertain the number of in-migrants from other districts of the presidency, states and other countries as well. According to 1931 Census, about 13 per cent of the in-migrants were from the other districts of the presidency, and only 0.77 per cent was from the other parts of the country and from abroad. About 86 per cent of the population in Coimbatore city, as per the enumeration, was from within the Coimbatore district.

However, there was a surge of in-migrants, whose numbers continued to rise over the period. For example, the total population of Coimbatore city was 286,305 in 1961, of which 126,802 persons, consisting of 55.71 per cent, were in-migrants. Of them, 42 per cent were from within Coimbatore district, 24 per cent from other districts of the Madras Presidency,[39] 32 per cent from other states of India and a little more than 1 per cent from overseas (see Table 3.2). The rate of proportion of in-migrants, however, came down in 1971.

This decline may be due to the growth of agglomeration areas around the city. About 31 per cent of the population alone was accounted as in-migrants. But, of the migrants we could see the same trend of in-migration. In the 1991

Table 3.2 In-migration details of Coimbatore city: 1931–71

Details/years	1931	%	1961	%	1971	%
Total migrants	–		126,802	44.29	291,540	30.60
From Coimbatore district	81,740	85.86	53,881	42.49	146,025	50.09
From other districts of the state	12,718	13.36	30,856	24.33	73,050	25.06
From other states	594	0.62	40,751	32.14	70,935	24.33
From other countries	146	0.15	1,314	1.04	1,530	0.52

Note: Urban Agglomeration concept was followed from 1971 Census onwards.
Sources: Census of India (various years).

Census, in-migration details are not available for Coimbatore city, but only for the agglomeration area.

In-Migration in Agglomeration Areas

Population growth did not leave untouched the urban agglomeration area, which saw a steady increase over the period. In 1971, the total number of population in the Coimbatore urban agglomeration area was 736,203 persons, of which, 291,540 persons (39.6 per cent) were in-migrants. Of the in-migrants, half of them had migrated from within the Coimbatore district, 25 per cent from other districts in the state, 24 per cent from other states in India and 0.52 per cent from other countries. The in-migration trend, however, has declined and the pattern also has changed in the subsequent decades. In 1991, the total population of the urban agglomeration areas was 1,100,746 persons, of which 301,430 (36.93 per cent) were in-migrants. Of the migrants, 38 per cent were from Coimbatore district: 40 per cent from other districts of the state; 21 per cent were of other states and a little more than 1 per cent from abroad (Table 3.3). In the beginning, the migrant population was largely from the native district, and later on this trend changed. Population growth with the increase of in-migrants led to emergence of slum settlements in Coimbatore city. Consequently, numbers of slums have increased with the passage of time. At present, there are forty-three slums within the corporation area.[40] According to the 2001 Census, 59,890 people (30,708 males and 29,182 females) are living in the slum areas.[41] It shows that economic transformation in the Coimbatore urban agglomeration areas has attracted in-migrants not only from the district but also, a large chunk, from other districts and states in recent years.

Table 3.3 In-migration details of Coimbatore Urban Agglomeration: 1971–91

	1971	%	1991	%
Total migrants	291,540	100	301,430	100
From Coimbatore	146,025	50.09	116,580	38.22
From other districts of the state	73,050	25.06	120,550	39.52
From other states	70,935	24.33	64,300	21.08
From outside India	1,530	0.52	3,580	1.17

Source: Census of India (various years).

Out-Migration

Though the in-migration trend has increased over the years in Coimbatore city and its agglomeration areas, it is difficult to assess the role of migration in population growth without quantifying the out-migration. Interestingly, out-migration was very low in Coimbatore district, and in comparison to the rate of in-migration, it was negligible during the study period.

Occupational Pattern

In Coimbatore city, though some traditional industries existed during the nineteenth century, rapid industrialization occurred only at the end of the first quarter of the twentieth century. For example, in 1931, the total population in Coimbatore city was 95,198 persons, of which 38,569 were workers and 57,381 non-workers. Of the workers, 4,368 (11.33 per cent) were in the primary sector, 9,360 (24.27 per cent) in the secondary sector and 24,839 persons (64.4 per cent) in service sector.[42] Since then, the city area has extended along with the growth of industries. In 1961, Coimbatore city, which was spread over about 69.56 sq. km, increased to 103.09 sq. km in 1971 and 105.6 sq. km in 1991. The total workforce also increased from 98,229 persons in 1961 to 110,281 in 1971 and 281,194 in 1991. The workforce was engaged mainly in the secondary and service sectors activities. Even in 1961, only 3 per cent of the total workers were engaged in the primary sector activities, and the percentage declined to 2.41 per cent in 1991. It indicates that the growing population in Coimbatore city is mainly involved in occupations other than agricultural activities. The workforce in the industrial sector accounted for 37–39 per cent and in the service sector for 58–60 per cent during the same period. This economic transformation was the prime reason

Table 3.4 Occupational classification of Coimbatore city and agglomeration: 1961–91

Year	1961	%	1971	%	1991	%
City						
Total main workers	98,229	100	110,281		281,194	100
Primary sector	2,729	2.78	1,893	1.71	6,778	2.41
Secondary sector	36,654	37.31	36,468	32.93	110,476	39.29
Tertiary sector	58,846	59.91	72,370	65.36	163,940	58.30
Urban Agglomeration						
Total main workers			238,284	100	382,387	100
Primary sector			27,450	11.52	27,176	7.11
Secondary sector			95,681	40.15	150,437	39.34
Tertiary sector			115,153	48.33	204,774	53.55

Sources: Census of India (various years).

for the rural people to move towards the urban areas. Not only in the city but also in the Coimbatore urban agglomeration areas, the process of economic transformation had taken roots over the period. For instance in 1971, 11.52 per cent of the workforce was engaged in the primary sector, but it had declined to 7 per cent in 1991. Almost the same proportion of workforce was engaged in the secondary sector at the same period (Table 3.4). It shows that industrialization had paved the way for the economic transformation of the agglomeration areas, which led to the movement of population towards the urban and sub-urban areas.

Tirupur

Tirupur city is popularly known as 'Dollar City', 'Knit City', 'Cotton City' and mainly 'Hosiery Centre'. The city is located in southwestern part of Tamil Nadu on the banks of Noyyal River about fifty kilometres east of Coimbatore. Now, a district headquarter, it lies on 11°07' Northern Latitude and 77°15' Eastern Longitude. The geographical extension of Tirupur city was a very recent phenomenon. Till independence and even some years later, Tirupur was a characteristic small town, and it became a town with the inclusion of Thennampalayam, Karuvampalayam and Valipalayam villages on 1st December 1947.[43] In 1971, the total geographical area of Tirupur town was only 11.92 sq km, but by 1991 it increased to

43.52 sq km. Similarly the Tirupur urban agglomeration area, which was 54.86 sq km in 1961, spread to 90.98 sq km in 1991.

Population Growth

Population growth rate of Tirupur city was moderate till 1921. In fact, it had declined between 1911 and 1921 due to endemic epidemics in 1917–18.[44] After that, it witnessed a sharp rise. The decadal population growth rate was more than 50 per cent between 1931 and 1961. It was very high at 83 per cent in 1941 (see Table 3.5). Though population growth rate had declined since 1961, the decadal growth rate was higher when compared to Coimbatore city. For example, the population growth rate of Coimbatore city was 15.45 per cent in 1981–91, whereas it was 42.63 per cent for Tirupur. A large number of people from the villages of Coimbatore district and other districts of Tamil Nadu migrated towards Tirupur mainly for unskilled work in the dyeing and bleaching industries. The fast-growing Tirupur city and its agglomeration areas require more water to meet the needs of a growing population as well as the large number of water-consuming industries.

Table 3.5 Population growth in Tirupur city and agglomeration: 1891–2001

Year	Town			Urban agglomeration		
	Area (sq. km)	Population	Decadal growth rate (%)	Area (sq. km)	Population	Decadal growth rate (%)
1881	–	3,681	–	–	–	–
1891	–	5,235	–	–	–	–
1901	–	6,056	–	–	6,056	–
1911	–	9,429	55.70	–	9,056	55.70
1921	–	10,851	15.08	–	10,851	15.08
1931	–	18,059	66.43	–	18,059	66.43
1941	–	33,099	83.28	–	39,195	117.04
1951	–	52,479	58.55	–	60,465	54.27
1961	27.20	79,773	52.01	54.86	97,965	62.02
1971	31.92	113,302	42.03	73.65	151,127	54.27
1981	43.52	165,223	45.83	90.98	215,859	42.83
1991	43.52	235,661	42.63	90.98	306,237	41.87
2001	–	346,551	–	–	542,787	–

Sources: Census of India (various years).

In-Migration

For Tirupur city, in-migration details are not available till 1961. The total population of Tirupur city in 1961 was 151,127, of which 63,820 persons, or 42.23 per cent, were migrants. Of the in-migrants, 79 per cent were from Coimbatore district, 13 per cent from the other districts of the state and 7 per cent from the other states of India (see Table 3.6). In 1971, in-migrants were largely from Coimbatore district itself following the spurt in the number of housing industries, which required heavy manual labour. The 1991 Census shows little detail about in-migration for both Tirupur and its agglomeration area.

In-Migration in Agglomeration Area

The in-migration trend was high in the Tirupur agglomeration area, where the total population in 1971 was 151,127, of which 63,820 (42.23 per cent) was in-migrants. Of them, about 80 per cent was from Coimbatore district, 13 per cent from other districts of Tamil Nadu and about 7 per cent from the other states of India. The rate of in-migrants also declined and the pattern also changed in the agglomeration area in the subsequent decades. In 1991 half of the in-migrants were from within the district, whereas 41 per cent were from the other districts of the state (see Table 3.7). Over the period, the proportion of in-migrants from Coimbatore district has come down remarkably.

A recent survey also suggested that a large proportion of migrant workers were from the neighbouring districts like Erode, Salem and Madurai as well as from other parts of the state.[45] Initially, it was the Backward Community people who were mainly engaged in these activities, with Scheduled Castes also getting engaged later on. Neetha states:

> Traditionally, the weaving community belonged to the backward caste (BC), "gounders", and initially the workers in all the units were mostly from this caste. However, with the growth of the industry and with the flow of the migrants the workers' caste composition has changed. At present scheduled castes, who were traditionally agricultural labourers, are seen joining the industry in large numbers though it is still dominated by the backward castes.[46]

It categorically shows that industrialization and the process of economic transformation had attracted in-migrants largely from other districts of the state in recent years. The declining rate of in-migration may be the reason for the low growth rate of population in Tirupur city as well as its agglomeration area in recent years.

Table 3.6 In-migration details of Tirupur: 1971

Details/years	1971	Per cent
Total migrants	62,820	100
From Coimbatore district	50,575	79.25
From other districts of the state	8,485	13.29
From other states	4,710	7.38
From outside India	50	0.08

Note: Urban Agglomeration concept was followed from 1971 Census onwards.
Sources: Census of India (various years).

Table 3.7 In-migration details of Tirupur agglomeration areas: 1971–91

	1971	Per cent	1991	Per cent
Total migrants	63,820	100	123,195	100
From Coimbatore	50,575	79.25	62,337	50.60
From other districts of the state	8,485	13.29	50,798	41.23
From other states	4,710	7.38	9,360	7.60
From outside India	50	0.08	700	0.57

Source: Census of India (various years).

Occupational Patterns

Until the first quarter of the twentieth century, Tirupur's economy was predominantly agrarian in nature, with almost all the workers engaged in primary sector activities. This trend changed since the second quarter of the twentieth century. From 1930 onwards, there was a shift towards the secondary and tertiary sectors. In 1961, a little more than half of the workforce in Tirupur city was into the secondary sector activities. It increased to two-thirds (65 per cent) of the workforce in 1991. As against this, the proportion of the workforce in the primary sector declined from 4.11 per cent in 1961 to 0.68 per cent in 1991. Whereas, in the service sector the proportion of the workforce declined from 45.34 per cent to 34.75 per cent for the same period (see Table 3.8). In short, within a period of six decades, Tirupur economy changed completely from the primary to secondary and tertiary sector activities. Not only Tirupur city but the agglomeration area too was absorbed into this remarkable rapid transformation. Between 1961 and 1991, the percentage of the workforce involved in the primary sector remained around 4 per cent (see Table 3.8). This indicates that economic

Table 3.8 Occupational classification of Tirupur city and agglomeration: 1961–91

Year	1961	Per cent	1971	Per cent	1991	Per cent
City						
Total main workers	29,804	100	40,598	100	103,725	100
Primary sector	1,224	4.11	1,409	3.47	704	0.68
Secondary sector	15,066	50.55	22,178	54.63	66,973	64.57
Tertiary sector	13,514	45.34	17,011	41.90	36,048	34.75
Urban agglomeration						
Total main workers			55,026	100	134,177	100
Primary sector			5,114	9.29	5,349	3.99
Secondary sector			28,772	52.29	84,626	63.07
Tertiary sector			21,140	38.42	44,202	32.94

Sources: Census of India (various years).

transformation of the agglomeration area had turned it into a centre of non-agricultural activities. Unlike Coimbatore city and its agglomeration areas, about two-third of the workforce in Tirupur is engaged in the industrial sector due to the presence of a very large number of dyeing and bleaching industries, and only one-third is in the service sector. Thus, it becomes clear that a large number of people are engaged in the secondary and tertiary sectors in the Coimbatore and Tirupur city as well as in their agglomeration areas. A major consequence of the urbanization process is the increased demand for water both in Coimbatore and in Tirupur.

Change in the Land Use Pattern

The land use pattern in the Tirupur Local Planning Area (TLPA)[47] witnessed a dramatic change in the past two decades. The total geographical area of TLPA is about 218.28 sq. km. In 1984, 190.41 sq. km (87 per cent) of TLPA was under agricultural use, 19.97 sq. km (9.15 per cent) accounted for residential use and 4.23 sq. km (2 per cent) under industrial use, with the rest occupied by commercial, educational and other public utilities (Table 3.9). In 2001, agricultural land use came down to 121.19 sq. km (56 per cent), with residential and industrial use touching 66.72 sq. km (31 per cent) and 18.37 sq. km (8 per cent), respectively. It clearly indicates that urbanization and industrialization have increased in the TLPA during the last two decades. Consequently, numbers of slums have increased in recent years. According to the 2001 Census,

Table 3.9 Land use pattern in TLPA: 1984–2001

Use	1984		2001 (proposed)	
	Area in sq. km	Per cent	Area in sq. km	Per cent
Residential	19.97	9.15	66.72	30.57
Commercial	1.67	0.77	4.18	1.91
Industrial	4.23	1.94	18.37	8.42
Educational	1.30	0.60	6.31	2.89
Public and semi-public	0.68	0.31	1.48	0.68
Agricultural	190.41	87.23	121.19	55.52
Total	218.28	100	218.28	100

Source: City Corporate Plan – Tirupur, *Tamil Nadu Urban development Project-II*, 1999, p. 29.

8,922 persons live in the slum areas of Tirupur.[48] However, Tirupur City Corporate Plan (1999) documents claim that there are 63,094 persons living in eighty-eight slums of Tirupur.[49]

Industrial Development in Coimbatore and Tirupur Cities

The process of industrialization emerged in Coimbatore city during the early twentieth century, with the coming up of various types of industries. But in Tirupur city, this took root only in the second half of the twentieth century, with the explosive growth of the hosiery industry.

Industrial growth influences water demand in two ways: water has to be provided for drinking and for the water-consuming industries. It also creates two serious problems. First, water has to be diverted from the irrigation sector, resulting in conflicts between the industrial and agricultural sector, and the second is untreated effluent discharges end up polluting both the groundwater and the surface water. In this section, let us see the trends of industrial growth and water-consuming industries both in Coimbatore and in Tirupur cities.

Industrial Growth in Coimbatore City

Coimbatore city has a heavy concentration of cotton, textiles, hosiery and knitwear and metal-based industries producing textile and other machinery and irrigation pumps.[50] Coimbatore district is well known for its cotton cultivation since the early colonial rule. However, the cotton industry was established only in 1847. Since 1907, when a local entrepreneur established a cotton mill in Coimbatore, several cotton industries sprang in the city subsequently. The growth and concentration of the textile industry in the district has helped the growth of industries largely engaged in manufacturing machinery and equipment used in the textile sector.[51] The Textool Company was established in 1944 at Ganapathy. Another unit engaged in the same line is the Lakshmi Machine Works at Periyanaickenpalayam established in 1962. These two factories continue to make a remarkable contribution in sustaining the supply of tools and machinery required for the textile industry.[52] Over the period, several industries were set up in Coimbatore city. In 1988, there were about 1,131 industries, of which 85 were foundry, casting and forging units; 79 manufacturing of electric motors and pumps; 92 other engineering product units; 164 textile machinery units and 582 units of other industries. The growth of these industries has attracted more labourers from the villages. Not only the direct employment opportunities increased in the city but a large number of indirect employment opportunities also opened up due to the industrial growth.

Apart from the emergence of large-scale industries, there was a spurt in the development of small-scale industries. For example, there were 4,763 small-scale industries in Coimbatore city in 1992. It increased to 10,075 units in 1996–97.[53] A large number of small-scale industries are related to textile production, and most of them are located in the Coimbatore Local Planning Area.[54] Every year, several small-scale industries are coming up in Coimbatore city.

Growth of Textile Industries in Coimbatore City

In Coimbatore city, though a few cotton industries were started in the middle of the nineteenth century, the number of cotton industries registered a vertical growth only after the second quarter of the twentieth century. Since then and till the end of the colonial rule, a large number of cotton textile industries have been established every year. About twenty-two textile mills, with a capital investment of Rs.97 lakhs, were established in the city between 1932 and 1939.[55] During the colonial rule itself, a large number of cotton industries were established in the Coimbatore city, making it the Manchester of South India.

In addition to the large number of cotton industries during the colonial rule, a number of cotton industries were established in the peripheral areas of Coimbatore city after independence. While there were 111 textile (94 spinning and 17 composite) industries in Coimbatore district, in 1975 it shot up to 195 (180 spinning and 15 composite) industries in 1990.[56] At present, around 100 textile mills are located in and around the city. The burgeoning textile industry in Coimbatore district led to the establishment of more industries and auxiliary units with the increase in demand for more labour. However, the industrial demand for water in Coimbatore is fairly small compared to the domestic demand, since the industries are basically not water-consuming ones. However, at present there are more than 600 electro plants and melting industrial units in Coimbatore discharging their effluents into Noyyal River.[57]

Industrial Growth in Tirupur City

Industrial activity in Tirupur city is mainly confined to hosiery industry engaged in the production of knitted fabrics. Compared to other industries, the hosiery units are more labour-intensive. For example, this industry requires a team of fifteen persons to complete a piece of banian.[58] Due to the availability of cheap labour, electricity, transportation, favourable climate, etc., Tirupur attracted businessmen from the different parts of the country. The unfavourable conditions in the knitting factories in the neighbouring districts led to opening of new firms in Tirupur during the early twentieth century.[59] Between 1966 and 1975, about 150 industrialists transferred their business centres from Calcutta to Tirupur.[60] The number of registered small-scale units of cotton textile and textile product (hosiery) units in Tirupur was only 1,143 in 1980, and it increased to 9,319 units in 1997.[61]

Since the late nineteenth century, Tirupur was a centre of textile business, dominated by yarn trade and cotton.[62] However, the Cotton Market Committee was established only in 1921 by the Tirupur Municipality.[63] Till the early twentieth century, Tirupur's economy was predominantly or completely dependent on agriculture and its allied activities. The first ginning mill was established in 1904. There were no major industries in Tirupur city till 1911, and even till the 1930s, there were only a few knitting and ginning mills. Since the 1930s, infrastructure facilities were developed. With the commissioning of Pykara electricity system in 1933, Tirupur city was electrified between 1936 and 1945. The Pykara electricity system proved to be a boon for the phenomenal growth of Tirupur. However, industrial growth was very slow till independence, in fact, till the late 1960s.[64] After independence, the hosiery industries engaged in the manufacture of banian products were launched, and in the subsequent decades, their number also increased. In 1991, about 3,900 different kinds of hosiery industries, viz. knitting mills, ginning mills, dyeing and bleaching mills, printing mills, etc. have come up in Tirupur city (see Table 3.10). However, this figure does not show the

Table 3.10 Industrial growth in Tirupur city: 1911–2001

Year/Type of industry	1911	1921	1931	1941	1951	1961	1971	1981	1991	2001
Knitting mills	–	–	5	22	35	250	415	1,300	2,800	2,500
Dyeing and bleaching mills	–	–	–	2	15	42	67	68	450	750
Printing on cloth	–	–	–	2	8	15	20	22	125	350
Lable looms	–	–	–	–	1	4	6	9	100	150
Card-board making	–	–	–	–	2	9	18	48	253	200
Calendering	–	–	–	–	4	12	23	41	95	200

Notes: For 2001, compiled from the different sources.
Calendering: It is a thermo-mechanical process, i.e. it involves use of heat and mechanical pressure, but no chemicals.
Lable Looms: Looms designed only to print labels.
Source: *Municipal Office*, Tirupur.

real picture as it covers only registered firms, leaving out other related subsidiary units manufacturing cartons, tapes, polythene bags and others.[65] In other words, the official data have not brought out much of the informal and unregulated activities giving a wide variation.[66] In addition to this, a number of small units have increased over the period. A large proportion of the knitwear firms employ ten to fifty workers.[67] The rapid increase in the number of hosiery units attracted a large number of migrant labourers who landed Tirupur in search of employment opportunities. Unlike the industries in Coimbatore city, which required some technical knowledge, industries in Tirupur are largely manual labour–oriented. Consequently, Tirupur absorbed a large number of migrants. Another facet of industrial growth in Tirupur was the setting up of water-consuming industries. Although there are a large number of water-consuming units in Tirupur, only 184 units were registered under SSI as water-consuming industries till 1997.[68]

The numbers of industries also increased since 1925. In 1995, there were 8,437 industrial units in Tirupur city. Of this, 713 were water-intensive units. The requirement of water for industrial use was ninety million litres per day. A large quantity of water is required mainly for the 526 dyeing units.[69] As on 1 January 1997 there were 851 water-consuming bleaching and dyeing units in Tirupur.[70] Between 1997 and 2001, the number of dyeing and bleaching industries has declined because of the closure of 164 units as ordered by the Madras High Court as they failed to control pollution. In the year 2000, there were 2,500 knitting and stitching units, 750 dyeing and bleaching units and 735 supporting units. A large quantity of salt is used in the dyeing process, and hence the wastewater (90 million litres per day) is highly saline in content and is contaminated with a variety of chemicals.[71] The increasing number of water-consuming bleaching and dyeing industries in Tirupur made the city one of the most demanding one for water over the period.

Meeting Water Demand in Coimbatore and Tirupur[72]

Coimbatore

Though Coimbatore city is located near the Noyyal River, drinking water has become a major problem since the late nineteenth century. In addition to the low rainfall, groundwater is also scarce due to the underlying hard-rock formations. Even the quality of available water is very poor.[73] The city was constituted as a municipality in 1866, with a population of around 35,000, and till the 1880s, water supply was managed with the existing wells in different parts of the city. Expenditure of the civic body was very meagre during the late nineteenth century.[74] Scarcity of drinking water emerged only towards the end of that century due to non-availability of sound groundwater sources. The available few water sources in and around Coimbatore were not of good quality. Initially, the government planned to use the nearby water sources. But these plans were not taken up either due to the higher cost or because the sources were not good enough for human consumption. However, the government had come up with several other schemes during the late 1880s, and till 1912, many of them were under consideration. Yet, they were not taken up due to prohibitive cost, bad quality of water and most importantly protests from farmers.[75] In short, as early as the 1890s, scarcity as well as quality of water forced the authorities to draft proposals to divert water from other basins. Consequently, in 1931 the government diverted the Siruvani River water, located at a distance of 36 km from the city. Since then, there has been rapid urbanization and industrialization in the region. But, the water sources were insufficient to meet this pace of development. The per capita availability of water declined since the 1930s. For instance, per capita water consumption, which was 126 litres per day in 1931, declined to 53 litres by 1961. Further, it came down to 36 litres per day in 1971 (see Table 3.11). In the meanwhile, the government had initiated several

Table 3.11 Trends of Siruvani and Pillur domestic water supply in Coimbatore: 1931–2001

Year	Quantity (in MLD)	Population (in millions)	Per capita consumption litres/days
1931	11.3	0.90	126
1941	12.5	0.13	96
1951	18.6	0.20	93
1961	14.8	0.28	53
1971	13.0	0.36	36
1981	60.0	0.70	85
1991	85.0	0.82	103
2001	153.0		150

Sources: Bergh, Gunilla and Pia Nordberg, *Water in Expanding Cities – A Case Study of Coimbatore, Tamil Nadu, India*, Royal Institute of Technology, Stockholm, Sweden, 1996, p. 23.
Menon, A. et al., *Tamil Nadu Urban Environmental Challenge – A Study of Eight Secondary Cities/Towns*, MIDS, Chennai, 1997, p. 173.
Coimbatore city Municipal Corporation – Engineering, 2001 in http://www.coimbatore- corporation.com/admin-engg_comm.asp (accessed in May 2006).

measures to enhance water supply from the Siruvani Water Supply Scheme at different times. For instance, to augment the supply, the government sanctioned Rs. 24.25 lakhs in 1942, and the scheme was completed in the year 1965. The second augmentation scheme, executed by Tamil Nadu Water and Drainage (TWAD) Board, was completed in 1976, and it helped to draw up to eighty-five lakhs gallons per day.

At present, about 95 per cent of the drinking water supply in Coimbatore district is met from distant river water sources through expensive water supply schemes.[76] There are two major sources of drinking water supply – Siruvani[77] and Pillur schemes. The Coimbatore Corporation maintains the distribution of water supply. At present, it is maintained at 110 litres per capita per day (lpcd). The entire supply of water from Siruvani is by gravity, whereas pumping is being done in the Pillur scheme.[78]

Till the 1990s, the government managed water supply for Coimbatore city from Siruvani water supply scheme. In 1985, there were 46,492 service connections in Coimbatore city.[79] Water distribution was largely carried out through metre basis for the houses besides a few under the tap basis, about 1,500 on non-domestic basis and about 800 through public fountains. The numbers of service connections rose in the subsequent years, and in 1991–92, they rose to 58,689. Of this, 264 were on tap basis, 56,060 on meter basis, 1,170 on non-domestic basis and 1,163 in public fountains.[80] At present, there are 85,318 domestic meter connections, 3,574 non-domestic meter connections, 120 tap connections (payment on monthly flat rate) and 3,412 public fountains in the Coimbatore Corporation area.[81] Total quantity of water supplied to Coimbatore city during 1991–92 was 8,349 lakhs litres: daily an average supply of 672.40 lakhs litres benefit the population of 1,135,549 at the per capita rate of seventy litres.[82] Increased urbanization and growth of urban agglomeration areas, especially during the 1980s and 1990s, forced the government to launch the new water supply schemes. The Siruvani Water Supply Scheme was also extended to supply water to the newly added areas of Coimbatore city, Satellite towns and sixty-five wayside villages in 1980s.[83] The corporation also maintains a fleet of fifteen water lorries/tankers for supplying water to areas not served by the Siruvani Water Supply Scheme and also to places where the supply is poor. To meet the new demand, the government initiated other water supply schemes.

Finally, in 1989 proposals were made to divert the Bhavani River water to Coimbatore city at Pillur, located about 95 km from the city. This scheme is designed to divert about 131.25 MLD of water, of which the Coimbatore Corporation's share stands at 65.97 MLD of water. Since 1995, water was provided through this scheme.[84] About 113.48 million cubic litres of water were diverted from Bhavani River at Pillur in two stages. In the first stage, it provided 125 million litres per day (MLD) in 1996 and 250 MLD in 2011 for the Coimbatore Local Planning Area, 20 town *panchayats* and 523 rural settlements on the way.[85] Since 1994, the Pillur water supply scheme has been providing water to the Coimbatore city. The total water supply both from the Siruvani and the Pillur schemes was 148.46 MLD in 1994. Of this, 137.59 MLD was used for domestic water supply and 10.87 MLD for industrial purposes. Apart from this, 1.33 MLD was provided for Sulur town *panchayats* and 1.80 MLD for Sulur Air Force.[86] At present, 153 MLD (87 MLD from Siruvani and 66 MLD from Pillur) is being provided to Coimbatore city at the rate of 150 litres per capita per day.[87] Augmentation of water supply to Coimbatore Corporation was realized with Pillur dam as a source up to MSR- Phase-I. The Tamil Nadu Water and Drainage Board (TWAD) prepared a scheme for augmenting water supply to Coimbatore Corporation at a cost of Rs. 90 crores. Under this, 232.25 MLD (101 MLD from Siruvani Water Supply Scheme and 131.25 MLD from Bhavani Water Supply Scheme) of water will be supplied. The Bhavani Water Supply Scheme provides water to Coimbatore city, 20 towns and 523 rural habitations, and the Pillur Water Supply Scheme provides water to Coimbatore Corporation.[88] In addition to this, water is also supplied to residents in unapproved layouts and new residential areas by twelve corporation-owned tankers, while private tankers supply water to 350 locations.[89] The corporation then planned to achieve an average gross supply of 150 lpcd by the year 2004, catering to 100 per cent of the population.[90] The average net supply available to the city population is expected to be 120 lpcd.

In 1996, the Avinashi-Athikadavu scheme was proposed to improve the irrigation facilities in the dry region of Erode and Coimbatore districts. In 2000, this scheme was modified into a drinking water scheme through the open canal system. The proposal was to divert the surplus water from the Bhavani to recharge groundwater sources in the Nambiyur, Uthukuli, Chennimalai, Perundurai and Bhavanisagar Panchayat Unions of Erode district and Annur, Avinashi, Karamadai, Sulur and Sarkarsamakulam Panchayat Unions of Coimbatore districts.[91] The Avinashi-Athikadavu Drinking Water Project was formulated at a cost of Rs. 270 crores. The government proposes to take up this project for implementation in phases by availing of assistance from financial institutions.[92]

Tirupur

Though the Noyyal River runs through the town, water problem in Tirupur was an acute one as early as the 1930s. Large-scale diversion of river water for irrigation coupled with contamination added to the water woes in the early twentieth century itself.[93] The river has twenty-three *anicuts* and twenty-eight system tanks for irrigating around 19,799 acres. From Tirupur to Orthupalayam, eight system tanks irrigate around 1,677 acres in the Noyyal basin. With about thirty-one irrigation *anicuts* built above, even the available little water was contaminated all the way down to Tirupur. Until the 1920s, water was managed mainly with seven public wells.[94] Every year, Tirupur city had spent a certain amount for repairing the wells to provide maximum water supply. With the attempts to provide adequate water supply failing to meet the demand of the growing population, in the 1920s, the government proposed a scheme to draw water from the Koilveli infiltration gallery, located about five miles away from Tirupur. Though it was designed to provide water supply to only 20,000 people at 22.73 litres of water per head a day,[95] it gave only 340,950 litres per day. This was so inadequate that it served not even one-third of the water demand. Consequently the government proposed several water supply schemes.[96] In 1949, the government sanctioned for the investigation of a water supply scheme with the Bhavani River as the source to serve Tirupur and seven wayside villages, viz. Pogalur, Kurukkalaiyampalayam, Annur, Karavalur, Nombiyampalayam, Avinashi, Karamadai and Tirumuganpundi. In 1962, water was diverted from the Bhavani River at Mettupalayam. The capacity of this scheme was 7 MLD, of which 4.5 MLD was supplied to Tirupur city. In 1993, the second scheme was developed with a capacity of 45 MLD, of which 24 MLD was supplied to Tirupur. As a whole, 28.50 MLD water from Bhavani River was diverted to Tirupur town.[97] The per capita water supply was 127 litres in 1996. At present, the knitwear industries are tapping about 600 tankers of water every day from 35 km radius of Tirupur town. Due to the ever-increasing water demand for the industries, a proposal was made for a new project to divert water at the confluence of Bhavani with the Cauvery jointly financed by industries in Tirupur.

In the early 1990s, the people of Tirupur and the Tirupur Exporters Association (TEA) represented to the government to improve the basic infrastructure facilities. In 1991, the government launched the Tirupur Area Development Project to provide all infrastructural facilities. For this purpose, the government set up a Special Purpose Vehicle (SPV) along with the Infrastructure Leasing and Financial services Limited (IL&FS) and TEA. In 1995, the New Tirupur Area Development Corporation Limited (NTADCL) was established through the SPV to provide the infrastructural facilities.

Due to the increase in demand for water, mainly for the industries, both the government and private entities jointly initiated a water project on Build, Own, Operate and Transfer (BOOT) basis. The three partners, TACID, TEA and IL&FS, together designed the Tirupur Area Development Project (TADP) as a public-private partnership. In 1995, the New Tirupur Area Development Corporation Limited (NTADCL) was launched with the cooperation of Government of Tamil Nadu, IL&FS and TEA. The NTADCL and Mahindra-led consortium signed an agreement for a private integrated water and sewerage project in Tirupur. The consortium comprised Mahindra Realty and Infrastructure Developers Ltd, a subsidiary of Mahindra and Mahindra Ltd, India; Bechtel Enterprises Inc, a US Water Transnational Corporation; and United Utilities International, UK.[98] The main objective of the project was to provide piped water supply to Tirupur Municipality and twenty-one wayside towns and village *panchayats* and water supply to the dyeing and bleaching industries in the Tirupur Municipality area. The project was launched in 2002, to provide water supply for the dyeing and bleaching industries and domestic consumers in Tirupur Local Planning Area (TLPA), comprising the Tirupur Municipality (TM), fifteen village *panchayats* and three town *panchayats*. In addition to this, water supply was proposed for five wayside *panchayats* Unions.[99] According to the project, 185 MLD of water will be drawn from River Cauvery at Anaiyinasuvam Palayam, near Bhavani town.[100] Of this, 115 MLD is for industries and the remainder 62 MLD for Tirupur Municipality and other neighbourhood villages.[101] This project was scheduled to be completed by April 2005.[102] Adoption of differential pricing system was a crucial aspect of this project. At present, it is proposed to be Rs. 2.25 per/kl for wayside *panchayats* Rs. 3.50 for town *panchayats* and Rs. 5 for domestic consumers. For industrial consumption, the cost would be Rs. 45.[103] Now, water charge for domestic consumption up to 24 kl/month is Rs. 2.00, and for above 24 kl/month, it is Rs. 4.00; and for non-domestic consumption, commercial use it is Rs. 6.00 kl and for industrial use Rs. 4.00 kl.[104] In short, the increasing number of industries in general and water-consuming industries in particular both in Coimbatore and Tirupur cities had created demand for more water for industrial use, which resulted in water scarcity and accompanying environmental problems in the Noyyal basin.

Industrial Water Demand – 1900–70

Until the early twentieth century, water from the Bhavani River and its tributaries was used only for irrigation and was never diverted either for domestic water supply to towns and villages or for industrial concerns. During the early twentieth century, water was diverted to provide water supply mainly to the Coimbatore Municipality and to some extent to the railways and other industries. However, in the second half of the twentieth century, it was further diverted to the small towns and villages.

Whether diversion of water to the industries created any scarcity on the agricultural front is an interesting question. If so, what had been the government's policy and the role of the judiciary towards effective water management in the Bhavani River basin? It is also important to have a comprehensive understanding of the adverse impact that discharge of industrial effluents had on the environment. Did the farmers protest against these diversions and environmental hazards, and what were the measures taken by the government to protect the farmers' interest and water quality in the Bhavani River basin? Probing these issues would throw some light to understand the problems of water management and environmental consequences.

The main objective of this section is to understand government policy regarding industrial water supply in a historical perspective between 1900 and 1970. This section consists of two parts. The first part focuses on the history of water diversion to the railways. The second part discusses water supply to industrial concerns and the attendant environmental issues in the light of the government policies.

Water Demand for the Railways

When water from the Bhavani and its tributaries was diverted to some extent for the railways at the end of the nineteenth century, the government had not visualized its implications on the agricultural sector. Initially, the government had collected the water charges at a flat rate without considering the quantity of water taken for the railways. Since 1898, the South Indian Railway Company had taken water from the Kallar River at Kallar in Coimbatore district through pipes.[105] From 1902 onwards, the South Indian Railway Company was taking 4,000 gallons of water to the Mettupalayam Railway station from the Odanthorai channel in Coimbatore district by paying a paltry sum of Rs. 6–10-6 per annum to the Revenue Department.[106] However, the railway company had been also informed that supply of water would be stopped any time if it affected irrigation of the *ayacut* under the channel.[107] In spite of this, there was no indication of any resentment among the farmers against the diversion of water to the railways.

The government did not pay much attention to collect even the meagre amount of water charges from the railways, and until 1926, the authorities had neglected it. In 1927, the government changed the mode of collection and fixed the tariff according to the actual quantity of water replacing the earlier flat rate. As such, the Railway Company was invariably charged Rs. 3 per 1,000 cubic yards for drawing water from the government sources.[108] It was the rate fixed for the South Indian Railway Company towards drawing water from the Odanthurai channel.[109] The tariff per annum was fixed on the basis that the three-inch pipe would irrigate about one acre land. It was further stated that this rate would be continued for the Railway Company subject to modification in every decade.[110]

Since October 1898, the South Indian Railway Company had been availing water from the Kallar River through pipes. The government meanwhile ordered that the water charges should be collected from the companies since the beginning (1898). But the railway companies did not oblige. In 1928, the government order stated that though the government had ordered in 1909, the railway companies were not charged as no agreements were entered into with them.[111] The company, however, requested the government to waive the balance due from them. Consequently, in 1931, the government ordered that the South Indian Railway Company should be levied only from 28th September 1927 and waived the earlier dues.[112] It shows that the government had wantonly neglected the need to regulate water supply to the railway companies until the first quarter of the twentieth century.

In those days, the Bhavani River water was diverted only through the old channels, viz. Arakkankottai, Thadappalli and Kalingarayan channels. As such, diversion of water to the railways may not have posed a serious threat to the agricultural sector. Even though there was no representation from the farmers' side regarding water diversion to the railways, the government had hiked the water charges. In 1948, the government raised the rates for water drawn for the railway company from irrigation sources and navigation channels to Rs. 6 per 1,000 cubic yards, subject to a minimum of Rs. 100 per annum.[113]

During the second half of the twentieth century, water supply to the railway company was regulated through installing metres and other measuring devices. In 1954, the government proposed to fix metres or other suitable devices to measure the quantity of water, which would be maintained at the government's cost. The railway was made responsible for the proper housing and safe custody of those devices installed. Rent for the metres at appropriate rates, cost of repairs or replacement due to the negligence of the railway would be adjusted in the accounts of the railway. Further, it should maintain and keep a log book, in which daily entries should be made about the quantum of water drawn.

Water Demand for the Industries

Since a long period, the traditional industries might have utilized the Bhavani waters, though in less quantity. Then, the water diverted for industrial uses might not have created any issue inviting the government's attention towards formulating a policy. For instance, in Karnool district of Andhra Pradesh, several factories had been drawing water from the Karnool-Cuddapah canal for periods extending up to forty years (before 1927) without paying any charges. Since the Bhavani River basin is also part of the Madras Presidency, the same might have been practised here as well. The available historical records do not give any indication that water supply to the industries was regulated due to the objections raised by the farmers. Different kind of water charges for the industries was introduced only in 1909.

In 1909, the government fixed the rate for industrial water supply at Rs. 3 per 1,000 cubic yards if taken by means of sluices or pipes, Rs. 80 for the same taken by hand, subject to a minimum charge of Rs. 50 per annum for both the cases, unless the concerns were specially exempted or concessional rates allowed by the government.[114] It shows that the water tariff was imposed neither to provide constant water supply to the farmers nor to protect the environment from industrial effluents but was solely aimed at garnering more revenue for the government.

During the second quarter of the twentieth century, water demand for the industries shot up in the Bhavani River basin areas. For instance, in 1925, the sanitary engineer had estimated that about 50,000 gallons of water per day would be utilized by the existing factories in Coimbatore town, generating revenue worth Rs. 9,000 per annum at a fair rate of Rs. 0-8-0 per 1,000 gallons per day.[115] Following non-compliance of the 1909 Government Order directing the authorities to collect the outstanding tariff, the government advised them to charge the industries for taking water from the government sources.[116]

In 1940, when the chief engineer (irrigation) proposed to raise the rate of water charges but the government deferred its implementation due to the Second World War.[117] Until 1945, the minimum rate was only Rs. 3 per 1,000 cubic yards. In 1945, though the government accepted the recommendations of the chief engineer (I), implementing them was further postponed until normal conditions were restored after the Second World War.[118]

Until 1946, water charges were collected at different rates based on the method of lifting and the quantity of water. In 1946, the government modified the earlier rules for supplying water to the industries from the government sources. The entire quantity of water actually used for boiling purposes was to be charged at the rate of Rs. 3 per 1,000 cubic yards. If used for cooling purposes without exceeding the fixed amount of water or beyond the permitted quantity the rate was one-fourth of the actual rate (Rs. 3 per 1,000 cubic yards). In that case the company should return the same quantity of water into the channel or river. It further stated that all expenses connected with the arrangements (metre and other devices) should be borne by the company. If the company draws more water than the prescribed quantity, the penal amount would be charged at the rate of Rs. 8 per 1,000 cubic yards. The charges for the estimated quantity of required water by the company should be paid in advance.[119]

In 1948, the water charges for industries were invariably fixed at the rate of Rs. 6 for 1,000 cubic yards even for cooling purposes.[120] The government order stated that the water cess for water drawn for all types of industrial uses from the government irrigation sources and navigation channels had been fixed at the rate of Rs. 6 per 1,000 cubic yards, subject to a minimum charge of Rs. 100 per annum and the rate being applicable to the rice mills also.[121] In the case of water taken for cooling purposes and returned undiminished and unpolluted to the government sources, a concessional rate was fixed at the rate of Rs. 1–8–0 per 1,000 cubic yards. So long as the water was not returned back to the channel, the water cess was to be charged at Rs. 6 per 1,000 cubic yards for industrial purposes. Hence, it becomes evident that only towards the end of the first half of twentieth century that the government evinced some interest about the question of environment protection.

In addition to the little emphasis on water quality and protection from pollution, the government had imposed some restrictions on the Industries considering the importance of irrigation for agriculture through the rivers and channels during the second half of the twentieth century. In 1950, the Solar industries and Traders Ltd, Punjai Lakkapuram, Erode, approached the executive engineer, PWD, Erode, seeking permission to take water from the Kalingarayan canal. But, they were refused permission on the ground that the canal water was intended only for irrigation purposes. However, the government granted permission to take water from the channel in the same year at the rate of Rs. 6 per 1,000 cubic yards under the following conditions.[122]

1. Pumping should not be done directly but with the help of a cistern to be built by the company at its own cost.
2. Cisterns shall be supplied by a six-inch-diameter sluice with a headwall tube built at the side to be selected by the PWD.
3. The sill level of the sluice would be kept about one feet above the bed level of the channel.
4. The company should agree to pay water charges fixed by the government from time to time.
5. During the period of scarcity and closure periods, water would not be allowed for industrial purposes.
6. Company should not change or modify any of the arrangements fixed initially.
7. In the event of infringement of any of the conditions, the pipe sluice would be blocked permanently and no water from the channel would be permitted.

The above conditions show that the government had initiated certain measures to regulate industrial water supply in order to protect the farmers.

The United Bleachers Ltd factory, located on the right bank of the river Bhavani, just near the railway bridge in Mettupalayam, required about one cusec of water, which amounted to 540,000 gallons per day. In 1954, its requirement was about 250,000 gallons per day for another six months. The company accepted to pay the usual cess of Rs. 6 per 1,000 cubic yards for the water consumed. The government permitted it to draw water for ten years from 1 March 1954 by sinking borewells in the river bed with the following conditions:

1. The company shall not use the water for any purpose other than processing in the factory.
2. The company shall pay charges at the rate of Rs. 6 per 1,000 cubic yards subject to a minimum of Rs. 100 per annum or any other rate fixed by the government from time to time.
3. After processing the effluent, water shall be treated properly before being let into the river.
4. The metres installed by the company at its cost should be open at all times for inspection by the officers of PWD or the Revenue Department.
5. The company should bear the cost for drawing water and also for letting it back.
6. The company shall not claim any right to draw water and the permission was liable to be cancelled at any time.[123]

Since independence, successive governments have paid little attention to the farmers and water quality while diverting water for the industries. Till 1977, no separate act was enacted to protect water from the discharge of effluents from the industries. In 1977, under the Water (Prevention and Control of Pollution) Cess Act 1977 (Act No. 36 of 1977), water charges were fixed for industrial purposes at the rate of ¾ *paise* per kilo litre for cooling, spraying in mine fits or boiler food; two *paise* per kilo litre for processing whereby water gets polluted and the pollutants are early bio-degradable and 2½ *paise* /kl for processing whereby water gets polluted and the pollutants are not easily bio-degradable and are toxic.

Ineffective Pollution Control Measures and Environmental Damages

Water-consuming industrial units have proliferated during the last two decades of the twentieth century. In 1980, there were only 26 units and they together consumed about 4.40 MLD, whereas the number increased to 325 and consumed about 40.89 MLD in 1990. In 1997, the number of units further shot up to 866 and consumed about 106.91 MLD.[124] Coupled with the steep rise in the number of water-consuming industries and their quantity of consumption, pollution load also increased during this period. In 1980, the pollution load was 10,252 tonnes of TDS, comprising 6,053 tonnes of chloride, 420 tonnes of sulphate, 482 tonnes of TSS, 413 tonnes of COD, 169 tonnes of BOD and 8 tonnes of oil and grease and it increased to 174,201 tonnes of TDS, 91,404 tonnes of chloride, 11,984 tonnes of sulphate, 54,592 tonnes of TSS, 4,928 tonnes of COD, 714 tonnes of BOD and 40 tonnes of oil and grease in 2000 (see Table 3.12). Between 1980 and 2000, the cumulative pollution load was 2,354,464 tonnes of TDS, 1,311,722 tonnes of chloride, 125,775 tonnes of sulphate, 97,152 tonnes of TSS, 90,160 tonnes of COD, 29,848 tonnes of BOD and 1,513 tonnes of oil and grease.[125] Although water requirement for the processing of per kilo cloth has reduced over the period, it has been increasing due to the mushrooming growth of the number of water-consuming industries. While 226.5 litres of water was required to process per kg of cloth in 1980, it has come down to 145 litres in 2000.[126]

Increasing number of water-consuming industries in the Noyyal basin has created serious environmental problems, particularly since the 1970s. After using the water for processing purposes, the industries let out the untreated effluents into the Noyyal River and other small streams – Nallar and Jamunnai – besides other water bodies and agricultural lands. A recent estimate by NTADCL quantifies the effluents discharged by the dyeing and bleaching units at 40 MLD.[127] The total volume of effluent discharge from the 851 bleaching and dyeing units was about 60 million litres per day.[128] While Noyyal has become an effluent drainage, the Orathupalayam dam downstream was turned into a storage tank of the toxic discharge. As such, groundwater has been contaminated beyond redemption, resulting in loss of productivity and decline in land value over the period. A study conducted by Madras School of Economics (1998) at Veerapandi and Orathupalayam villages near Tirupur revealed that about two-third of landowners had left their lands uncultivated either in part or in full due to non-availability or poor quality of water; 90 per cent of landholders attributed fall in productivity to water pollution and 43 per cent reported decline in land value during the last decade.[129] Another study by Jacob (1996) concluded that the indiscriminate discharge of industrial waste effluent has led to groundwater pollution. Even the industries could not use that water. Further, it shows that the open wells had a higher level of contamination than the borewells.[130] At present, about 102 MLD wastewater, containing bleaching powder, sulphuric dyes, inorganic catalysts and other chemicals are being discharged every day.[131] According to a recent report, there are 800 bleaching and dyeing units in Tirupur, using 60,000 kilos of chemicals and over 115 million litres of freshwater per day.[132] In addition to this, water consumption is very high when compared

Table 3.12 Different kinds of pollution load generated in Tirupur: 1980–2000 (Quantity in Tonne/Year)

Years	TDS	Chloride	Sulphate	TSS	COD	BOD	Oil and grease
1980	10,252.33	6,052.62	419.95	481.86	412.56	169.34	8.30
1981	12,681.97	7,402.87	555.51	589.50	516.99	203.82	10.04
1982	15,690.13	9,135.25	698.64	726.94	643.15	250.31	12.35
1983	18,863.26	10,937.06	858.91	870.66	776.06	297.97	14.74
1984	22,685.28	13,116.61	1,050.26	1,043.50	938.42	355.55	17.60
1985	25,901.92	14,778.20	1,279.57	1,177.99	1,081.22	393.57	19.66
1986	38,836.94	22,131.07	1,927.47	1,765.33	1,619.73	588.86	29.45
1987	53,291.43	30,332.01	2,654.59	2,422.02	2,218.01	806.79	40.41
1988	67,745.93	38,532.95	3,381.70	3,078.72	2,816.29	1,024.72	51.36
1989	82,594.08	46,972.88	4,122.14	3,754.42	3,429.89	1,249.58	62.66
1990	91,628.22	52,204.13	4,545.69	4,166.81	3,814.32	1,389.89	69.55
1991	119,000.25	67,753.73	5,912.57	5,412.61	4,943.61	1,804.23	90.37
1992	147,063.45	83,793.70	7,275.16	6,696.12	6,097.70	2,234.97	111.92
1993	175,129.72	99,835.53	8,637.87	7,979.79	7,251.90	2,665.77	133.48
1994	203,557.62	116,096.89	10,012.80	9,280.93	8,420.20	3,102.95	155.33
1995	230,397.52	131,098.73	11,447.50	10,488.05	9,532.84	3,494.97	175.27
1996	236,307.32	134,217.50	11,827.09	10,746.17	9,772.28	3,572.09	179.42
1997	242,396.85	137,413.97	12,227.79	11,009.82	10,023.31	3,649.92	183.61
1998	199,583.66	101,908.48	12,647.69	5,720.51	5,643.91	1,014.61	57.97
1999	186,655.17	96,603.48	12,307.52	5,147.60	5,279.74	863.44	49.06
2000	174,200.78	91,404.03	11,984.10	4,592.40	4,928.05	714.30	40.35
Cumulative Total	2,354,463.83	1,311,721.71	125,774.52	97,151.75	90,160.18	29,847.65	1,512.90

Computed from PCB Data, 2000; Source: Appasamy 2000, p. 63.

to international standards. It is around 200–400 litres of water per kg of finished product in Tirupur, while it is only 120–150 litres at the international level.[133] Since the early 1990s, pollution control initiatives have been initiated, but they were not implemented till recently. For example, in 1991, Tirupur Dyers Association formed the Tirupur Effluent Treatment Company Pvt. Ltd (TETCO) to establish four effluent treatment plants with the support of both the state and central governments.[134] Though there was no development on this front, the number of the units has increased several fold. In 1994, the association had accepted to establish eight Common Effluent Treatment Plants (CETPs) for the 300 dyeing units, with others having independent plants before January 1996. But they have not established the treatment plants. In the meanwhile, Karur Taluk Noyyal Irrigation Farmers Association filed a writ petition at the Madras High Court in 1996, seeking to close all these industries. And, the high court ordered the Tamil Nadu Pollution Control Board (TNPCB) to issue notices to these polluting industries and prepare a status report on the ETPs. In November 1997, the TNPCB submitted the status report, saying that more than half of the units had not started the ETPs. According to the report, of the 866 dyeing and bleaching units in Tirupur, 288 were covered by 8 CETPs, 404 had Independent Effluent Treatment Plants (IETPs) and 114 had closed down.[135] Significantly, the court was told that work on the eight CETPS, with which 288 units were connected, were still under progress and only 78 units had completed 100 per cent work on ETPs and 243 units have completed only 75 per cent of the works on ETPs. All other units will be closed. And, in March 1997, the High Court ordered the closure of 160 units, which had not started any work on ETPs. In January 1998, 108 units were closed. On 11 February 1998 in the presence of counsel for the petitioner, joint chief environmental engineer and assistant environmental engineer of Tirupur agreed to complete 8 CEPTS and 386 IETPs on or before 11 May 1998. Accordingly, on 10 March 1998 the high court granted time till 11 May 1998, to 609 dyeing and bleaching units to establish the CETPs and individual plants.[136] Further extension of six months was denied by the High Court in April 1998. Consequently, Tirupur Dyeing Factory Owners Association (TDFOA) and Tirupur Exporters Association (TEA) filed a special leave petition in Supreme Court seeking an interim stay on the Madras High Court Order, but it was turned down on May 14. The Supreme Court upheld the decision of the high court to close the 860-odd dyeing and bleaching units by 11 May 1998.[137]

Even after establishing the CETPs, the dyeing and bleaching units failed to treat the effluents at the prescribed level. At present, there are about 300

Individual Effluent Treatment Plants (IETPs) and eight[138] CETPs in Tirupur. According to TNPCB's latest record (during August 2000), 424 units have their own treatment plants, while 278 units have joined CETPs, 164 units, which are not connected either to an IETP or to a CETP, have been closed down on the order of the Madras High Court.[139] The total effluent generated by the 278 units connected to the 8 CETPS and the 424 individual units was about 83.14 MLD. Of this, about 37.98 MLD was treated by the CETPs and 45.16 MLD by the individual plants.[140] But these industries are not treating them effectively.[141] The Pollution Control Board found that the units covered under seven CETPs discharged the treated effluents without removing the salts used in dye-fixation that had led to groundwater pollution and ecological damage in the Noyyal River basin.[142] The dyeing and bleaching units in Tirupur are using around 350 tonnes of salt.[143] Nearly 6,500 tonnes of salt and 570 tonnes of bleaching powder are used every month for processing.[144] In April 2002, the TNPCB has served notice to the seven CETPs to bring down the total dissolved solids (through segregation of salts used in dyeing) to the permitted level of 2,100 ppm in treated effluents by May 31. Further, it warned that failure to adhere to the deadline would invite severe action, including closure of the units.[145] Studies reveal that the effluents from these industries have also caused serious health problems, like skin diseases and stomach ailments. The cattle and livestock in these areas also suffer from skin diseases and became impotent or infertile in recent years.[146] In the downstream of Noyyal basin, farmers of Perundurai and Kangeyam taluks of Erode district complained against discharge of effluents by dyeing and bleaching units engaged by the knitting and garment manufacturers in Tirupur and sought compensation for crop loss suffered on account of contaminated groundwater.[147] From the above, it becomes evident that effluent discharges have led to huge social costs as witnessed by fall in agricultural productivity and fish stock, contamination of drinking water, health problems and deterioration of entire natural ecology and environment of this region.

What Went Wrong? Institutional Failures at Different Levels

In the Bhavani and Noyyal River basins, demand for water increased within the sector and among the various sectors from the early twentieth century.[148] Coupled with this, water pollution has aggravated the problem further.[149] Given the nature of the problem in these river basins, questions arise as to what were the drawbacks of water governance and how the institutions have failed in managing them. It is apparent that the institutions have failed at multiple levels. At the apex level, without taking into account the quantum of surplus of these river basins, water was diverted for additional agricultural areas and other purpose at different points of time. For instance, initially, diversion was carried out for domestic water supply from Siruvani in 1924, then, Pillur in 1989 and later from Cauvery in 2002. Options other than diversion from these basins were never considered to meet the demands. At the micro-level, the institutions have failed to protect the used water, particularly that of domestic (drainage) and industrial (effluent) sectors. While the cities and towns invariably discharge the untreated drainage, industries too were letting out effluents into the river basins. Though the post-colonial government has enacted different acts to protect water, the institutions that are responsible have failed to implement them. Precisely, mismanagement of water resources at the apex level and failure of institutions at the different sectoral levels culminated in intensifying the competing demand for water, particularly during the post-independence period.

Impact of Competing Demand on Agriculture

It is evident that the availability of water for agriculture sector has shrunk progressively in the Bhavani and Noyyal River basins since the early twentieth century. Besides the diversions to other sectors, expansion of cultivation and other technological development within the agricultural sector also sharpened the problem.[150] On the one hand, diversion of water for domestic and industrial sectors reduces the availability of water for agricultural, and on the other hand, the diverted water of these sectors gets discharged in the form of drainage and effluents, affecting the quality of water, further reducing the availability of water for the agricultural sector.

Conclusion

In the Noyyal River basin, water diversion for Coimbatore and Tirupur cities commenced in the early twentieth century due to the process of urbanization and industrialization. Initially, water was diverted primarily for domestic purposes and later was extended to meet industrial demands. In the Noyyal River basin, water from Siruvani, a tributary of Bhavani River, was diverted to Coimbatore city. Consequent to rapid urbanization and industrialization both in Coimbatore and Tirupur cities, greater demand for water has emerged not only for the domestic purpose but also for water-consuming industries. In the Noyyal River basin, local water supply sources were not adequate to meet the burgeoning demand of Coimbatore and Tirupur. As a result, the Pillur diversion was taken up for Coimbatore city and the Annur diversion for Tirupur city from the Bhavani River.

This diversion from Bhavani River to the Noyyal basin to meet the urban demand of Coimbatore and Tirupur has decreased the availability of water for agriculture. During the years of low rainfall, the problem could be accentuated. Conflict may therefore arise between the agriculture and urban sectors. The cost of meeting urban demand for water increases as more distant sources have to be tapped and again water has to be taken to long distances. The wastewater from the urban sector brings a social cost as that causes serious pollution problems and affects downstream agriculture and other uses. It is also interesting to note that in the case of both Coimbatore and Tirupur, providing water itself spurs greater urbanization, which only increases the demand for water. Clearly, water has to be used more prudently by conservation, recycling and reuse and should be priced at its true value. The government can no longer afford to finance large schemes to transport water from outside the basin. The latest proposal is for the industries to share the infrastructure cost of building a pipeline from the confluence of the Bhavani with the Cauvery.

Both the industries and railways had used the river water without any restriction, and neither the farmers nor the government did consider it an issue until the second half of the twentieth century. During the second quarter of the twentieth century also, the government's main concern was revenue and it completely neglected the impact on the environmental and the attendant problems. It was only after independence that the government paid some attention, though inadequate, for the protection of water in the Bhavani River. In short, until the 1970s, the government had failed to give much attention to the diversion of water to the industries and discharge of effluents into the river and its channels. Also, the farmers too were oblivious of the long-term effects of industrial water supply and effluent discharges in the Bhavani River and its tributaries. More attention should also be paid to effluent treatment and recycling so that the increasing quantum of wastewater does not end up causing further damage to the downstream users. Diverting water from other basins for domestic and industrial needs and discharging it as effluents not only aggravate the situation in the context of competing demand for water but will be a great threat to the ecology and environment and also to the sustainability of the natural resources in general and water resources in particular in the Bhavani and Noyyal River basins of Tamil Nadu.

4

Water Supply Schemes and Conflict

Diversion of water for purposes other than agriculture, viz. industrial and domestic supply, had led to conflicts in water management. The very idea of water diversion from the Bhavani and Noyyal River basins, which emerged at the end of the nineteenth century, was concretized only during the second quarter of the twentieth century. This chapter attempts to analyse the history of water conflicts between the agricultural and non-agriculture sectors, viz. industrial and domestic sectors, in these basins between 1890 and 1970.

Invariably, providing potable water is a crucial one for all the growing cities and towns. Drinking water supply was initially met through exploiting the existing water sources like wells and tanks. Coimbatore presents a distinctive picture when compared to other cities since the city's drinking water supply depended upon the wells, which were inadequate to meet the demand and the water was also salty. Population in Coimbatore city was 53,000 in 1901 and it had increased to 565,293 in 1971 (figures for the 1981 city boundaries). Here, the first textile unit was established by the British in 1888. Then, a local entrepreneur established a mill in 1907. Since then, a number of other industries too got established. In 1995, the city had about 150 large-scale textile units, 350 small spinning mills, 20,000 power looms, 40,000 handloom units, 2,000 knitting units, 500 steel-casting foundries and 350 electric-motor foundries. In addition to that several other industrial units also came up. Due to population explosion and industrial growth, demand for water had increased over the period. For example, water consumption in 1931 was 11.3 mld, distributed for 0.09 millions people at the rate of 126 litres per day. In 1971 this increased to 13 mld, supplied at the rate of 36 litres per day for 0.36 million people. In 1991, this went up to 85 mld and was distributed at the rate of 103 litres for 0.82 million people. To meet the increasing demand, the municipality tried to extract water from the tanks and

This is to acknowledge that the earlier version of the chapter was published in *Rethinking the Mosaic: Investigation into local water management,* along with Professor Paul P. Appasamy.

streams adjoining the city. Due to the non-availability of good quality drinking water in these sources, diversion of water from the Bhavani, Noyyal and their tributaries was actively considered at the end of the nineteenth century.

Tirupur town, though located on the banks of Noyyal River, however, was facing a severe water crisis because of the growing population and expansion of industries since the 1930s. The total population of Tirupur, which was 6,056 in 1901, rose to 128,228 in 1971 (figures for 1991 boundaries). The per capita water supply was 127 litres in 1996. The number of industries also has increased since 1925, and in 1995, there were 8,437 units, of which 713 were water-intensive. With the requirement of water for industrial use at 90 million litres per day, a large quantity was needed mainly for the 526 dyeing and bleaching units.

Has the diversion of water from the Bhavani and Noyyal River for domestic water supply led to any conflict between farmers and the municipality, municipality and the public works department, and municipality and the urban people? Was there any opposition to the municipality from urban people over fixing water tax? Was there any clash of interest between the municipality and farmers besides the Public Works Department and the state? Apart from these, another issue demanding detailed attention is whether the farmers had protested against these diversions. If so, how the government had dealt these issues and what assurances were made to the farmers in the basins? And what was the policy adopted by the government to resolve these conflicts? These queries may throw some light on understanding water conflict in its entire dimension between the different sectors and departments of the government both in Coimbatore and Tirupur town.

The idea of diverting Bhavani River water to Coimbatore Municipality's water supply scheme was initiated in the 1890s. Simultaneously diversion of the surplus water into the Noyyal River basin for irrigation was also discussed. Whether the Noyyal River basin farmers had raised any demand to divert the Siruvani water for irrigation has to be seen in this context. The nature of conflicts that erupted between the Coimbatore municipality and Public Works Department while diverting Siruvani water for agricultural purposes and how they were resolved is also an interesting one.

This chapter, while addressing the above-mentioned queries, also discusses whether the government had considered the importance of irrigation and the traditional rights of the farmers in the Bhavani and Noyyal Rivers and their tributaries and channels during 1890–1970. This chapter consists of three sections besides the introduction. The second section deals with the history of drinking water supply scheme of the Coimbatore city and Tirupur town. The third section narrates the chronology of water diversion from the Bhavani River basin to the Noyyal River basin for agricultural purposes. The fourth section analyses the conflicts, and the last section ends with the concluding observations of this chapter.

History of Coimbatore Water Supply Schemes

Constituted as a municipality on 20th November 1866, Coimbatore was spread over about ten sq miles consisting of ten revenue villages, viz. Coimbatore, portion of Telungupalayam, Ramanathapuram, Krishnarasapuram, Sanganur, Anupparpalayam, Puliankulam, Kumarapalayam, Savaripalayam and Ganapathi. Though located near the adjoining Noyyal River, the drinking water problem was an acute one because groundwater was scarce due to low rainfall (see Table 4.1). The quality of water was also very poor and the groundwater contains lime, probably magnesium and other salts as well. The tanks in and around the city

Table 4.1 Statement of rainfall at Coimbatore: 1892/93–1908/09

Year	Rainfall (in inches)
1892/93	15.12
1893/94	22.43
1894/95	16.24
1895/96	17.53
1896/97	27.17
1897/98	13.44
1898/99	25.11
1899/1900	24.89
1900/01	25.11
1901/02	28.04
1902/03	32.01
1903/04	31.83
1904/05	14.38
1905/06	17.54
1906/07	33.32
1907/08	19.87
1908/09	26.77

Source: G.O. No. 145 Mis W PWD [B&R], 15-11-1917, Tamil Nadu State Archives, Chennai (hereafter TNSA).

are either situated at elevated places ordinarily not suited for drawing water or are dependent upon poor (highly unreliable) water sources. The existing well water, being hard in nature, could not be used for boilers, dyeing, cloth and other manufacturing purposes as well as for domestic consumption. The examination of different well waters in Coimbatore city in the 1890s showed that the water had lost its characteristics and was contaminated (see Table 4.2). However, the municipality did not consider any other source of water supply for the town. Until the 1880s, the Coimbatore Municipal Council had managed through repairing pumping from the existing wells in the different parts of the city (see Table 4.3). No attempt was made to bring water from the rivers and other sources.[1]

The towns and villages neighbouring Coimbatore and those along the Bhavani and Noyyal Rivers were starved of sufficient and good quality drinking water and were dependent upon the nearby wells and public tanks. As mentioned earlier, groundwater was hard and its availability was also very limited. Due to the growing population, industrialization and the process of urbanization, water problem was very acute in most of the towns and villages located along these rivers between the late nineteenth and early twentieth centuries. Insufficient and bad quality of water had caused the spread of cholera and other diseases. For example, in Coimbatore city, ninety-six persons were affected by epidemics in 1926–27, of

Table 4.2 Results of chemical and bacteriological examination in different wells of Coimbatore city: 1890.

Details	District jail well	Main gate well	Jail garden well
Total solids grams per litre	1.610	1.730	1.580
Volatile solids per litre	0.320	0.390	0.320
Chlorine per litre	0.398	0.390	0.355
Total hardness Clarks scale	49.000	49.000	49.000
Permanent hardness Clarks scale	15.750	26.250	22.750
Free Ammonia Ml grams per litre	1.160	0.080	0.160
Albunmnoid per litre	0.120	0.040	0.080
Nitric acid per litre	11.250	11.250	15.000
Apparent quality of the water as inferred from the results obtained on examination	Bad	Bad	Bad

Source: G.O. No. 53 Mis L&M (M), 16-1-1893, TNSA.

Table 4.3 Expenditure on Coimbatore municipal water supply: 1888/89–1899/1900

Year	Amount (in rupees)
1888/89	946
1889/90	1,456
1890/91	455
1891/92	1,200
1892/93	269
1893/94	795
1894/95	NA
1895/96	NA
1896/97	NA
1897/98	510
1898/99	479
1899/1900	357

Note: NA = Not Available.

Sources: G.O. No. 1190 Mis L&M (M) 14-8-1890, TNSA; G.O. No. 1294 Mis L&M (M) 13-8-1891, TNSA; G.O. No. 1106 Mis L&M (M) 23-8-1893, TNSA; G.O. No. 282 Mis L&M (M) 8-3-1894, TNSA; G.O. No. 1195 Mis L&M (M) 4-9-1894, TNSA; G.O. No. 1029 Mis L&M (M) 20-7-1899, TNSA; G.O. No. 1148 Mis L&M (M) 11-8-1900, TNSA.

Table 4.4 Different sources of Coimbatore water supply proposals/schemes

Year of proposal made	Name of the scheme	Water sources	Dropped/Finalized	Remarks
1888	Muthikulam Scheme	Bhavani River	Dropped in 1890	Prohibitive cost
1892	Noyyal River Scheme	Noyyal River	Dropped in 1893	Prohibitive cost
1901	Chitrachavadi Channel and Rajavaikkal of Noyyal River	Chitrachavadi Channel and Rajavaikkal of Noyyal River	Dropped in 1901	Bad Quality of Water
1907	Kistnambadi Tank Scheme	Chitrachavadi Channel of Noyyal River	Dropped in 1908	Protest from Farmers and other down stream villages

(continued)

Year of proposal made	Name of the scheme	Water sources	Dropped/ Finalized	Remarks
1909	Sub-Artesian Springs, Singanallur Scheme	Sub-Artesian Springs, Singanallur Valley Scheme	Dropped in 1890	Prohibitive cost and poor financial conditions of the Municipality
1912	Siruvani I	Siruvani River	Finalized in 1924	Best water at low cost of the scheme
1928	Anayar and Periyar Scheme	Anayar and Periyar Streams	Finalized in 1929 and 1930	Temporary water supply
1956	Siruvani II	Siruvani River	Finalized in 1970	Supply of water increased
1980	Pillur Scheme	Bhavani River	Finalized in 1989	Supply of water increased

Source: Extracted from Section Two.

whom, fifty-nine died. In 1927–28, 86 of the 127 affected had lost their lives.[2] Consequently, the government initiated several steps to divert water from Bhavani, Noyyal and their tributaries. Let us see a brief account of the different water supply schemes (see Table 4.4) for Coimbatore city before analysing the other issues.

Muthikulam Scheme

In the history of Coimbatore water supply schemes, Siruvani is the oldest one and has been mentioned in an inspection note of Colonel Montgomery in 1879.[3] But the government did not consider the proposal till the late 1880s, when the Coimbatore Municipal Council took up various possible schemes. In the late 1880s, the government proposed construction of a multi-purpose dam across the Bhavani at the junction of Siruvani (i.e. a tributary of the Bhavani) for drinking water supply to Coimbatore and also to irrigate about 2,000 acres in the Noyyal basin. In 1890, the scheme was dropped because (1) diversion of water from Siruvani (during low flow periods) could affect the large irrigation channels which take off from the river between Mettupalayam and Bhavani town, and (2) supply across the chain of hills between Mettupalayam and the Noyyal River would require a huge investment for excavating or tunnelling.

Hence, the government decided that diversion of the west-flowing streams into the Noyyal basin was impracticable.[4]

Noyyal River Scheme

At the same time (1892), the government planned to bring water from the head sluice of the Kurumymookoor channel some miles above the Vellalore *annicut* of Noyyal River. This proposal also did not take off because the proposed location of the filtration gallery had valuable coconut topes and lacked approach routes either to deliver materials for construction or to store fuel afterwards. Further, a huge amount was required to compensate the coconut topes and to establish the roads. In addition, the quality of the Noyyal River water also was found to be bad and contaminated (see Table 4.5). Ultimately, the proposal was discarded considering the prohibitive cost.[5]

Muthannankulam Tank Scheme

In 1901, Coimbatore Municipal Council proposed to store the Chitrachavadi and Rajavaikkal water for the purpose of water supply to Coimbatore at the Muthannankulam tank, located at the northern-end of the town. As the tank

Table 4.5 Results of chemical and bacteriological examination of Noyyal River water: 1890

Details	Noyyal River water
Total solids grams per litre	0.540
Volatile solids per litre	0.080
Chlorine per litre	0.060
Total hardness Clarks scale	28.00
Permanent hardness Clarks scale	0.700
Free Ammonia Ml grams per litre	0.200
Albunmnoid per litre	0.120
Nitric acid per litre	0.450
Apparent quality of the water as inferred from the results obtained on examination	Bad

Source: G.O. No. 53 Mis L&M (M), 16-1-1893, TNSA.

Table 4.6 Results of chemical and bacteriological examination of Chitrachavadi Channel water: 1906.

Details	Chitrachavadi Channel water
Total solids grams per litre	38.000
Chlorine per litre	4.970
Total hardness Clarks scale	28.000
Permanent hardness Clarks scale	8.500
Free Ammonia Ml grams per litre	0.009
Albunmnoid per litre	0.008
Nitric acid per litre	Nil
Oxygen absorbed (Tidy's process)	0.068
Nitrates	present
Sulphates	present
Phosphates	Nil
Iron, poisonous metals	Nil
Apparent quality of the water as inferred from the results obtained on examination	Contaminated

Source: G.O. No.1337 Mis L&M (M), 27-6-1907, TNSA.

was situated at an elevation higher than that of the town and spread over about 9.75 acres, a proposal was made to enlarge the tank to store water for a period of three to five years. This proposal was also dropped, since it received the drainage from the outskirts of the town and because of the anticipated objection to fill this tank from the Noyyal River, which already had too many demands on it. Also, the quality of water at the tail-end of Chitrachavadi channel was bad and unfit for drinking (see Table 4.6). Finally the scheme failed to take off.[6]

Kistnambadi Tank Scheme

In 1907, the government proposed to construct a tank near the Kistnambadi tank, where the Chitrachavadi channel from Noyyal finally discharges its flow. This scheme was proposed to harness the surplus from the Kistnambadi tank let into the rivers to fill the next lower Selvambadi tank, which is deprived of a weir of its own and was directly connected with the Kumarasamy tank. There is a surplus weir to the Kumarasamy tank, and the whole amount of water flowing over this weir would be available for the proposed new water supply tank.[7] But this proposal received stiff opposition from the government agricultural farm and the farmers of the Chitrachavadi channel and other downstream villages.[8] The agricultural farm objected to it for the following reasons: (1) lands for the proposed storage tank would be used for the farm, the institute and the residential buildings for the staff, (2) more than half of the wetland acquired for experimental work would be taken away and (3) water supply for the wetlands would be affected in bad years.[9] In addition to that a petition submitted by eighty-six landholders of Chitrachavadi and other villages stated that they had been suffering on account of inadequate rainfall, while uncertain supply from the Chitrachavadi channel for their paddy crops and topes would force them to leave a large extent of land fallow for several years. Further, citing that they had been availing remission frequently, they requested reduction in the land assessment rate or an exemption from any increase of assessment for the next two settlement periods. Given the facts above, they asked the government to reconsider the proposed storage tank for the Coimbatore water supply scheme.[10]

The quality of Kistnambadi tank water was also bad and contaminated (see Table 4.7). The government then decided to abandon the scheme because the storage reservoir would have to be necessarily enlarged at a considerable additional cost so as to hold supply for twelve months. Even then there is no guarantee that supply would be sufficient throughout the year.[11]

Table 4.7 Results of chemical and bacteriological examination of Kistnambadi tank water: 1906

Details	Kistnambadi tank water
Total solids grams per litre	39.000
Chlorine per litre	5.325
Total hardness Clarks scale	20.000
Permanent hardness Clarks scale	0.500
Free Ammonia Ml grams per litre	0.010
Albunmnoid per litre	0.012
Nitric acid per litre	Nil
Oxygen absorbed (Tidy's process)	0.108
Nitrates	Present
Sulphates	Present
Phosphates	Nil
Iron, poisonous metals	Nil
Apparent quality of the water as inferred from the results obtained on examination	Contaminated

Source: G.O. No. 1337 Mis L&M (M), 27-6-1907, TNSA.

Sub-artesian Springs and Singanallur Scheme

In 1908, the government contemplated to study the possibility of securing sufficient water supply from the newly discovered artesian springs near Coimbatore and elicited suggestions for other schemes with a source of supply other than Noyyal River at a moderate cost.[12] In 1909, the sanitary engineer had found only three possible sources, viz. sub-artesian springs, Sanganurpallam valley, and Singanallur tank. In 1909, the government was requested to investigate the sub-artesian and Singanallur tank schemes.[13]

In 1910, the government deferred the study on the sub-artesian sources of water supply until the financial conditions of the council improved.[14] In 1912, investigation of the Singanallur tank scheme was abandoned owing to its prohibitive cost and unreliable prospects of water supply.[15] In the same year, the government ordered an investigation of Siruvani and Bhavani rivers as sources of water supply to Coimbatore city.

Siruvani Scheme–I

In 1912, a preliminary investigation was conducted for four possible schemes, viz. Siruvani River scheme, Sub-artesian supply, Bhavani River scheme and Singanallur tank scheme.[16] The initial cost and probable annual maintenance for the different schemes were as follows:

Scheme	Probable initial cost (rupees in lakhs)	Probable annual maintenance cost (rupees in lakhs)		
		Siruvani bund on ½ the capital cost at 5.96% for 30 years	Maintenance, pumping charges, etc.	Total annual maintenance
Siruvani River water supply	15.95	47,530	5,000	0.52
Sub-artesian supply	7.50	22,147	161,500	1.84
Bhavani River	21.00	62,770	402,500	4.65
Singanallur	26.25	72,353	57,500	1.30

The Siruvani River water was reported to be of excellent quality and the best among those examined in connection with the investigation (see Table 4.8). This water was uncontaminated except by wild animals in the hill areas.[17] Considering the many advantages, the sanitary engineer recommended the Siruvani River scheme to the Coimbatore Municipal Council for consideration.

The Coimbatore Municipal Council reported that the high cost of the proposed Siruvani water supply scheme could not be met with its own resources. Hence, it recommended to look into the feasibility of a combined hydro-electric scheme, which would be financially viable. In 1913, the sanitary engineer submitted an alternative approximate estimate for a water supply scheme for Coimbatore, combined with a hydro-electric project. The scope and nature of the scheme was to provide water supply to 70,000 people in Coimbatore town and another 20,000 in Podanur railway shops and colony. The power generated would be for electricity supply to Podanur workshops, colony, Nilgiris Railways, Coimbatore colony and industrial concerns, and electrification of at least Coonoor, Wellington and Ootacamand. It would also increase the area of wet cultivation in the Bodampatti valley and indirectly benefit cultivation under the

Table 4.8 Results of bacteriological and chemical examination of Siruvani water: 1923

Bacteriological examination	
Total chlorines per c.c. on agar at 37 IC	1,200
Lactose fermenters present in how many c.c.	1 C.C & upwards
Result of Vibrios test	No Vibrios in 100 c.c.
Nature of lactose fermenters isolated and number of species	Two of class II and 8 of class III. 3 species
Chemical examination	
Physical appearances: colour and transparency	slightly yellowish but clear
Smell	No
Quantitative:	(in parts per 100,000)
Total solids	4–6
Temporary hardness	Nil
Permanent hardness	1.0
Chlorine	0.3
Ammonical Nitragen	Trace
Albuminoid	0.0

Source: G.O. No. 2158 Mis LSG (PH), 23-10-1925, TNSA.

Noyyal River basin system.[18] Since 1913, this combined project remained under consideration. Subsequently, the power scheme was dropped.[19]

In 1919, the sanitary engineer submitted independent plans and estimates for the Siruvani water supply scheme. These envisaged irrigation of 2,000 acres in the Noyyal River basin, continuous water supply to 100,000 people at the rate of 20 gallons per head per day and 375 gallons per minute per day for industrial concerns. The government, in 1924, sanctioned Rs. 41 lakhs on the basis of sharing the cost on a 50:50 ratio with the municipal council. The foundation stone was laid by Honourable Viscount Goschen of Hawkhucs, Governor of Madras, on 10 October 1924. Work on this scheme was started in 1925.[20] As a special case, the government was prepared to allow its grants to be spent first and ordered that the expenditure would be incurred in the following manner:

Year	Amount (rupees in lakhs)
1924–25	0.50
1925–26	7.50
1926–27	14.75
1927–28	12.25
1928–29	6.00
	41.00

It also warned that, if the expenditure exceeded the estimated amount, that should be met entirely from the municipal funds. Otherwise, the scheme would be stopped.[21] In 1926, the government ordered that the Coimbatore municipality need not pay any charge for drawing water from the Siruvani River for drinking water supply till it affected irrigation.[22] In 1930, the government revised the estimate to Rs. 4,374,808, and it was shared between government and the municipality into Rs. 2,357,024 and Rs. 2,017,784, respectively.[23] In 1932, the government sanctioned the revised estimates aggregating to Rs. 4,641,650 for the complete scheme pertaining to Coimbatore water works.[24] The Siruvani scheme was completed and drinking water supply was made available since 1931.

Anayar and Periyar Scheme

Before the completion of the Siruvani scheme, drinking water scarcity was very severe in Coimbatore town. Hence, in 1928 the government ordered to arrange for advance water supply from the government sources, viz. Anayar and Periyar streams.[25] In 1929, the government sanctioned Rs. 36,240 for this scheme, and it was further hiked to Rs. 40,485 in 1931.[26] Water was diverted from Anayar River into the gravitation main by means of a temporary dam, which was supplemented by the Periyar stream. This scheme was expected to supply five gallons of water per head per day for a population of 70,000.[27] From 2 March 1929, water was drawn from Anayar and from 18 April 1927 in the Periyar stream. The total quantity of water drawn from both the sources was about 3 lakh gallons per day.[28]

The farmers of Palladam and Coimbatore made representations to divert the surplus water of Siruvani to the *ayacut* under the Noyyal River basin. In 1949, the government sanctioned Rs. 67,660 for raising the height of the Siruvani dam by four feet under the 'Grow More Food' scheme. The storage level was increased, facilitating discharge of more water into the tunnel for irrigation purposes in the Noyyal basin. During September 1950 and June 1951, a quantity of 25 to 40 cusecs was released.[29] This was mainly used by the *ayacuts* under the Chitrachavadi channel. In July 1951, following damage in the tunnel supply of water for Noyyal basin, irrigation was stopped by the municipality. Till 1955, no attempt was ever made to divert the west-flowing rivers such as. Kanhirapuzha, Tuppanadpuzha, Ambankadavuthodu into the Siruvani River.[30]

Siruvani–II

After the reorganization of states in 1956, the Tamil Nadu Government approached the Kerala Government to divert more water from Siruvani for drinking water purposes and also for extending irrigation in the downstream villages. But the Kerala Government refused permission for this.[31] Then the subject was included in the agenda for the meeting of the Southern Zonal Council held in April 1960, where it was decided that the chief ministers of both the states should settle the matter between themselves.[32]

In the meanwhile, in 1956 the chief engineer, PWD (Gl), prepared a proposal to increase the capacity of the reservoir from 2.4 MCF to 425 MCF to meet the increasing demand for more water to Coimbatore town, irrigation of downstream villages and the Noyyal basin through construction of a new dam across Siruvani. The approximate cost was estimated to be at Rs. 144 lakhs (114 lakhs for drinking water supply and Rs. 30 lakhs for irrigation).[33]

The agreement made between Tamil Nadu and Kerala provided for the supply of 1,300 million cubic feet of water every year, i.e. 223 million gallons daily.[34] The scheme for augmenting Siruvani water supply to fivefold over that of the then rate of supply was inaugurated on 15 September 1970 at a cost of Rs. 6 crores.[35] In 1977–78, the government sanctioned Rs. 1,616 lakhs towards the initial cost and Rs. 35 lakhs for annual maintenance.[36] Part of the works of this scheme, costing Rs. 701 lakhs in Kerala, was executed by Kerala PWD, with the Coimbatore municipality bearing the entire amount. The remaining works in Tamil Nadu costing Rs. 915 lakhs were undertaken by the Tamil Nadu Water and Drainage Board (TWAD). The 'Siruvani Water Supply Improvement Scheme' of the TWAD Board was estimated to cost Rs. 22 crores. This was taken up with loan assistance from the LIC besides the state government's resources.[37]

Pillur Scheme

In 1989, the Pillur Reservoir Project was constructed across the Bhavani River to generate electricity as well as to extend water supply to Coimbatore, 20 towns and 523 hamlets situated in 99 village *panchayats*.

This was the early history of the present Coimbatore water supply schemes. In this chapter the proposed schemes were also discussed to comprehend the reason as to why some of them did not materialize.

Tirupur Water Supply Scheme

Water problem in Tirupur is an acute one though the Noyyal River runs through the town. There are two main reasons for this: (1) There are about thirty-one irrigation *anicuts* across the Noyyal above Tirupur, and (2) even the available little water was contaminated all the way down to Tirupur.[38] Due to low rainfall, water problem was usually severe during the summer. The average rainfall for twenty years (1909–29) was only 25.72 inches (see Table 4.9). Until the 1920s, water for Tirupur was supplied mainly through seven public wells.[39] Every year, Tirupur municipality had spent a certain amount for repairing pumping from the wells to provide maximum water supply. The attempts to provide adequate water supply could not meet the demand of the growing population of the Tirupur municipality. And until the 1920s, the government too did not initiate any steps towards providing sufficient drinking water.

Table 4.9 Statement of rainfall at Tirupur station: 1909–29

Year	Rainfall (in inches)
1909	25.77
1910	31.45
1911	17.82
1912	26.74
1913	17.74
1914	17.08
1915	32.60
1916	23.72
1917	31.20
1918	25.16
1919	23.88
1920	22.75
1921	26.70
1922	36.08
1923	16.69
1924	24.24
1925	27.20
1926	16.70
1927	20.49
1928	27.78
1929	22.52

Source: G.O. No. 316 Mis LSG [PH], 10-2-1933, TNSA.

In 1919, the Koilveli valley water was examined and found to be hard and bacteriologically not hygienic (see Table 4.10). Yet, this source of water was recommended for the Tirupur municipality because of the absence of any other perennial supply.[40]

In the 1920s, the government proposed a scheme from the Koilveli infiltration gallery, located about five miles away from Tirupur town. This scheme was designed only for 20,000 people at five gallons of water per head per day.[41] It consists of two stages: (1) construction of an open infiltration gallery and collecting wells and a full power test, and (2) construction of a gravitation main, service reservoir and distribution system, land acquisition, diversion of road, etc.[42] In 1920, the sanitary engineer reported that the first part be taken up first,

Table 4.10 Results of chemical examination of Koilveli Springs

Physical appearances, colour and transparency	Slightly yellowish but clear
Smell	None
Quantitative:	
Total solids parts per 100,000	45.000
Temporary hardness per 100,000	17.500
Permanent hardness per 100,000	10.000
Chlorine per 100,000	1.420
Free ammonia per 100,000	0.003
Albuminoid ammonia per 100,000	0.003
Nitric nitrogen per 100,000	0.225
Qualitative:	
Nitrates	Nil
Sulphates	Present
Phosphates	Nil
Iron, poisonous metals	Nil
Microscopic examinations of suspendedmatter	Practically no deposit

Source: G.O. No. 1327 Mis LSG (PH), 8-8-1923.

and depending on its viability, the later part could be taken up.[43] In 1923, the cost of the first part was estimated at Rs. 1.05 lakhs, and in 1927, the government approved an approximate estimate of Rs. 0.67 lakhs.[44] Before sanctioning this scheme, the government ordered to ensure the possibilities of the water supply scheme by 'full power test', and in 1928, it sanctioned Rs. 51,000 for the purpose.[45]

In 1931, the revised estimate of Rs. 64,300 was sanctioned for a full power test.[46] Again, in 1937, the government approved Rs. 184,000 for the Koilveli water supply scheme.[47] But this scheme was kept under suspension till a drought season.[48] Later, the scheme's expenditure was scaled down to Rs. 182,370–10-2, of which, Rs. 91,185 was the government's share and the rest as municipal contribution.[49]

The Koilveli water supply scheme provided only 75,000 gallons of water per day and was distributed through some twenty public taps. This was inadequate and served not even one-third of the water demand of Tirupur municipality.[50] Consequently, the Tirupur municipality looked up for alternative schemes for sufficient water supply.

In 1949, the government sanctioned investigation of a water supply scheme with the Bhavani River as the source to serve the Tirupur municipality and seven wayside villages, viz. Pogalur, Kurukkalaiyam palayam, Annur, Karavalur, Nombiyampalayam, Avinashi and Tirumuganpundi.[51] Later, Karamadai, a wayside village, was also included in its ambit.[52] The Tirupur municipality had agreed to adopt the scheme with the eight wayside villages.[53] In 1949, the sanitary engineer recommended the provision of the gravitational supply from the Coonoor River as the most suitable and economical scheme for Tirupur. He estimated the cost at about Rs. 106 lakhs, with an annual maintenance charge of Rs.138,000.[54]

The sanitary engineer of Coimbatore reported in 1953 that the minimum flow of Coonoor River was fifty-six cusecs and that only five cusecs were required for the Tirupur water supply. These five cusecs would not affect the riparian and irrigation interests under the Lower Bhavani Project (LBP).[55] He further reported that the estimated cost of the scheme would be Rs. 91.25 lakhs. Based on these recommendations, the Tirupur water supply scheme was sanctioned in 1955, with Coonoor River as the source.[56] This scheme was inaugurated by the chief minister on 7 July 1955.

In the meanwhile, chief engineer (irrigation) had stated that the results of gauging conducted in the Coonoor River revealed that water supply would be available for some more days after meeting existing irrigation needs and that it was not possible to tap water from the river for water supply without being detrimental to irrigation.[57] Consequently, the government suspended this water supply scheme.

The people of Tirupur municipality protested against deferring the execution of the water supply scheme at the advanced stages. As a result, the municipality pressed the government to proceed with the work in the Bhavani River at Mettupalayam as a source. According to them, even after the change over to the Bhavani River, the portion of the scheme beyond the Bhavani bridge would remain the same as designed and approved for the scheme with Coonoor as the source.[58] Finally, in 1956, the government recommended to continue the scheme and a loan of Rs. 25 lakhs was also sanctioned.[59]

Inter-Basin Water Conflicts

Lack of water supply in the Noyyal River basin forced the farmers of Palladam and Coimbatore taluks of Coimbatore district to demand more water for irrigation.[60] Following this, the idea of diverting Bhavani water into the Noyyal basin emerged during the last quarter of the nineteenth century, when the government was considering about the domestic water supply scheme for Coimbatore city. But then, the proposal had not taken shape considering the prohibitive cost.[61] Though the farmers had constantly made representations to reconsider the decision, the government had refused to budge.[62] However, the proposal was discussed by the farmers as well as the government institutions at that time. Since 1923, the proposal to utilize the surplus water coming through the tunnel for irrigating the Noyyal basin has been under consideration. It was expected that the excess water running through this tunnel between 1st June and 15 December was sufficient for direct irrigation of 1,600 acres of paddy, and if provided with a storage facility in the Noyyal basin, the acreage could be doubled.[63] Meanwhile, the Siruvani water supply scheme materialized in 1931. A huge quantity of tunnel water was found to be in excess at that time after the supply of drinking water to Coimbatore city.

Seized of the issue regarding utilizing for irrigation any of the water passing through the Siruvani tunnel, the government stated that:

> the Coimbatore Municipal Council is informed that the Chief Engineer for Irrigation has reported that sufficient reliable information is not available as to the quantity of water which may be drawn through the tunnel and as to the surplus quantity which will be available for irrigation in the Noyyal valley and that in order to divide the area for which water would be available for direct irrigation, the gauging of the stream for two years has been ordered. He has also reported that only after the receipt of the results of the two years gauging of the Siruvani, the Superintending Engineer has submitted the findings on the investigation of a channel in the higher reaches of the Noyyal and that it will be possible to formulate proposals for the most profitable use of the surplus water passing through the tunnel for purposes of extension of irrigation.[64]

But the diversion for irrigation had not taken place till 1944. Until then, the government was considering about various alternative proposals and decided to postpone the diversion of Bhavani water into the Noyyal basin till a decision on the Lower Bhavani Project was reached.[65] In September 1944, the PWD had diverted the Siruvani water into the Noyyal basin for irrigation purposes only for fourteen days without the previous consent of the Coimbatore Municipal Council. Taking offence, the municipality claimed that the government should compensate for the water diversion for the fourteen days.[66] This was turned down on the ground that 'there was no occasion to agree to the request for payment of compensation to the municipality for diversion of water from the Siruvani reservoir into the Noyyal basin for irrigation purposes'. It further said: 'It is not, however, obligatory on the part of the government to consult the Municipal Council in regard to the utilisation of the surplus water of the reservoir after meeting the requirements of the town water supply.'[67]

The question of diversion again cropped up after the Lower Bhavani Project was finalized in 1946. The farmers who had been pressing the government, in 1946 demanded that (1) the usual flow of water in the Chitrachavadi channel need not be restricted, and (2) sufficient water may be allowed through the tunnel in the Siruvani River for storage in irrigation tanks in and around Coimbatore. In the same year, the Executive Committee meeting of the Madras Chamber of Agriculture passed a resolution urging implementation of the farmer's demand.[68] But the executive engineer reported that the free flow of water in the Chitrachavadi channel was not disturbed except from 1 to 21 April in every year, for taking up the annual repairs, and added that it was not possible to interfere with the drinking water supply scheme. Further, he suggested that there was a separate proposal for diverting the Siruvani River itself into the Noyyal basin for irrigation purposes.[69]

In the meanwhile, members of the Madras Legislature and the Central Legislative Assembly from Coimbatore district were discussing about an irrigation scheme for utilizing the Bhavani water for Avinashi, Palladam and Dharapuram taluks. Various alternative proposals were examined, and it was finally decided to postpone the scheme till a decision was reached on the LBP. In 1947, V. C. Palanisamy Gounder, MLA, in a letter to the PWD minister, urged him to issue very urgent instructions to the chief engineer, irrigation, to have the proposed plans for raising the Siruvani dam estimated expeditiously and sanctioned at an early date.[70] After finalizing the LBP, the government decided to increase the height of the Siruvani dam by four feet to divert the water through the tunnel for the Noyyal basin. In 1949, the government issued the necessary order with a view to enhance water supply to an existing *ayacut* of 3,500 acres under the Noyyal River.[71]

In 1948, the Coimbatore Municipality passed a resolution to divert the surplus water through the tunnel between June and September for irrigation purposes stipulating the following conditions: (1) The diversion shall be without prejudice to the rights of the municipality for the supply of thirty-five gallons per head per day. (2) The municipality reserves the right to stop the diversion if and when found that the supply has prejudicially affected. (3) The government shall investigate and ascertain the stability of the foundations of the dam before the scheme is put through. (4) The government may pay out of the irrigation funds a contribution to the municipality towards the maintenance of the water works, and (5) should there be any change to any portion of the water works, including the tunnel consequent on the release of the surplus water, the government shall reimburse the municipality all expenses incurred.[72] The above conditions were substantially observed, and the scheme was sanctioned and allowed to be proceeded with. Only two (4&5) remained to be settled.[73] After the completion of the works to raise the dam's height, the municipality permitted to divert twenty to forty cusecs water through the tunnel from September 1950 to June 1951. This water was mainly utilized by the existing *ayacut* under the Chitrachavadi channel. In July 1951, a slight damage occurred in the tunnel, leading to a temporary breakdown of water supply for Coimbatore. Consequently, the municipality refused to allow water through the tunnel for irrigation purposes, stating that the water supply for the town was disturbed due to increased draw through the tunnel.[74]

However, to achieve the objective of ensuring water supply for irrigation and to reach an agreement with the municipality, the two outstanding conditions were examined in consultation with the chief engineer, sanitary engineer and the Municipal Council besides the Health and Local Administration Departments. It was suggested that the Siruvani dam, approach channel, tunnel, etc. might be taken over by the PWD, certain safety measures be carried out in the tunnel to prevent any possible collapse and that the average annual expenditure of Rs. 23,000 incurred on maintenance works be recovered from the municipality as its contribution towards the cost of maintenance. Finally, the government realized that if the PWD took over the maintenance, the difficulty in letting down water for irrigation purposes could be solved.[75] In 1955, the district collector discussed about the surplus water diversion at the District Board Meeting and the board approved the inclusion of the scheme in the Second Five-Year Plan.[76]

The idea of inter-basin water diversion, which emerged at the end of the nineteenth century, did not materialize till the water supply scheme was launched for Coimbatore city. Not only famers of Noyyal basin, elected representatives of the Coimbatore region too had discussed the issue almost for half century. Farmers of the Bhavani River did not object to the diversion of water into the Noyyal basin. However, when the municipality diverted the Bhavani water for drinking water supply, the question of inter-basin diversion was extensively discussed. The conflict that erupted between the municipality and PWD was over the former's demand for a certain amount of compensation from the irrigation revenue. The PWD, which had refused to concede the demand stating that the scheme was not meant for the irrigation purposes, approached the municipality for diverting the surplus water into the Noyyal basin. The municipality turned down the PWD's plea on the ground that the scheme was constructed for drinking water purposes. However, the PWD convinced the municipality and had the water diverted to the Noyyal basin.

The inter-basin water diversion debate continued till the early 1950s, but nothing took place due to the conflict between the municipality and the state. When they arrived at a decision on diversion, there was no surplus water to satisfy the needs of the increasing population and industrial development in Coimbatore city. Then, the attention was shifted mainly to the water supply scheme.

Inter-Department Water Conflicts

Due to water diversion, conflicts arose between different sectors – domestic water supply and industries – and various departments – local bodies and public works department, local bodies and state, local bodies and urban people and farmers and the state.

(i) Conflicts between Municipality and State Regarding Funds

Though not directly related to water, divergence of views and conflicts between the municipality and the state emerged due to diversion of water for domestic supply, particularly over the contribution of funds for the water supply scheme. The Coimbatore Municipal Council had demanded that the government contribute certain amount from the 'irrigation funds' for the water supply scheme on the basis that the Siruvani water would be used for the irrigation purposes. Refusing to concede this, the government pointed out that there was nothing new in Siruvani water being made available for irrigation as it was only a diversion from the Siruvani to Coimbatore water supply scheme. Further, it assured that no storage would be provided for irrigation. Hence, the government categorically made it clear that no contribution would be given from the irrigation funds.[77]

Later in 1926, the Coimbatore Municipal Council insisted that the government pay a reasonable cost from the 'irrigation funds' for the diversion from the Siruvani to Noyyal. This too was turned down.[78] The municipal council again sought a reconsideration of the government's decision, but the response was that, 'a contribution from irrigation funds can be considered only if and when it is found that irrigation is benefitted by the water supply scheme.'[79]

In 1945, the Coimbatore municipality formally claimed compensation for the diversion of water from the Siruvani reservoir into the Noyyal basin for irrigation. But the government was firm in its refusal, saying 'there is no occasion to agree to the request for payment of compensation to the municipality for diversion of water from the Siruvani reservoir into the Noyyal basin for irrigation purposes'.[80]

The conflict between the municipality and the state regarding funds stemmed from the state's approach towards the local bodies. When a local body demanded a share from the 'irrigation funds', the state refused, stating that the scheme was not meant for irrigation. But, when it found surplus water, the government appropriated it for irrigation purposes without paying any monetary compensation to the local bodies. The state thus treated the local bodies as 'secondary citizens' so far as the sharing of irrigation funds and compensation for the surplus water diversion was concerned.

(ii) Conflicts between Municipality and State Regarding Water Charges

Until the sixth decade of the nineteenth century, the question of charging any tax for drinking water supply from the government sources did not arise in the Madras Presidency.[81] Even then, there was no uniformity on water tariff for the water supplied to the local bodies from the government sources. A few municipalities and Madras Corporation have paid the charges on the basis of quantity, and some paid only a fixed amount irrespective of the quantity drawn, while others paid nothing (see Appendix 4.1). In 1868, the charge was fixed for the very first time at Re. 1 for 1,000 cubic yards for the Madras Corporation, arrived at by dividing the quantity of water required for maturing a crop on an acre of land which was estimated at 7,000 cubic yards with the water rate per acre being Rs. 7.[82] The same rate had been adopted in the case of Cocanada, Masulipatam, Ellore and Chidambaram. In some other municipalities, viz. Berhampur and Karnool, a fixed charge was made irrespective of the quantity of water taken.[83] In 1930, the government passed an order stating:

> so far as existing water-supply schemes of local bodies are concerned, no charge for water taken from government sources shall be levied where none has been levied hitherto. But, in fact any future time, in connection with improvements to existing schemes or carrying out of new schemes, any considerable quantity of water has to be diverted from irrigation sources, it will be open to the government to decide what, if any, charge shall be levied on that account.[84]

Charging any tariff for the urban water supply scheme was never discussed while considering various sources of water supply to the Coimbatore municipality since the 1890s. In 1926, the government passed an order stating that 'the Coimbatore municipality will, for the present, be permitted to take water from the Siruvani River for its water-supply scheme, free of charge, but if and when irrigation is affected the question of charging for the water will be considered'.[85] But the municipality refused to accept the government order and pointed out that the question of charging for the water supply had never been indicated by the government right from the inception of the Siruvani scheme. Even while finalizing the scheme, the government had not mentioned about it, the municipality contended.[86] To the municipality's request for a reconsideration of the decision, the government responded that when such a contingency arose, the council representations would be considered.[87] But the municipal council did not accept the terms and conditions. In 1934, the government issued an order stating that 'if a local body getting its supply free of charge from a government source and sells water for non-domestic purposes, it should pay to the government one-third of the total amount realised by it every year from such sales'.[88] In 1935, the government said that concession was given only for the time being and there was no reason to exempt the council from payment of the charge in G.O. No.1297 I, 15-6-34.[89]

The municipality claimed that while sanctioning the scheme, the chief engineer had accepted that the cost of maintenance would be meted out from the income derived through the sale of water for non-domestic purposes so long as it did not affect irrigation. Since irrigation had not been affected at present, the government, it said, was not entitled to levy a charge on the water sold for non-domestic or industrial concerns. Therefore, the council considered filing a suit seeking a declaration that the Government of Madras was not entitled to claim any share of the revenue from the sale of water for non-domestic consumption. This prompted the government to direct the collector to take appropriate steps in case a suit was filed.[90] Consequently, the municipality gave up the litigation and paid the amount to the government.[91]

Later, when the government ordered to divert water from Anayar and Periyar streams (both tributaries of Noyyal) for enhancing water supply to Coimbatore municipality in 1928, the question of levying was discussed. The government claimed that the Anayar spring water would not flow down during the dry season even if not diverted for other purposes, and in the Periyar stream also, free flow of water was not taken but only the sub-soil water was being tapped from its bed. Based on this, the government argued that the water supply to Coimbatore city would not affect irrigation.

(iii) Conflicts between Urban People and Municipality Regarding Water Tax

The Coimbatore Municipality proposed to hike the property tax (from 7½ per cent in 1924) to 15½ per cent at a consolidated rate on an annual rental value of all buildings and the land within the municipal limits from 1 October 1925 to meet the cost of the Siruvani water supply scheme. The existing property tax of two *annas* for every eighty sq yards was increased to four *annas*. Out of the 15½ per cent and 4 *annas*, 8 per cent and 2 *annas*, respectively, would be taken as water and drainage tax. Social organizations and the public at large protested against this. A meeting of tax payers was held in twenty wards of the city between February and March 1925. Of this, eighteen wards completely rejected the proposed hike for Siruvani water supply scheme with only two wards accepting it with certain conditions.[92] Six public meetings were also held in different places of the city. Petitions containing thousands of signatures were sent to the chairman from the wards protesting against the enhanced tax. Several suits were filed in the district *Munsif* court challenging the hike, and a lower court as well as an appellate court had held that the council levy was illegal.[93]

The people agitating against tax hike mainly demanded that: (1) the government should bear entire centage charges; (2) the government should bear three-fourth of the cost of the scheme; (3) interest on the loan be reduced and the repayment period be extended to fifty years; (4) the agriculture and forest colleges, police recruitment school and central jail be included in the municipal limits; and (5) water tax on the annual income be reduced to 5 per cent.[94] The government refused to concede to the demands except for reducing the centage charges. Water and drainage tax in Coimbatore city was very low when compared to the prevailing rates in the fourteen other municipalities, the government pointed out (see Appendix 4.2). If reduced below 8 per cent, the municipal council would not be in a position to finance its share of the cost of the scheme.[95]

In 1927, the government order said that if the municipal council intended to do the drainage works, the tax rate would be enhanced and its extent would be determined when the question of financing the scheme was taken into consideration.[96] Following protests from the people against the proposed tax hike for the drainage scheme, the municipal council passed resolutions clarifying that there would be no need for additional taxation. To substantiate its stand, the council cited that the total value of buildings has steadily increased and it would be more before the completion of the water supply scheme. For example, the property tax was increased from Rs. 46,662 in 1915–16 to Rs. 103,000 in 1926–27.

The government, however, did not mention anything regarding the payment of water charges for drawing water from the Kalingarayan channel and Cauvery River since the inception of the water supply scheme to the Erode municipality. The government accorded permission to take water from the Kalingarayan channel for the Erode municipal water supply scheme under the condition that no damage would be done to the channel. Even here there was no mention about the charges for water supply scheme. Since 1919–20, the municipality had drawn water from the Cauvery River without paying any charges. The government also did not demand any charge for taking water. In 1930, the government ordered that the municipality has to pay the water charges from 1920 to 1929 at the rate of Re. 1 per 1,000 cubic yards. The municipality requested the government to remit the charges, since its financial condition was not comfortable. Finally, the government ordered that no charge be levied from the Erode municipality for water drawn either from the Cauvery or from Kalingarayan channel.[97]

(iv) **Water Conflicts between Farmers and State**

Water diversion for domestic water supply had created conflicts between the farmers and the state in the Bhavani and Noyyal River basins. The ryots of Chitrachavadi channel had protested against the diversion of water from Anayar and Periyar streams. Disregarding the ryots' objection, the government passed an order in favour of the Coimbatore municipality, without any levy. However, the municipality was warned that if there was any adverse effect on irrigation, the government might at any time cancel the permission granted to tap the subsoil water from Anayar and Periyar streams.[98]

In 1949, the government proposed to take water from the Coonoor River to provide drinking water to Tirupur. Opposing this, the farmers of Nellithurai, Thekkampatti and Odanthurai villages submitted representations to abandon this scheme, apprehending that this would drain the irrigation sources.[99] They feared that about 2,000 acres of paddy and betel-nut groves would be affected and about 2,000 agricultural labourers, dependent on these lands, would be deprived of their employment. Further, they pointed out that they were suffering for want of more water for irrigation. Consequently, in 1956, the government ordered that the work on the Coonoor River water supply scheme should not be proceeded with until further orders. It also sought another report from the chief engineer, PWD (GL) on the availability of water for the Tirupur water supply scheme from the Coonoor River.[100]

In April 1956, representatives from the municipality and government had participated at a conference held at the Assembly Chambers. The proceedings stated that 'the requirements of the municipality being only 3 cusecs, about 100 acres of the tope can be purchased by the municipality and the water to be utilised by this, diverted for water supply'.[101] Then the government decided in favour of the Tirupur municipality water supply scheme, stating that the small quantity of water would not affect irrigation. Disregarding the farmers' protest against water diversion, the government had mostly favoured the drinking water supply schemes of the two cities and villages of the Bhavani and Noyyal River basins. Clearly, the scales were tilted in favour of the latter.

Conflicts between Municipalities and State

Though no conflict arose from the farmers owing to diversion of water to the industries, it was, however, there between the local bodies and state regarding the collection and sharing of water charges. In 1924, the government had specifically stated that the maintenance cost of the Coimbatore Municipal Water Supply Scheme could be met from the proceeds of the sale water for industrial purposes. [102]

In 1934, the government made it clear that if the local body which received its supply free of cost and sold it for non-domestic purposes, it should then pay one-third amount of the total sales every year to the government.[103] In response, the Coimbatore Municipality reiterated that the government should reconsider the decision. Rejecting that plea, the government pointed out that the municipal council could not be allowed to enjoy the entire income from the sale of water for industrial purposes.[104] If the municipality drew water partly from government sources, it has to pay according to the proportion of water drawn from all those sources.[105]

In 1937, the municipal council emphasized that 'the government was not entitled to levy any charge whatsoever on the water sold by the council to individuals, non-domestic or industrial concerns'.[106] Based on this, the council intended to challenge the government in the court. The government too directed the collector to take steps to meet the threat from the municipal council.[107] However, in 1940, the Coimbatore Municipal Council gave up the litigation and paid the sum of Rs. 6,263-13-0 due to the government up to and including the half year ending 31-3-1939.[108]

Till independence and even sometime after that, the government considered water supply to industries only from the monetary point of view. Conflicts seldom arose in the agricultural sector against diversion of water to the industries. Only from the 1970s onwards, issues concerning industrial pollution came to the fore in the Bhavani River basin.

Conclusion

In the Bhavani and Noyyal River basins, the idea of inter-basin water diversion and augmenting domestic water supply emerged at the end of the nineteenth century. Since then, river water was diverted for non-agricultural sectors. These diversions remained the bedrock of the conflicts between the agricultural and non-agricultural stakeholders, viz. domestic and industrial sector, not only in terms of quantity of water diversion but also from the environmental point of view. Initially, the notion of water diversion for the Coimbatore water supply scheme was envisaged during the 1890s, when water diversion for the Noyyal basin was also discussed. In the early twentieth century, a small quantity of water was diverted for the railways and industries. At that time, neither the quantity of water nor the quality of water was an issue. For, neither the railways, which took water for the steam engines, nor the industries have then created environmental hazards.

The Bhavani and Noyyal River basins had three important stakeholders since the early twentieth century, viz. agricultural, domestic and industrial sectors. So far, we have analysed the conflict between domestic water supply and the agricultural sector arising out of water diversion for the former. In the 1930s, when water was diverted for the Coimbatore water supply scheme, the clash of interests rose to the fore between the municipality and the people. Those demanding drinking water were not ready to pay the cost, complaining that the rate of water tax was too high. The municipality had to impose the tax on the water users to mop up resources for maintenance, payment of water charge share to the state and recovery of the investment on the water supply scheme. Considering these factors, the appropriate tax rate could be made based on the value of water.

Lack of coordination among the government departments also had led to unnecessary conflicts in water distribution, management and its sustainability. Though the municipality had accepted the terms and conditions of the government relating to domestic water supply, it had refused to supply the surplus water to the agriculture sector. When the government pressed for diverting the surplus water for irrigation, the municipality contended that the government had not paid the expenses for the domestic water supply scheme. Consequently, this led to a tussle between the municipality, PWD and the state government. Hence, coordination among the government departments and different stakeholders becomes necessary for efficient water management.

Though the government had placed certain conditions to the municipality that water supply for domestic purposes would be restricted if agricultural operation was affected, it had acted only to the contrary whenever the farmers protested against diversion/scarcity. The government did not consider those protests with the seriousness they required, saying that only a small quantity of water was diverted for domestic purposes. As a whole, diversion of water supply had indeed affected cultivation, which was not taken into account either by the municipality or by the state.

In the agriculture sector, too, the increasing demand for water arose due to changing cropping pattern and mechanization of the water-lifting devices, leading to water scarcity. In addition to that, the discharges of industrial effluent polluted the quality of water, turning in toxic. Given this situation, how to accommodate the new demands in the dynamic process of economic transformation of the different stakeholders is an important question.

Hence, an equitable share should be allotted among the stakeholders for the maximum utilization of water; and within that proportion, the increasing demand should be managed. This could prevent the conflicts cropping up due to the ever-rising demand on the scarce water resources from the different sectors of the economy. The government should endeavour to take appropriate steps to encourage and educate farmers to cultivate less water-consuming crops in areas afflicted by water scarcity to meet the growing demand in the non-agricultural sectors and within the agricultural sector. It should frame scientific norms ensuring equitable distribution of water among the different sectors and for the efficient utilization of water. Once the share was fixed, the increasing demand of water in that sector should be met within that proportion. All the same, it should also look into sustainability, considering the future needs through constructing tanks along with plans for effluent and drainage treatment. Unless this is accomplished, the constantly increasing demand for water mainly from the domestic and industrial sectors with their attendant effluent and drainage discharges would not only reduce the water supply for irrigation but also pollute the water resources. Ultimately, sustainability of the scarce water resources could become a great question in future.

Appendix – 4.1 List of local bodies, sources of water supply and rate of charges in Madras Presidency: 1927

Name of the local bodies	Sources of supply	Rate of charges
Berhampur Municipality	Ichapur canal	Rs. 1,225
Cocanada	Samalkota canal	Rs. 1 per 1000 c.yds
Masulipatam	Bandar canal	Rs. 1 per 1000 c.yds
Ellore	Kistna-Ellore canal	Rs. 1 per 1000 c.yds
Madras Corporation	Red hills tank	Rs. 1 per 1000 c.yds
Karnool	Karnool-Cuddapah canal	Rs. 1 per 1000 c.yds
Anantapur Municipality	Wells excavated in the bed of Pandameru River charge	do not pay any
Adoni	Gangalamanchi tank	do not pay any
Bellari	Wells excavated in the bed of the Hagari River	do not pay any
Chengalput	Wells excavated in the bed of the Palar River	do not pay any
Canjeeveram	Wells excavated in the bed of Vegavathi River	do not pay any
Tanjore	Vennar	do not pay any
Mannargudi	Vadvar Municipal channel	do not pay any
Nagapatam	Vettar	do not pay any
Chidambaram	North Rajan channel	do not pay any

Note: 1,000 cubic yards = 168,750.

Source: G.O. No. 250 Mis LSG (PH), 10-2-1927, TNSA.

Appendix 4.2 Property tax and water and drainage tax in different municipalities in Madras Presidency: 1926 (in per cent)

Name of the municipality	Property tax	Water & drainage tax	Total
Cuddapa	8¾	8¾	17½
Rajamundry	8½	8	16½
Masulipatam	9½	9	18½
Nagapatanam	8½	8½	17
Coonoor	10	8	18
Tanjore	8¾	8	16¾
Tuticorin	8½	5½	14
Trichinopoly	8½	9½	18¼
Vellore	7	8	15
Ootacamund	9	6½	15½
Conjeeveram	8	8½	16½
Ellore	8½	8	16½
Vizagapatam	8½	8	16½
Tirupathi	8½	7	15½
Bellari	9¾	6½	16
Berhampur	8½	8	16½
Kumbakonam	9	5½	14½
Nellore	9½	7	16½
Dindigul	7½	6	13½
Cocanada	7½	6	13½
Chidambaram	8	8	16
Gudur	10	5	15
Coimbatore	7½	8	15½

Source: G.O. No. 1845 Mis LSG (P.H.), 23-9-1927, TNSA.

5

Canal Irrigation, Technology and Conflict

In addition to the competing demands among the different sectors, within the agricultural sector technological transformation – use of electric and oil-engines pumpsets – mechanization and introduction of hybrid seeds have created more demand for water, especially during the green revolution period and after.[1] The increasing competition had increased frequency of the conflicts, besides aggravating their intensity.[2] Due to these mounting pressures, sustainability of this scarce resource had become an increasingly difficult task in recent years.[3] With these contesting claims among the different irrigators and different sectors, customary rights and existing law have been negotiated over the period.[4] In this context, the present chapter attempts to analyse the conflicts consequent to the emergence of competing demand for water in the agricultural sector and the role of politicians, judiciary, different groups of people and changes effected in the statute in negotiating water rights during the process of technological transformation in a historical perspective (1930–70).

The twentieth century had witnessed conflicts of greater magnitude among the nations and within countries in sharing river waters. For instance, India and Bangladesh were locking horns over sharing the Ganga water, and in India, the four southern states – Karnataka, Tamil Nadu, Kerala and Pondicherry – are engaged in a bitter and prolonged dispute over the Cauvery water. Sometimes conflicts emerge at the local level between individuals and groups, between the river basin people of various states and also directly and indirectly between the states.[5] Due to politicization between the states and at times at the centre, even the intervention of the Supreme Court, tribunals and the union government has not helped resolve the conflicts, as is evident from the Cauvery water disputes.[6] Within the states, more precisely in the basins or channels, diversion of water for domestic and industrial supply had led to conflicts among the different water-

The earlier version of this chapter was published in *Environment and History*, 2001.

using communities even as early as the close of the nineteenth century itself.[7] In the canals, a major conflict was the one between the tail-end farmers and head-reach farmers of main canals, branch canals, distributaries, minors and field water courses.[8] This was due to the excess area planned under irrigation.[9] It had been estimated that only 80 per cent of the canal potential created since independence was being used.[10] And, in the early stages, as soon as the headwork was over, the whole supply was distributed even before the completion of the canal system. Ultimately, the head-reach farmers claimed more than the share of water originally planned and also increased unauthorized cultivation.[11] This, coupled with the cultivation of water-intensive crops also in farm lands adjoining the canals, resulted in unequal distribution to the tail-end.[12] Consequently, a collective response prominently emerged from the tail-end farmers, afflicted by perennial scarcity and uncertainty of water supply.[13] Wade had also analysed the correlation between water scarcity and different forms of collective action at the village level.[14] The common methods of representing the grievances are submitting petitions, filing police cases, seeking court intervention, etc., by the individual, group of people and the officials of the Public Works and Revenue Departments against the individual, group of people and other officials. Most of these grievances were kept unresolved for a long period.[15]

In contrast, in the tank system, the tail-end farmers have the weakest water management institutions. In the distributaries, risk and scarcity depend upon the water supply, while in the tank system, the water demand is being determined by the soil type.[16] Yet, in some cases where there are no local water users associations, whenever a conflict arose over water distribution, the farmers used to take it up with the officials. Even if the associations existed, they were reluctant to intervene between the quarrelling farmers.[17] The tail-end farmers getting less proportion of water than the head-reach farmers during periods of scarcity indicates that the 'tail-enders tend to be the poorer'.[18] The tail-end farmers were thus forced to arrange for their own supply through wells and tubewells.[19] Even in the tank system, conflicts emerged between the tail-end and head-reach farmers, with the aggrieved having moved to the courts for adjudication.[20] Be it water conflicts or risks and disputes over water flow in the tank system, the court judgments were guided generally 'on the basis of "natural" water flow, customary use and entitlement by grant'.[21]

In addition to the above, installation of electric and oil-engine pumpsets created new forms of conflict not only in well and tank irrigation but also in the canal irrigation.[22] Folke, who attempted to analyse water conflicts from the point of view of political economy, found that in the context of unequal social relations, the dominant castes had an upper hand both in having access to water resources and in emerging unscathed in water conflicts.[23]

Conflict resolution, administrative, judicial or political, would not be immune to newer forms of conflicts attendant to the development process.[24] Hence, water conflicts are an integral part of development. Studies on tank irrigation system have concluded:

> 'Traditional' systems are often inequitable and do not meet the needs of poorer, lower castes or tail-enders or female farmers. The caste-based roles involved in tank management can re-enforce social hierarchy and increasingly result in dispute, withdrawal and system collapse. Indigenous water allocation systems have not been adaptable to changes, especially those in the pattern of wet-land ownership or changes in cropping (e.g., the demands from new cash crops). Such changes have generated social conflict and the breakdown of water management systems.[25]

It was further substantiated by Rajagopal: 'Appropriation of water becomes more problematic when the tail reaches belong to minority/Scheduled Castes and when they are less powerful than head reaches economically and politically.'[26]

The role of the bureaucratic/administrative machinery in water management has been emphasized prominently in recent researches.[27] Studies on canal water management have largely focused on the role of bureaucrats, their corrupt practices in association with the politicians in fleecing the farmers and the transfer mechanism being practised by the administrators. These aspects were extensively analysed by Wade with reference to Andhra Pradesh.[28] Until the early 1970s, irrigation policies, which mainly focused on technological upgradation, have neglected the institutional considerations.[29]

Due to technological development, either more area was brought under irrigation or cultivation of water-intensive crops was extended, leading to conflicts among the farmers. When attempts were made to impose restrictions/penalties to contain newer demands, intervention of politicians or the farmers seeking judicial remedy tied down the hands of implementing authorities.[30] To retain their vote banks, the politicians either favoured their caste groups or were forced to support the illegal extractors in the various canal systems.[31] Subsequently, these issues were addressed at the government level either to regulate irregular water extraction or to effect policy changes. Only a few evidences are available, throwing some light on the role of politicians in the distribution of water at the local level right down from the canals.[32] Further, he says that 'the authority of the irrigation bureaucracy weakened through increased "political interference".'[33]

Intervention by politicians had crippled and made ineffective the functioning of government officials in various canals.[34]

Here an attempt has been made to analyse the role of politicians in resolving water conflicts in favour of their relatives and their own castes as well as their attempts at changing the policies and the role of the judiciary in dispute resolution in the context of technological transformation in the agrarian system during the colonial and post-colonial period (1930–70).

What is technological transformation? Transformation means a complete change. Sometimes it is being used do denote 'change' and/or 'transition'. According to Schultz, 'the notion of "technological change" is in essence a consequence of either adding, or dropping, or changing at least one factor of production'.[35] But in this chapter, it is employed to convey the complete change from traditional water-lifting devices to totally mechanical devices, viz. oil-engines and electric-pumpsets.

Until independence, power generation was mostly taken up by the state governments and to a little extent by the local governments and private companies.[36] In Tamil Nadu, power generation commenced at the early twentieth century both in the private and in the government sectors. At the close of the first quarter of the twentieth century, there were two concerns – one at Madras (at present known as Chennai) and another at Ootacamund (Udhagamandalam) in Nilgiris district – which distributed power supply to the public, mainly for household purposes. In 1927, the Electricity Department was established in Tamil Nadu,[37] and subsequently the Pykara and Mettur projects were started. In 1938–39, both the Pykara and Mettur power stations supplied electricity to Coimbatore, Erode, Tirupur, Udumalpet and other northern parts of Tamil Nadu for irrigation.[38]

Electricity supply for lift irrigation was a basic step in the introduction of modern technology in agriculture, which exploited extensively the sub-soil water resources. Because, mechanized sources of farm operations are less costly than human and animal labour.[39] Electric water-lifting devices are more economical than diesel engines both in terms of capital and in terms of operational costs,[40] with longer life expectancy.[41] The low cost of both the energized pumpsets and tubewells led to a rapid exploitation of groundwater resources.[42] For example, in the Bhavani River basin, water extracted from 30 to 40 feet in 1950s had gone deeper by 700–1,000 feet in the 1990s.[43] In 1933–34, there were only eight pumpsets connected with electricity. It increased to 11,189 in 1949–50, and further to 225,192 in 1964–65.[44] At the end of the Fourth Five-Year Plan (1974), the total number of pumpsets in Tamil Nadu had gone up to 681,205 (including 708,339 tubewells in 1978).[45] Of this, 134,475 pumpsets (about 20 per cent) were situated in Coimbatore district.[46] The number of electric pumpsets would be naturally high in Coimbatore and Erode regions, where, besides production of power, electric motor foundries were concentrated.

Manufacture of technologically upgraded water-lifting devices – centrifugal pumps – were started by two industries, viz. PSG and OPF, in Coimbatore around 1952.[47] In 1956, there were three large-scale and eight small-scale irrigation pumpset industries in Coimbatore city. These developments facilitated the farmers of neighbouring areas to install pumpsets with electric motors. Cost of irrigation per unit of water was also less for electric pumpsets than oil-engines and other traditional water-lifting devices.[48] The cost of lifting 1,000 gallons of water ranged from 0.2 to 1.4 paise per unit for electric pumpsets, 1.4 to 2.7 paise for oil-engine pumpsets and 1.8 to 4 paise for the traditional bullock mhote.[49] In other words, the cost of irrigation with bullock power was Rs. 200 per acre, diesel pumpset Rs. 83 and electric pumpset only Rs. 56.[50] Further, bullocks could not be relied upon to draw water from deep wells.[51] Consequently, there was an increase in the consumption of electricity than the other sources of energy due to increasing efficiency in transmission and utilization.[52]

The Tamil Nadu government's policy emphasized rural electrification with special concessions for the agricultural sector. In fact, both the central and state governments encouraged 'power supply for irrigation in order to make and keep the country agriculturally self-sufficient'.[53] As already mentioned, electric pumpset industries in Coimbatore commenced production in 1940s and their number had swelled to 139 in 1974. Every year large number of electric motors were produced. For instance, in 1973–74, 93,989 centrifugal pumps and monoblocks, and 41,160 electric motors were produced. The concentration of pumpset industries in and around Coimbatore district could be attributed to developed well and canal irrigation and massive rural electrification through the Pykara system. 'And there were, around Coimbatore, rich and progressive farmers (cotton growers) ready to invest in irrigation pumps.'[54] '[T]he impact of mechanisation on the use of animals is more pronounced than on human labour. Much the same is true of Coimbatore, which has also experienced a phenomenal expansion in the use of energised pumpsets and a significant growth in the use of tractors, though not of mechanical threshing.'[55] Around the 1980s, there were 162 revenue villages within the command area of Lower Bhavani Project (LBP), which account for 11,822 energized wells, 7,399 wells fitted with oil-engines and 6,154 wells with bullock-baling.[56]

Rapid increase in groundwater exploitation for irrigation, domestic, industry, livestock and other uses led to conflicts in many areas.[57] Legal rights to water resources varied between the people and the government. Except private wells and tubewells, the government had powers to regulate artificial tanks and lakes, natural tanks and lakes, public wells and tubewells, over which the farmers have either customary rights or usufruct rights.[58]

Groundwater extraction rights were customarily associated with land ownership.[59] 'Land owners generally regard wells as "theirs" and view others as having no right to restrict or otherwise control their right to extract water.'[60] But recently, though the judiciary had acknowledged the customary rights, the government proclaimed absolute rights over all natural waters.[61]

> [T]here is no fundamental right of access to water. Land owners have an absolute right to the water under their land ... The amount of water it is legally possible to extract does not depend on the amount of land owned. Any land owner can abstract any amount of water ... The rights granted under such a legal framework are inappropriate in a socialistic society and does not suit the interests of the nation as a whole. Since the attachment of water rights to land ownership can violate the fundamental right of life, the current water rights structure needs to be modified to ensure equitable distribution of this resource, particularly for those who do not own land.[62]

'The increased exploitation of groundwater by their richer neighbours and the consequent depression of the groundwater table is making the use of traditional water-lifts increasingly difficult.'[63] For example, in Puliampatty village, the spinning mill owners established twenty borewells each about 1,000 feet in ten acres of land. Consequently, the adjacent poor farmers' cultivated lands dried up and became desertified.[64] The swelling number of tubewells has particularly affected the dugwells, mostly owned by the small farmers.[65] The simultaneous increase in wells and pumpsets resulted in a drastic rise in groundwater extraction.[66] Recently, the large-scale installation of tubewells with energized pumpsets also had caused a sharp decline of sub-soil water.[67] Installation of higher horse power pumpsets also aggravated the situation, as the water table got depleted at an alarming rate. Given the disappointing performance of the canal systems in terms of the failure in providing a more controllable, predictable and reliable water supply, most of the farmers were prepared to install tubewells for timely and precise water management to achieve more yields and profits.[68]

Arguing that irrigation is a 'technological' input in production, Bharadwaj suggests that 'the interaction between the irrigation technology and the social relations [impinges] on the dynamics of development of the region as a whole'.[69] In this context, the present study attempts to analyse technological transformation and the attendant issues in Tamil Nadu between 1930 and 1970. In other words, it attempts to contextualize the dynamic process of changing water-lifting techniques and its consequences on irrigation management over the period.

An interesting but also essential feature is to understand the role of politicians in the making of policies concerning water, particularly those aimed at effecting technological advancement in water-lifting devices, viz. electric and oil-engine pumpsets.

How have the massive installations of new water-lifting devices created the water conflicts and what was the role of the politicians in their creation/ resolution? What was the role of the various castes among the water-using communities in the course of the conflicts and that of the judiciary in conflict resolution? What were the government policies in effecting changes in water management during the colonial and post-colonial period? To answer these queries, here an attempt has been made and the main objective is to study the water conflicts due to technological transformation; cropping pattern; the role of bureaucrats, politicians – Member of Parliament and Member of Legislative Assembly – and judiciary; and the changes in government policies pertaining to both the old Kalingarayan channel and new Lower Bhavani Project canal areas in a historical context (1930–70). It also looks at how the representatives of the ruling party had favoured those belonging to their own caste/community and attempted to modify the rules and regulations to suit them at the cost of the tail-end farmers. It further proceeds to identify the root causes of water conflicts and how they were resolved, either by means of judicial/administrative intervention or by the politicians. In short, it attempts to understand the water conflicts in their various facets and the colonial as well as post-colonial state's capacity in accommodating the demands.

This chapter consists of four sections. The problem was introduced in the first section. The second section analyses the conflicts, which are a corollary of technological transformation, political intervention and government policy in the Kalingarayan channel between 1930 and 1970 along with the role played by the judiciary. The third section discusses the conflicts together with technological transformation, cropping pattern and the government's policy and legislations aimed at dispute resolution in the LBP canal between 1950s and 1970s. The last section ends with the concluding observations of this chapter.

Water Conflicts in the Kalingarayan Channel

Since the early thirteenth century, the Bhavani River water was diverted for irrigation purposes through the Kodiveri[70] and Kalingarayan *anicuts*. A rough-stone *anicut* known as Kalingarayan *anicut*, built by an ancient Tamil king during the early thirteenth century and located just before the Bhavani River confluence with the river Cauvery, diverts the water to its right in the Kalingarayan channel. Also known as *Konavaikkal*, it irrigates about 13,460 acres of wet crops through 769 sluices.[71] All the command areas, enjoying riparian rights, are located only on the left bank of the channel.

The channel takes off on the right side of the Kalingarayan *anicut*, extending up to fifty-eight kilometres and irrigating wet crops in about 13,460 acres which alone had riparian rights.[72] However, riparian rights were not considered by the government due to the ever-increasing demand for water over the period. Sengupta stated: 'Neither riparian nor prior appropriation rights of private parties, of farmers and companies alike, are secured.'[73] Until 1933, water from this channel was not used by the right-bank non-*ayacut* highland farmers for cultivation.[74] No account is available about water management until the early nineteenth century. The available accounts were related to cropping pattern, maintenance and repairs, indicating absence of any restriction on the type of cultivation in the Kalingarayan channel *ayacut* area.

As in other irrigation systems, in the Kalingarayan channel also water distribution and maintenance were managed by the *ayacutdars* under the *kudimaramattu* system, which existed even prior to the colonial period.[75] *Kudimaramattu* was a contribution of labour for petty repairs to irrigation works, which the farmers were bound to give since time immemorial. Also known as 'village labour', 'communal labour', 'maintenance works', 'village repair' and 'community management', this existed even during the pre-colonial period.[76] The main responsibilities of the *Kudimaramuttu* system were: (a) To fill up gullies or other inequalities caused by rain and cattle upon the bunds of the tanks and channels; (b) to check the growth of the prickly-pear and any similar rank and pernicious weed on bunds; (c) to clear away such underwood from the tankbunds as may be considered by the range officer to be injurious; (d) to clear away the deposits from tank sluices and from the river and spring channels to afford a sufficient opening for supply of water for flow; (e) to clear and repair the earthwork of petty and branch channels, and clear away the accumulations which obstruct the flow; (f) to keep in order the supply channels of tanks in such extent as was sanctioned by local custom; (g) to watch the bunds to prevent breaches, leakages and other accidents and to open and close the *calingulas*[77]; (h) to construct ring dams at breaches and, where required, undertake temporary strengthening of tank bunds during the season of cultivation; and (i) to inform the officers about uncovering the sluices in tank bunds for repair.[78]

Actually, the *Kudimaramattu* works were done by the *Nirkkatti*, a water distributor of a village who has to maintain the reservoir, inspect often the toom or outlet from the tank to fields to prevent unnecessary and unusual expense of the water and his duty was to distribute impartially to each field under the orders of the village headman in quantities proportionate to the extent of land and stage of the crop.[79] Unauthorized diversion was restricted by the local organization by imposing penalties. Maintenance of the channel was undertaken by the farmers themselves. In other words, 'the great majority of the indigenous irrigation works were locally managed'.[80] In most cases of tanks in Tamil Nadu, maintenance of distribution network and regulation of water use were well defined, of course, informally by the village-level organizations, and for some tanks, even the written rules were also found.[81] In short, the *Kudimaramattu* system ensured better distribution of water and maintenance.

In contrast, the colonial government, which undertook irrigation management in the later period, neglected both distribution and maintenance of the channel and tank systems.[82] Consequently, the traditional water management system was eroded in South India particularly during the colonial period.[83] Mosse further says that 'decline of tank systems did not result from a collapse of community co-operation or a "tragedy of the commons", but rather from the wider political and economic changes brought by colonialism'.[84] Because, 'the principles of indigenous resources management are not easily transferable to new development contexts, and ... many aspects of "traditional" tank management are anyway undesirable'.[85] Anyhow, due to these changes, a number of conflicts arose in water management. Jose says: 'The rising prominence of centralised bureaucracy and the consequences it has on the functioning of agrarian societies, manifested through the breakdown of traditional labour sharing arrangements, non-participation of the beneficiaries in decision-making on management of the system and the rise of conflicts among water users at various points.'[86] In the Madras Presidency, the government's involvement in tank repairs and restoration was insignificant or negligible till the early twentieth century. 'Although in south India the colonial government had to create a whole department for tank repairs, in hundred years it never developed into anything more than a mere financing and labour employing agency.'[87]

In the Kalingarayan channel, the government permitted lifting water through *picottas*[88] for extension of irrigation in the uplands of the non-*ayacut* area on the right bank which did not have riparian rights in the early twentieth century.[89] However, the government had imposed certain restrictions, which included that the water lifted should be used only for dry crops without exceeding the permitted *ayacut* area, i.e. 500 acres. No conflict, however, erupted as long as water was lifted from the channel through traditional methods for the dry crops. Contrary to the regulations, the right bank head-reach farmers started installing electric and oil-engine pumpsets during the 1940s, and cultivated wet crops, mainly paddy, in the 'permitted' non-*ayacut* area under this channel.[90] The increased volume of water lifted by these non-*ayacut* farmers caused scarcity for the tail-end *ayacut* farmers, leading to conflicts in the 1940s.

In the Kalingarayan channel, water was used by means of sluices in the traditional manner, and whenever water level fell below the requirements in the channel, the turn system[91] was followed. The turns would 'be regulated by the Sub-Divisional Officer's written orders on each occasion which shall also be communicated to the Tahsildar, but should it be necessary for the Section Officer or Sub-Overseer to anticipate his orders by reason of urgency, this disposal shall be immediately committed to writing and shall be forwarded to the Tahsildar for information and to the Sub-Divisional Officer for approval'.[92] In 1933, the chief engineer permitted extension of the command area by 500 acres and allowed the upper-reach highland non-*ayacut* farmers of the right bank to lift water from the channel through bullock lifts for dry crops. The farmers also accepted to pay the land rent at the rate of 25 per cent of wetlands. However, this did not affect water supply to the tail-end *ayacut* farmers, and in fact, no dispute had occurred due to lifting of water by the head-reach highland farmers. Because, unlike most of the channels which culminate at a dead end, the Kalingarayan channel finally joins the River Cauvery. The unused or 'surplus' water was allowed to drain off into the Cauvery.

During the 1940s, although the collector had refused permission for oil-engines, economically well-off right-bank head-reach highland non-*ayacut* farmers had installed about fifty pumpsets and oil-engines and extended irrigation besides cultivating wet crops.[93] This led to scarcity of water supply to the tail-end farmers, who in turn protested and gave petitions to the local authorities and a memorandum to the revenue minister, Government of Madras, seeking necessary action and asking for adequate water for cultivation. The local government officers directed the head-reach highland farmers to remove their unauthorized energized pumpsets. But, they did not oblige and decided to challenge the order in the court. Thus, the changing mode of water lifting for irrigation and cropping pattern in the head-reach non-*ayacut* areas of the Kalingarayan channel during the second half of the twentieth century had brought attendant conflicts. Further, it paved the way for the rich and large landholders to become richer, while the tail-end farmers suffered to meet their needs. Appropriation of water by rich and large landholders led to wide inequality between the head-reach and tail-end farmers.[94] Though this appropriation of water might have brought about agricultural development in general, it inevitably created inequalities between the head-reach and tail-end farmers. Consequently, the poor farmers could not claim their rights through the legal means due to lack of finance and political patronage.[95] On 6 July 1953, the farmers of the tail-end[96] villages who irrigated lands fifty-three miles below in Erode taluk of Coimbatore district complained that they did not get adequate water supply. They pointed out that this was due to the right-bank head-reach non-*ayacut* farmers illegally lifting more water through electric and oil-engine pumpsets for raising wet crops between miles twenty and forty on the upland villages[97] (see Map 2). They pointed out that even though water was passing at the maximum level at mile twenty, adequate supply was not there for the tail-end farmers. Further, they argued that irrigation on the right side of the channel, which did not have riparian rights, should be closed down.[98]

In 1933, the collector had permitted the upland head-reach non-*ayacut* farmers to lift water only through bullock lifts for dry crops. They had used the channel water until the 1940s as per the government's directions. In 1946, some of them applied to the sub-divisional officer for water ticket.[99] But he had stated that no water ticket was necessary as the lands were in the collector's approved list.[100] In 1950, the collector, while conceding baling through *picottas* or by any other power appliance, said *tirwa*[101] would be fixed on that basis. However, since 1948–49, farmers in the upland villages using electric and oil-engine pumpsets had extended the area under wet crops. Faced with inadequate water supply, the tail-end farmers since late 1940s continued to press for the removal of unauthorized pumpsets installed by the head-reach upland farmers. In response, the Tahsildar served show-cause notices on 24 September 1952 and 17 November 1952 to remove the unauthorized pumpsets. But only a few farmers obliged. Even when the Collector passed an order to this effect, the upland head-reach farmers did not heed.[102] Consequently, the Tahsildar of Erode filed twenty-six criminal complaints against those who had failed to comply.

Initially, the penal assessment of one time water rate was levied under the Board of Standing Orders (BSO). According to BSO 4(11), 'Whenever water is irregularly taken from any Government source or work to any land for purposes of irrigation, the Collector, divisional officer, tahsildar or deputy tahsildar may impose enhanced rates of water-cess in accordance with such rules as may from time to time be made by Government on their behalf.'[103] The Irrigation Act 1865 also empowered imposition of penalty. According to Section 1(b) of the Irrigation Cess Act:

> Whenever water from any such river, stream, channel, tank or work, by direct flow or percolation or by indirect flow, percolation or drainage from or through adjoining land, irrigates land under cultivation, or flows into a reservoir and thereafter ... irrigate any land under cultivation, and in the opinion of the Revenue Officer empowered to charge water-cess, subject to the control of the Collector and the Board of Revenue, ... it shall be lawful for the State Government ... [to] prescribe the rules under which, and the rates at which, such water-cess shall be levied, and alter or amend the same time to time.

The Board of Standing Order (4) framed the rules for levy of enhanced water cess for irregular irrigation. Accordingly on the first occasion it would be twice the normal water cess; on the second occasion, five times, on the third, ten times; and on the fourth or any subsequent occasion, twenty times.[104] Based on the above, the penalty was imposed. Yet, illegal irrigation indulged in by the head-reach upland farmers could not be stopped. On the contrary, the number of unauthorized pumpsets had only increased. Even now, the government imposes penalty for unauthorized pumping in the Bhavani River basin. However, illegal pumping in the Kalingarayan channel has been regularized over the period, following representations to this effect from the farmers concerned to the government through farmers' associations and political leaders.[105]

The collector had authorized the tahsildar to launch prosecution before the sub-magistrate, Erode, against these twenty-six ryots, and subsequently chargesheets were filed.[106] The farmers could not file cases against the government authorities after the 1945 amendment to the Irrigation Cess Act. According Section 4(1) of the Tamil Nadu Irrigation Cess (Amendment) Act, 1945:

> No suit or any other proceeding shall lie against the State Government, or any officer or servant of the said Government, or any authority subordinate to them, or any person acting under the authority of or with the permission of the said Government, officer, servant or authority, in respect of any act done or purporting to be done under section 1 of the said Act before the commencement of this Act if such Act could have been done under the said Section 1 as amended by this Act, and the State Government and all officers, servants, authorities and

persons aforesaid are hereby indemnified and discharged from all liability in respect of all such Acts.

Hence, the farmers filed writ petitions in the high court, Madras, under Article 226 of the Constitution of India.[107] Before the government could move the court (in 1953), the head-reach upland owners had filed two writ petitions[108] in the high court, against the collector of Coimbatore and tahsildar of Erode taluk, challenging the levy of penalty of twenty times of the normal water cess for illegal irrigation. The collection of penalty was stayed by the high court.

An interesting point to be considered here is that K. Periyasami Goundar, member of parliament (MP), from Erode, had acted in favour of the head-reach upland farmers to help them retain their unauthorized pumpsets.[109] Because, the MP of the Congress Party, which was in power both at the centre and in the state, himself was a landlord and his relatives and partymen also had lands at Palanigoundanpalayam below Pasur village (head-reach). Despite the Kalingarayan channel coming under his constituency, the MP supported the head-reach upland farmers since most of them belonged to his caste, the dominant Goundar community.[110] It was further substantiated by case studies. A study by Mariasusai (1999) shows that despite several petitions and police complaints made by the individuals, group of people and officials of the Public Works and Revenue Departments, against the violations and appropriation of water by the head-reach farmers, the officials were unable to take any action. Even if the court cases went in favour of the petitioners, the court directives were not enforced due to caste and political patronage for violators.[111]

Eleven peasants together filed a writ petition against the collector of Coimbatore and tahsildar of Erode taluk. Except one, all the other litigants were of the Goundar caste.[112] Though the tail-end farmers also belonged to the same community, they could not exert any influence in the administration because the member of legislative assembly (MLA) representing the tail-end villages, K. R. Nallasivan, was of the Socialist Party. The ruling party (Congress) politicians obviously would have more influence in the administrative power structure. As a result, the local administration was unable to remove the unauthorized pumpets. It evidences that partisan political intervention to protect the illegal water users, with utter disregard to the problems of the tail-end peasants, had led to fierce disputes among farmers in the Kalingarayan channel. A study by Mariasusai (1999) reveals that in the LBP canal, politicians hailing from the dominant caste extended support to their own caste people whenever they violated the rules for fetching water. Further, they have helped influence to regularize the violations through their power and linkage with the government. The study clearly shows that the dominant caste landholders, particularly large landholders, violated the rules and regulations with political patronage in the river basins. On the contrary, it was very much evident that those who do not have political support, particularly the lower-caste people, small and marginal farmers, were forced to suffer by denying their democratic rights is very much evident.[113] With the support of politicians, the head-reach upland farmers attempted to regularize their unauthorized pumpsets. Taking up their cause, K. Periyasamy Gounder, MP, in a petition on behalf of fourteen farmers from the upland villages,[114] stated that their lands were being irrigated by means of bullock lifts from the channel since the last twenty-five years. In reality the farmers, however, had switched over to mechanized irrigation instead of bullock lifts. The Public Works Department (PWD) authorities did not object to the installation of electric and oil-engine pumpsets. The chief engineer had fixed 500 acres as the limit to which irrigation on the right bank of the channel in the upland villages would be allowed. Then followed the demand that the existing pumpsets be regularized and the intended prosecution and levy of penal assessment be also stayed.[115]

In April 1953, seventeen persons from the upland villages[116] filed a case against the State of Madras and Vadakkupudupalayam, Vengamputtam, Pallakattuputhur and Kodumudi villages, stating that the defendants had no absolute right to supply of water and contended that due to the installation of pumpsets, there was no increase in the area under cultivation. The head-reach upland farmers claimed that their lands were under the *mamool* list,[117] for which they had spent huge amount for levelling, waterways and for constructing engine rooms. Further, in support of their claim, they cited out the notice of the collector dated 5 July 1950, stating that baling might be done by *picottas* or by any other power appliance with the *tirwa* being fixed on that basis. Based on the above, they sought the following relief: (1) a declaration that they were entitled to take water for their lands with pumpsets (2) restrain the defendants by an injunction from interfering with the plaintiffs working on the pumpsets, (3) the government pay back penalties levied on the plaintiffs during the last five years (1945–50) and (4) direct the government to pay damages for the illegal interference in working with the pumpsets.[118]

The collector, in a rejoinder, had reported that all the lands were not in the *mamool* list. They were classified as dry land and the government was not under any obligation to supply water to them (see Table 5.1). According to the collector, though entered in the *mamool* list, the permission to these lands for lifting water was liable to be cancelled at any time without assigning any reason. The farmers had installed unauthorized oil-engines, taking away a major share

Table 5.1 Details of illegal river pumping from the Kalingarayan channel as on 2 July 1953

Name of village	Whether included in the *mamool* list	Whether water ticket has been obtained	Whether complaint under sec. 430 IPC has been filed	Mode of irrigation whether by pumpsets	Whether pumpset is permitted by unauthorized pumpsets
Nanjai Uthukuli	yes	no(not necessary)	yes	yes	no
P. Kolanalli	yes	no	yes	yes	no
N. Uthukuli	yes	no	yes	yes	no
Kolathupalayam	yes	no	yes	yes	no
Kolathupalayam	no	no	yes	yes	no
P. Kolathupalayam	yes	no	yes	yes	no
Modakurichi	yes	no	yes	yes	no
N. Uthukuli	yes	no	yes	yes	no
Pasur	yes	no	yes	yes	no
P. Kilambady	–	no	not prosecuted	–	–
P. Kilambady	–	no	not prosecuted	–	–

Source: Letter from the Collector, Coimbatore, to the Secretary to Government through the BOR, 22 July 1953, Tamil Nadu State Archives, Chennai (hereafter TNSA).

of the water to the detriment of the downstream agriculturalists. The revenue authorities held that irrigation with the help of oil-engines was in contravention of the conditions. Inclusion in the *mamool* list per se does not confer any right to water supply by the government to the owners of the dry lands. Out of the nearly forty-two cases of pumpsets, head walls and pipe sluices had been constructed only in a few cases. Hence there was no means of controlling water supply to the pumpsets.[119]

Based on the collector's report the government had passed the following order:

> All the lands which are claimed to be in the mamool list are not in fact in the mamool list. Even in the case of lands in the mamool list, supply is permitted only when normal quantities of water are available and government are at liberty to restrict supplies and exclude lands from the list. The lands referred to both by the M.P and in the suit notice are all dry lands which have been allowed to take water only by the baling by bullock lifts. The conversion of bullock lifts into mechanical lifts was unauthorised. The use of mechanical lifts involves the draining away of available supplies, much to the detriment of owners of lands lower down who are entitled to supplies, particularly owners of registered wet lands. Complaints have in fact been made by ryots in the lower reaches that their supplies have been badly affected by the use of mechanical lifts by the ryots of upper reaches.
>
> There is no case whatever for intervention. In the case of the Raja, Komarapalayam and Pugalur channels in the Trichi and Salem districts, the Government directed the removal of all unauthorised pumpsets. In this case also the action taken to remove the pumpsets was sound. The stay orders in respect of prosecutions for the non-removal of the pumpsets may be vacated, the prosecution allowed to proceed and the threatened suit may be awaited.[120]

The government, following representations from the tail-enders, directed removal of unauthorized electric and oil-engine pumpsets by the head-reach non-*ayacut* peasants whenever shortages arose for the tail-enders. However, the administrators failed to comply with the directive due to the intervention of politicians, who acted in favour of the farmers violating the existing rules and regulations on water use in the Kalingarayan channel. Having violated the rules and regulations, they had sought legal protection for the unauthorized pumpsets. The high court stayed the government from removing the unauthorized pumpsets. Until the judgment was delivered, the administrators were unable to implement the government order.[121] The writ petitions of the head-reach upland farmers were dismissed by the Madras High Court in 1953.[122] According to the court,

> the power to penalise irregular irrigation was incidental to the right and duty of the government to regulate supply of water from source of irrigation like in Kalingarayan channel which belonged to the Government, to ensure adequate supply of the water available for distribution to all those to whom the Government was bound to supply water, for example, to the holders of lands registered wet within the *ayacut* of that source of irrigation, and secondly, to those entitled to supply of water under the permits granted to them, permanent or temporary, that is, general or special. Such control and regulation of the supply of water were recognised by immemorial usage as the right and duty of the Government.[123]

The writ petitions were dismissed with a cost of Rs.100 each in favour of the respondents (government). Even afterwards, neither the government authorities removed the unauthorized pumpsets nor the tail-end farmers pressed for the implementation of the court order.

The head-reach upland farmers made further attempts to regularize their unauthorized pumpsets and the non-*ayacut* area of the channel. The MP who supported them might have influenced the administration to keep off and not to implement the rules. Following politicization of the water conflict in the channel, the administrators were unable to implement the orders, whether judicial or administrative.

In 1955, the government restricted installation of additional electric and oil-engine pumpsets.[124] However, the views of the local politicians of the ruling party getting reflected in state-level politics facilitated their entry into the government's policy. Consequently, in the same year, the government ordered that the collector could permit installation of pumpsets where permits were previously given for bullock lift and registered for baling wet lands in consultation with the executive engineer. Penalty need not be levied in these cases and any penalty imposed already should be completely reimbursed. Even the non-registered wetland holders could be allowed to install pumpsets and the collector should regularize them at the earliest. For these also, penalty need not be levied and any penalty already levied should be completely cancelled. If more area than the permitted limit for bullock lifts was cultivated through the pumpsets, the penalty amount would be imposed until such was regularized by the collector. Even in that case, the penalty amount levied should be restricted to ten times and all penalty cases should be withdrawn.[125] Even afterwards, neither were the unauthorized pumpsets that were installed removed nor was their installation restricted. Subsequently, the unauthorized pumpsets were further regularized in 1984.[126] In 1997, there were about 753 unauthorized pumpsets irrigating about 2,160 hectares.[127] It appears that the government's policies regarding this dispute had changed due to political compulsions at the local level as well as the need to accommodate the competing demands to ensure development both in the agricultural and in the industrial sectors.

In most of the years, water supply in the old Bhavani channels, including the Kalingarayan channel, did not receive the prescribed quantity. Consequently, the availability of water supply also declined.[128] In these circumstances, with 'water conflicts' having emerged already within the agriculture sector, the government permitted water supply for the industries. In the 1950s, Solar Industries and Traders Ltd. of Punjai Lakkapuram, Erode, was permitted to pump two lakh gallons of water per day (equivalent to about 0.4 cusec) from the Kalingarayan channel. After using this water for industrial operations, the factory had planned to utilize the same for irrigating about thirty acres of its land.[129] Since the tail-end farmers were already suffering due to scarcity of water as a result of installation of pumpsets by the head-reach upland farmers, the government permitted lifting of water for industrial purposes with the following conditions: (1) pumping should not be done directly from the Kalingarayan channel but through a cistern; (2) the cistern shall be supplied by a six-inch-diameter sluice with head wall; (3) the sill level of the sluice will be kept about one feet above the bed level of the channel; (4) the company should agree to pay the charge at the rates fixed by the government from time to time; (5) during scarcity and closure periods, water would not be supplied; and (6) the company shall not change/modify any of the arrangements for pumping fixed initially.[130] Ultimately, the age-old riparian rights of the farmers in the Kalingarayan channel were either transgressed or conveniently ignored by the government while extending irrigation under Kalingarayan channel between the 1930s and 1970s. In other words, the growing demand to increase productivity through advanced technology led to water conflicts. Though the judiciary had looked at these conflicts from the 1865 Act, mass representation and political intervention had brought about changes in the government policy to accommodate the process of transformation in the traditional irrigation system. The water conflicts in the Kalingarayan channel expose the fact that the government had disregarded riparian rights of the tail-end farmers to accommodate technological transformation in the water-lifting devices, extension of irrigation into new areas in the head-reach and the growing demands in the industrial sector.

Water Conflicts in the LBP Canal

The Lower Bhavani Project (LBP) dam is located on the Bhavani River just below the confluence of Moyyar, about ten miles west of Satyamangalam town and about twenty-three miles northeast of Mettupalayam between 77° 8' east longitude and 11° 28' north latitude in Coimbatore district of Tamil Nadu. The original design of LBP was distinct from the other basins to extend irrigation mainly for the dry crops, besides a small extent of wet crops. The main dry crop recommended for cultivation in half of the *ayacut* area in the LBP was cotton.[131]

A dam across the Bhavani River was conceived by the eminent engineer Arthur Thomas Cotton in 1834. 'The general plan was to form large tanks in the Nilgris and Annamalais, to irrigate and water the entire Coimbatore district, and a large part of Malabar and throwing additional waters into the Cauvery for the improved supply to the deltas in the districts of Trichinopoly and Tanjore, and to have canal communication between the eastern and western coasts of southern India in its final stage.'[132] Since then various proposals were discussed at different periods, viz. 1857, 1866, 1880, 1897, 1908, 1925, 1926, 1928, 1932 and 1933, but none of them was ever taken up until 1946.[133] Initially, a proposal for two reservoirs, viz. Upper Bhavani Project (UBP) proposed for dry crops and Lower Bhavani Project (LBP) for wet crops, was discussed. Ultimately, the proposal of UBP was dropped in favour of the LBP in 1946.

In the 1932 proposal, the main canal was designed to be seventy-three miles long with a command area of 19,840 acres.[134] Whereas, in the 1946 scheme, it was decided to extend the main canal by another fourteen miles and the gross command area to 292,555 by excluding the existing wet irrigation. The actual *ayacut* area was confined to 207,475 acres and the remaining 85,080 acres was excluded.[135] About 15,170 acres in different villages was not taken up for irrigation due to two reasons: (1) irrigation would harm the tobacco crop, and (2) there were a large number of wells with oil-engines in those villages.[136]

Prior to the LBP, the farmers of Coimbatore district mostly cultivated the rain-fed food crops – such as *cholam, cumbu,* ragi, paddy; oilseeds and; groundnut – and the commercial crop – cotton. They also raised cereals, sugarcane, fodder, orchards and gardens. The main source of irrigation was wells though canals and tanks, and other sources irrigated to a little extent.[137] More than half of the farmers in the district were holding lands below five acres, of which only half of the area was under cultivation, indicating that most of them were engaged in agriculture for their subsistence.[138] Agriculture was mostly dependent on the seasonal rains.[139]

According to Vaidyanathan (1978), structural changes in agriculture had taken place in Coimbatore district between the mid-1950s and 1960s due to the expansion of canal irrigation as well as a change in the quality of irrigation.[140] Vaidyanathan's study found that 'The percentage of land area leased-out has fallen from 20.5 per cent to 3.8 per cent and that leased-in from 10.3 to 5.3 per cent, thus showing a reduction in the net area leased-out.'[141] He further says that hired labour increased from 26.2 per cent to 84.9 per cent in the district for the same period.[142] This might be due to 'the small farmers and tenants dispossessed of their holdings have swelled into the ranks of the agricultural labourers dependent on wage employment'.[143]

The original idea was to stop the canal at its eighty-ninth mile and let it into Kattuvari, a tributary of Noyyal River.[144] The irrigable extent of about 207,475 acres proposed under this scheme was then localized in three taluks – 46,960 acres in Gobichettipalayam, 18,542 acres in Bhavani and 141,973 acres in Erode of Coimbatore district.[145]

In 1947, the farmers of Dharapuram taluk made a strong representation to the government to extend the LBP canal up to the Noyyal basin, which was frequently affected by drought and famine.[146] In the same year, the government decided to extend the canal and water supply to 25,000 acres in Dharapuram taluk on the right side of the Noyyal valley and curtailed an equal extent of irrigable area in the upper reaches of the LBP. This canal, known as the Dharapuram canal, extends for about thirty-five miles. The government, which ordered to extend the LBP canal to provide irrigation for 25,000 acres, had actually brought only 20,500 acres in Dharapuram taluk and the remaining 4,500 acres fell within Karur taluk of Tiruchirappalli district.[147] The LBP canal was thus extended to cover the three taluks in Coimbatore district (40,500 acres in Gobichettipalayam taluk, 17,000 acres in Bhavani taluk, 125,000 acres in Erode taluk) and one taluk in Tiruchirappalli district (20,600 acres in Karur taluk).[148]

Constructed mainly for irrigating dry crops, the LBP with a length of about 124 miles, including the approach channel, was intended to irrigate about 207,000 acres. Of this, 197,000 acres was to be under dry crops, especially cotton and millets, and about 10,000 acres, mostly water-logged areas, under wet crops. Irrigation facilities were extended since 1952.

In September 1952, 6/2[149] miles from down the head of the LBP canal was opened up for irrigation to cover an extent of 5,000 acres.[150] In 1953–54, it was extended up to 43/2 miles for irrigating about 30,000 acres and 15,000 acres, respectively, for the first and second crops. In 1954–55, irrigation was extended further down to 123/3 miles, with the command area being expanded up to 114,910 acres, including the area already given water supply.[151] Since 15 September 1955, 167,400 acres, which fell under the main and extension canals, were opened up for irrigation. The entire canal area was supplied with water in 1956.[152] Since then, water supply fluctuated every year and declined over the period in the LBP canal (see Table 5.2). But there was a remarkable increase in the cultivation of water-intensive crops between 1955–56 and 1962–63 (see Table 5.3).

Flouting the government direction, the farmers invariably cultivated wet crops right from the opening up of the LBP canal. Even in the subsequent decade, farmers in the taluks irrigated by the LBP canal largely cultivated water-intensive crops like paddy, sugarcane and turmeric (see Appendix 5.1). Then, the government lifted the restrictions on water supply from one half between 1 January and 15 March for cotton crop, and even millets could be raised, unless noticed, before 1 January. Following these measures, the farmers in the LBP canal area continued to raise the crops of their choice without any hindrance.

Table 5.2 Quantity of water released in the LBP canal: 1954–55 to 1970–71 (in M.cft)

Year	Quantity
1954–55	19,585
1955–56	22,381
1956–57	27,164
1957–58	37,584
1958–59	37,403
1959–60	44,991
1960–61	43,599
1961–62	50,414
1962–63	47,332
1963–64	30,787
1964–65	50,004
1965–66	8,447
1966–67	27,472
1967–68	25,778
1968–69	24,541
1969–70	31,857
1970–71	19,568

Source: Executive Engineer, Bhavanisagar.

Table 5.3 Changing cropping pattern in the LBP canal: 1952/53–1962/63

Crop	1952–53	1953–54	1954–55	1955–56	1956–57	1957–58	1958–59	1959–60	1960–61	1961–62	1962–63
Paddy	–	1,271	12,510	17,190	32,529	61,898	66,557	72,797	82,446	115,714	130,094
Cotton	–	1,416	26,825	36,015	43,136	29,031	19,886	8,989	7,887	3,648	5,208
Millets	2,947	4,138	24,995	27,971	39,787	44,134	48,226	22,489	15,981	16,655	10,499
Other crops	–	2,358	8,709	20,737	21,011	53,127	74,541	50,141	42,077	45,753	33,150
Area cultivated	2,947	9,183	73,019	101,913	136,463	188,190	209,250	154,416	148,391	181,720	178,948

Source: Government of India, *Report on Optimum Utilisation of Irrigation Potential, Lower Bhavani Project (Madras State)* (New Delhi: Committee on Plan Projects, 1964), 36.

Table 5.4 Planned and existing cropping pattern in LBP in 1959–60 (in acres)

Crops	Planned Area	Originally Per cent to total	Existing Area	1959–60 Per cent to total
Paddy	10,000	4.8	93,313	53.4
Cotton	97,000	46.9	8,778	5.0
Dry crops	100,000	48.3	72,636	41.6
Total	207,000	100	174,727	100

Source: Government of India, *Evaluation of Major Irrigation projects – Some Case Studies*, 1965, 207.

In 1958, the area under paddy cultivation increased to 16,000 acres as against the original estimate of 10,000 acres. In the subsequent years, this went up to an astounding 130,000 acres in 1962.[153] This would become apparent when compared with the original proposed area (see Table 5.4). Due to increased wet cultivation, the operation of the project was shifted into a 'diversified dry-wet project' as against being an 'all dry' project.[154] In 1959, 'seasonal sluice turn system' was introduced. Under this system, water supply was normally allowed in two separate seasons – from 15 August to 15 December and from 15 December to 15 March.[155] In the first season (15 August to 15 December), the farmers could raise any crop without restriction, whereas in the second season, only dry crops were allowed to be irrigated. Raising of any wet crop was completely prohibited and if cultivated would attract heavy penalty.[156]

Since 1959, though cultivation of water-intensive crops was prevented during the dry season, the head-reach farmers, in particular, had never followed this. Although the violators could be penalized by the collector, enforcement was inadequate either because of political intervention or due to administrative inefficiency. When enforced, corrupt village administrative officers either made it a personal collection or reduced the penal amount.[157] The government too caved in and stopped both the levy and collection of penalties when the farmers protested.[158] Consequently, the area under water-intensive crops area increased every year, leading to scarcity of water, particularly for the tail-end areas. Rapid expansion of paddy cultivation resulted in the farmers at the tail-end of the canal not receiving sufficient water supply.[159] In 1963, the government imposed a ceiling on paddy cultivation and brought it down to 60,000 acres.[160] One of the main reasons was that about 40–50 per cent of the *ayacut* area was affected by seepage and about seventy-two hamlets consisting of 1,488 families were affected.[161]

Since the entire area was planned to be irrigated by 'Intermittent Turn System', farmers of the uplands in the LBP canal flouting the prescribed rules and regulations ultimately led to water conflicts among the *ayacutdars*.[162] The head-reach farmers had primarily created the grounds for these conflicts. They never followed the turn system, cultivated wet crops and put up cross-bunds in the canals. Consequently, the tail-end farmers were deprived of sufficient water and the intermittent turn system too caused serious hardships to them.

In 1956, farmers of different villages in the lower reaches besides the Member of the Legislative Assembly (MLA) and the Ryots Association in the LBP canal gave several petitions complaining that some of the more influential landowners in the head-reaches had not allowed water to their fields as per the turn system by violating the time schedule. Peasants from the lower- reaches of the distributaries also joined the petitioners. Of the thirty-five petitions submitted during the year 1955–56, seventeen were about ryots' non-cooperation, unauthorized paddy cultivation, cross-bunding in canal and non-excavation of field *bothies*[163] (see Map 2). The rest (eighteen) pertained to inadequate water supplies (see Appendix 5.2). Responding to about half of the petitions, the government, camouflaging the whole issue, simply stated that the problem was due to insufficient water in the LBP canal.[164] Hence, turn system was abandoned and a 'zonal irrigation' system was introduced from 1959.[165]

When the issue came up for discussion in the Tamil Nadu Legislative Assembly, the government directed the Revenue Department to take necessary action to prevent unauthorized paddy cultivation and illegal irrigation. It also proposed to provide the remaining sluices in the distributaries and sub-distributaries with proper shutters.[166] However, the lascars were not very fair in the distribution of water.[167] It indicates that despite the government initiating several measures for better water management, the lower-rung staff not executing them proved to be one of the main reasons for the poor water management.

Despite the insufficient quantity of water, the head-reach farmers installed pumpsets and extended wet crop cultivation, accentuating the water conflicts in the LBP canal.[168] Taking into account all these factors, the government in 1955 ordered that no new electric pumpset or oil-engines should be installed in the *ayacut* areas for lifting water from the wells and any grant or loan should not be sanctioned for pumpsets in the canals or wells. Farmers installing pumpsets were warned of maximum penal assessment and prosecution without prior permission of the government.[169] Because the water table had declined steadily in the LBP areas except those places adjacent to the canal between 1959 and 1963.[170] The upland farmers raised wet and garden crops, such as turmeric, tobacco and chillies. It affected the approved distribution of the project waters and supply to the regular *ayacut* areas, especially in the tail-end of the LBP.[171]

In 1956, the government provided certain concessions to the tail-end farmers of Dharapuram taluk for installing pumpsets for lifting water from their private wells but not directly from the government irrigation sources.[172] However, they demanded removal of the unauthorized pumpsets used by the head-reach farmers and regulation of water supply in the appropriate manner.

The government, then, permitted them to apply for pumpsets for lifting water from the LBP canal while attaching certain conditions. In 1954, the chief engineer (irrigation) agreed that the Electricity Board could provide power supply to the pumpsets in both the *ayacut* and non-*ayacut* lands in the LBP. He made a proposal containing certain conditions, including that the horse power should not exceed more than two and that it should be used only for dry crops.[173] The government, instead, suggested to increase it to 5 HP, stating that the horsepower limitation would not benefit the farmers. But the chief engineer pointed out that increase in the horse power would adversely affect the overall irrigation interests and might induce the farmers to cultivate wet crops and other garden crops. With this comment, he finally agreed to increase the horse power if restricted to a fixed number of pumpsets with pumping permitted only during the non-irrigation season.

Based on the above recommendations, the Revenue Department directed the Electricity Board to supply power throughout the year for lifting water from wells both in the *ayacut* and non-*ayacut* areas in the LBP, subject to the following conditions: (1) pumpsets should not exceed more than 5 HP, (2) number of pumpsets should be restricted to 200, (3) power supply should be used only for dry crops and (4) electricity would be cut off if water was used for purposes other than that for which it has been specifically sanctioned.[174]

In the meanwhile, the farmers from the villages of Mettupalayam and Mangalapatti in Dharapuram taluk and Monjanur in Karur taluk submitted petitions seeking to extend electricity supply to their villages either by increasing the number of wells already fixed for the tail-end lands or in the *ayacut*. They also assured that increasing the number of pumpsets would not affect the *ayacut* area.

The question of extending electricity connection for pumpsets in Dharapuram taluk was discussed in the Legislative Assembly in 1955. Despite the chief engineer's protest against any blanket increase in the number of pumpsets anywhere in the LBP area, there was a consensus for extending electricity to the villages. The minister for agriculture said that only certain villages were permitted for pumping water.

The chief engineer (irrigation) suggested that pumping from wells very near the water courses which drain themselves into the Noyyal River might be permitted in a limited way and submitted a detailed proposal to the government. The tail-end farmers protested against these recommendations. In 1956, the government directed that power supply be granted for pumping from wells in a narrow belt of 6,300 acres in the tail-end villages of Nathakakkadiyur, Palayakottai and Muthur villages of Dharapuram taluk and Anjure village in Karur taluk. Further increase in the number of pumpsets, the government said, would be considered only after monitoring the development of the LBP.[175]

In 1954, the government banned digging of new wells and deepening of existing ones in the LBP area.[176] However, the Community Development authorities actively encouraged the above and until 1956, about 549 wells were sanctioned by them.

In the LBP area, the government restricted to 200 the number of pumpsets for lifting water from the main and extension canals.[177] 'Under the hire purchase scheme for oil-engines and electric motor pumpsets, ryots were granted loans.'[178] In 1956, the project engineer, Erode, sanctioned more number of oil-engines and electric pumpsets under the 'hire purchase system' to the tune of Rs. 1,220,600 (see Table 5.5). Installations of pumpsets were mostly financed by the farmers themselves and also through the medium-term credit provided by the co-operatives.[179] In fact, a large number of small farmers purchased the electric motors with the assistance of the State Cooperative Land Development Banks in Coimbatore district. For example, between 1968 and 1971, Rs. 4 crores per year was disbursed for the purchase of electric and diesel pumpsets.[180]

The government laid down a policy stipulating that 'no pumpset should be allowed to be installed on any of the channels in the Cauvery and Bhavani basins except under permits which could be granted only after the availability of water was ascertained and the requirements of the authorised and unauthorised pumpsets are apportioned'.[181] However, in 1957, the government permitted the widow of late freedom fighter Tirupur Kumaran[182] and her family members to install pumpsets for pumping water from the Pugalur channel to irrigate about 9.97 acres of land in Vengambur village of Erode taluk.

Table 5.5 Number of pumpsets and oil-engines in the LBP area in 1955–56

Particulars	No. of oil-engines	Electric motors	Total
Ayacut Area	345	85	430
Non-Ayacut area	53	130	183
Total	416	215	631

Source: G.O. No. 1401 Mis, PWD, 29 March, TNSA.

The contradictory policies adopted by the various government departments, like Cooperation, Agriculture and Electricity, at different levels also were directly responsible for the water conflicts. If the higher authorities permitted certain number of pumpsets in the channel, the lower-rung officers of the same department flouted the instructions. For example, while the CE (I), Madras, ordered not to install more than 200 pumpsets in the LBP basin, the project engineer, Erode, had in fact provided credit facilities for more number of pumpsets. In 1956, the Public Works Department minister, who discussed these issues, concluded that it was difficult for the government to restrict installation of oil-engines by the farmers. But he admitted that the government should not extend loans for deepening the existing wells and encourage pumping in the *ayacut* area. The discrepancies within the government departments at different levels led to unnecessary water conflicts in the LBP canal. In 1963, the government had directed the Electricity Board to adhere to certain conditions while extending power supply for pumpsets to lift water from wells in and around irrigation project *ayacut* areas in general. The conditions were: (1) electricity supply should not be given if the well was located within a distance of two furlongs from the canal and one furlong from the distributary. (2) The capacity of the pumpsets should not exceed more than 5 HP. (3) If electricity was supplied to wells within the *ayacut* area, water thus lifted should not be supplied outside the *ayacut* area. (4) Only permitted crops should be cultivated in the *ayacut* area. In other words, it was to ensure that the cropping pattern remained the same without change.[183]

In 1965, the government gave exemption from the above rules to pumpsets other than those in the LBP area if water lifted from the pumps situated in the *ayacut* area was not used for the non-*ayacut* area.[184] In 1967, the above relaxation was extended to the LBP area but only during the off-season. Then, the government imposed certain restrictions for providing electricity connection to pump water from the existing wells in the LBP. They were: (1) Pumping should be done only from the well and not from the canal. (2) Pumping will be permitted during the off-season alone. During the irrigation season, i.e. from 15th August to 14th March, or as may be notified from time to time, pumping will be heavily penalized. (3) To enforce Condition 2, the farmers were required to enter into an agreement with the TNEB (State Electricity Board) by giving consent for disconnecting power supply during the irrigation season. (4) In the case of main and branch canals the capacity of the pumpsets should not exceed 10 HP depending upon site conditions. In the case of distributaries the capacity should not exceed 5 HP up to a distance of fifty metres and 10 HP beyond that subject to the site conditions. (5) If the well, with electricity connection, falls within the *ayacut* area, water should not be supplied beyond the *ayacut* area. (6) Conversion of oil-engines into electric pumpsets shall also be governed by the above conditions. But this relaxation was not applicable to wells irrigating non-*ayacut* lands, for which the original limitation of two furlongs and one furlong continued to exist.[185]

Installation of pumpets in the main river and channels was permitted under these conditions: (1) Pumping can generally be allowed during August to December; (2) capacity of pumpsets should not exceed 3 HP, and the size of the pipe also should not exceed three inches; (3). food crops alone can be grown; (4). the area should not exceed 5 per cent of the registered *ayacut* under the channel.[186]

In the LBP canal area, no new well could be dug or deepened within the prohibited distance of two furlongs from the main canal, and those dug after 1963 were not given electricity supply. This was applicable for the branches and distributaries also.[187] These measures were aimed at ensuring normal flow in the canal to protect the tail-end farmers.

Until the LBP canal water was used for the prescribed crops within the stipulated area of cultivation, no major conflict ever arose among the farmers right from the head-reach to the tail-end, including the rich and the poor as well as large and small farm-holders. Conflicts cropped up following the installation of energized pumpsets and consequent extension of the area under irrigation and changing cropping pattern from dry to wet crops (mainly paddy) in the Bhavani River basin.

Conclusion

Broadly, the colonial government's policies had not given due importance for the welfare of the Indian population. Although it had built a few dams, they were perhaps either individual initiatives or mostly in the expectation of higher revenue assessment. For, the British had never intended to create a proper irrigation infrastructure to enhance agricultural productivity. For instance, the idea of constructing a dam across the Bhavani River which emerged in the 1830s, could not materialize till the close of the colonial rule. Of course, during the post-war period, the 'Grow More Food Campaign' was introduced, under which minor irrigation schemes were promoted. In the Madras Presidency, electricity generation which commenced at the beginning of the twentieth century itself was not augmented till the end of the colonial era. The colonial administration was never concerned about effectively utilizing the water resources, and even if it had attempted ever, it was aimed at more revenue. Further, it did not encourage modern technology like pumpsets and oil-engines to extract water for agriculture. Consequently, attaining self-sufficiency in food-grain production became the casualty during the colonial period.

After independence, extension of irrigation facilities was taken up as a prime objective to increase food-grain production by leaps and bounds. In addition to that, power generation was given importance. Irrigation and its related inputs, like electricity, oil-engines and electric pumpsets, credit facilities and hybrid seeds were never a priority of the colonial government unlike the post-independent government.

Until the early twentieth century (the 1930s), in the Bhavani River basin, water was not diverted either for agricultural or for domestic and industrial purposes except the three diversions in the old channel, viz. Arakkankottai, Thadappalli and Kalingarayan, established during the pre-colonial period. In the 1930s, water was diverted to meet the domestic demands of Coimbatore city from the Siruvani River a tributary of Bhavani. In 1931, 11.3 million litres of water per day was diverted to Coimbatore city from Siruvani River but it had gone up to 13 million litres per day in 1971. The quantity further increased to 85 lakh gallons per day in 1976.[188] In addition to that, water was diverted to Tirupur in 1962 from the Bhavani River at Mettupalayam and subsequently to sixty-five wayside village *panchayats*.[189] Water was also diverted from the Bhavani River to the Noyyal River basin[190] and, to some extent, for the railways and other industries. These diversions have been a prime cause for the different kinds of conflicts since the early twentieth century.[191] For example, for the 752 and odd dyeing and bleaching units in Tirupur city, 60 MLD groundwater per day was transported from the nearby rural areas through truck-tankers.[192] In addition to the increasing consumption by the domestic and industrial sectors, there was a growing demand for water within the agricultural sector due to more area being brought under irrigation, changing cropping pattern, mechanization of agriculture, other technological transformation, etc. over the period.

The close of the colonial era witnessed the process of technological transformation taking roots in the old Kalingarayan channel through the gradual replacement of traditional water-lifting devices by electric and oil-engine pumpsets. The change in water-lifting devices in the channel and the river, besides transforming the dynamics of farm operations, led to water conflicts in the Kalingarayan channel of the Bhavani River basin during the second half of the twentieth century. From the beginning of the post-colonial period, phenomenal changes took place in the LBP canal in terms of area under irrigation, changing cropping pattern, installation of pumpsets and oil-engines, which sharpened the conflicts.

An interesting observation is that the rules and regulations framed by the government at a given time were modified or changed over the period in tune with the process of transformation emerging within the agrarian system as well as in the other sectors of the economy. Political intervention has also had its cascading effect on conflict management over water disputes. The rich and large farmers attempted to legitimize their illegal farming operations with the connivance of the politicians and by dragging the issues to the courts. Politicization further made it difficult for the authorities to enforce the regulations, thus creating grave disadvantages to those sections of farmers who lacked political patronage.

Politics played an important role both in the planning of the scheme and in water management. Apart from supporting those violating the prevailing rules, the politicians have also made strong representations about the farmers' 'grievances' to the government to effect policy changes. Interestingly, the political leadership which represented the farmers' problems was biased in favour of their own region, community, relatives and party workers and sympathizers. Though the tail-end farmers also belonged to the assembly segments of his parliamentary constituency, the MP had undermined their legitimate interests since those assembly segments were represented by legislators of rival political parties. Finally, politicians of the ruling party obviously enjoyed an upper hand in influencing the policy decisions concerning water management.

This study clearly found that riparian rights of the farmers were not considered by the government while attempting to accommodate the ever-increasing demand for water from various sectors. All the more, it is appalling to see that the legal system is not coherent and in tune with the dynamic process of transformation in the agrarian system as well as in the other sectors of the economy. Transformation and attendant conflicts in the LBP emerged around the 1940s, but the judiciary viewed these problems based on the Irrigation Cess Act of 1865. The successive governments and the political leadership, unable rise above its myopic vision, never foresaw the issues and responded only belatedly. The state came up with only knee-jerk reactions and betrayed a lack of a sustainable policy which addressed the competing demands arising out of the dynamic process of economic transformation. The water conflicts analysed in a historical perspective also exposed the limitations of the legal system in accommodating the process of transformation and the vested interests behind political intervention which always favoured a particular region and caste, paving the way in deepening the crisis in the developing countries.

Appendix 5.1 Cropping pattern in Bhavani, Erode, Gobichettipalayam and Dharapuram taluks of Coimbatore district in 1971 (irrigated crops only)

Crops	Bhavani		Erode		Gobichettipalayam		Dharapuram	
	Area in acres	Per cent to total cropped area	Area in acres	Per cent to total cropped area	Area in acres	Per cent to total cropped area	Area in acres	Per cent to total cropped area
Rice	9,916.26	35.72	26,868.51	50.89	21,546.16	47.53	11,032.62	25.58
Cholam	1,369.28	4.93	4,668.54	8.84	2,239.71	4.94	8,292.77	19.23
Cumbu	3,075.36	11.08	1,459.85	2.77	3,284.32	7.24	2,074.65	4.81
Ragi & other cereals	3,692.06	13.30	1,673.34	3.17	3,642.47	8.03	5,612.62	13.01
pulses	89.49	0.32	82.47	0.16	100.53	0.22	1,633.09	3.79
Total food grains	**18,142.45**	**65.36**	**34,752.71**	**65.83**	**30,813.19**	**67.97**	**28,645.75**	**66.43**
Condiments	1,383.97	4.99	3,004.17	5.69	2,687.39	5.93	1,371.67	3.18
Orchards	72.12	0.26	689.94	1.31	339.91	0.75	300.84	0.69
Vegetables	871.87	3.14	227.80	0.43	305.06	0.67	262.90	0.61
Cotton	958.90	3.45	5,852.91	11.09	3,447.47	7.60	4,934.06	11.44
Sugarcane	3,964.60	14.28	2,320.70	4.39	3,600.23	7.94	1,454.33	3.37
Groundnut	1,328.92	4.79	3,768.87	7.14	1,847.37	4.08	3,376.90	7.83
Coconut	105.65	0.38	479.96	0.91	148.55	0.33	262.24	0.61
Gingelly	228.94	0.82	720.18	1.36	11.46	0.23	377.19	0.87
Other oilseeds	88.83	0.32	106.47	0.20	62.51	0.14	60.80	0.14
Coffee	–	–	0.12		0.11		0.14	
Tea	0.55	0.01			0.25		0.06	
Others	611.55	2.20	866.34	1.64	2,069.59	4.57	2,077.91	4.82
Total non-food crops	**9,615.90**	**34.64**	**18,037.46**	**34.17**	**14,519.90**	**32.03**	**14,479.04**	**33.57**
Gross cropped area	**27,758.35**	**100**	**52,790.17**	**100**	**45,333.09**	**100**	**43,124.79**	**100**

Source: Agricultural Census 1970–71, Coimbatore District: District, Taluk and Panchayat Union Tables, Government of Tamil Nadu, 1976, 36–37, 122–23, 160–61 and 190–91.

Appendix 5.2 List of petitions from the lower-reach farmers and the nature of problems in LBP channel

Sl. No.	Date of petition	Name of village	Name of distributory	Nature of problem
1	9-1-1956	Thadapalligramam	Tail-end at mile 23/0 of LBP Main Canal	Insufficient water supply
2	22-12-1955	Lakkampatti	Tail-end of branch distributory at 30/4 of main canal	defective distribution under the tail dam
3	11-10-1955	–	Tail-end of branch distributory at mile 3–4-600 of Kugalur distributory	Trouble in the internal distribution of water among the ryots
4	15-12-1955	Nagadevampalayam	Tail-end of distributory at mile 35/6 of main canal	Insufficient supply due to cultivation in the upper reaches
5	–	–		–
6	28-11-1955 9-1-1956	Vairamangalam	Tail-end of right side parallel channel of Mettupalayam distributory at mile 51/7 of main canal	
7	23-2-1956	Vairamangalam	Do	Large-scale paddy cultivation
8	24-8-1955	Surampatti	Tail-end of erode distributory at mile 56/4 of main canal	Field *bothies* not excavated
9	–	–	Tail-end of branch distributory at mile 5–4-480 of Erode distributory	Bunding by upper ryots
10	6-10-1955	Muthampalayam	Tail-end branch distributory at mile 1/0 of Unjalur distributory, at mile 63–0 of main canal	–
11	–	Ryots association of LBP at Erode	Muthampalayam branch distributory at mile 1/0	Non-cooperation by ryots
12	2-2-1956	Letter from Tahsildar, Erode	Tail-end of branch distributory at 5/0–200 of Erode distributory	Cross bunding by upper ryots

Sl. No.	Date of petition	Name of village	Name of distributory	Nature of problem
13	11-1-1956	Kanagapuram	Branch at 1/0–49 right of Unjalur distributory	Non-cooperation by ryots
14	-	Thuyyampundurai	Branch at 3–7–390 of Unjalur distributory	Scarcity of water
15	16-1-1956	do	do	do
16	7-10-1955	Avalpundurai	Branch at 4-3-570 of Unjalur distributory	do
17	29-1-1956	Erode	Sub-branch at 1–2-70 LBP of 5–0-30 branch of Unjalur distributory	Cross bunding by upper ryots
18	25-1-1956	Pudur	Tailend of branch distributory at mile 5–0–30 of Unjalur distributory	Large-scale paddy cultivation of upper reach
19	16-1-1956	Ryots	Tail-end branch of distributory at mile 8/2 & 9/0 of Unjalur distributory	Throttling the sluices in the upper reaches
20	27-12-1955	S.D.C's Letter	Branch distributory at mile 1–6–160 of distributory at mile 70–1-145	–
21	24-10-1955	Palayamkottai	Sub-branch at 2-1-66 of the Branch at 0–8-42 of Chennasamudram distributory	Not following the time schedule by the Upper ryots
22	30-9-1955	Velampalayam	Tail-end of the sub-branch at 0–3-70 of the branch at 1/5 of chennasamudram distributory	Insufficient water supply
23	22-11-1955	do	do	do
24	15-12-1955	Elamathur	Sub-branch at 2–5–40 left to kagam branch of Chennasamudram distributory	do
25	15-12-1955	Sivagiri	Sub-branch at 0–2-380 of the branch at 5–3-360 of Chennasamudram distributory	do

Sl. No.	Date of petition	Name of village	Name of distributory	Nature of problem
26	18-1-1956	Kollenkovil	Sub-branch at 0–3-20 of the branch at 5/7 of Chennasamudram distributory	Unauthorized cuts and cross bunding
27	14-10-1955	K.R. Nallasivam, MLA	Branch at mile 9–7 of Chennasamudram distributory	
28	27–10-1955	Ramasamy Goundar	do	Insufficient water supply
29	11-1-1956	Ryots of LBP Association, Erode	Branch at 10/4 of Chennasamudram distributory	Existence of cross walls
30	5–11-1955	Ichipalayam	13/2 branch od Chennasamudram distributory	Insufficient water supply
31	29-1-1956	do	do	do
32	-	From Ryots	Distributory at mile 76/5 & 78/7 of main canal	Non-observation of time schedule
33	13-10-1955	K.R. Nallasivam, MLA	Distributory at mile 78/6 & 78/7 of main canal	Non-cooperation among the ryots
34	12-10-1955	Justice Ramasamy Goundar	Tailend dam at 1–7-300 of branch at 0-3-500 at Anjur distributory	Insufficient water supply
35	12-10-1955	do	Branches at 0–3-500, 1–1–60 and 2–0-200 of Anjur distributory	do

Source: G.O. No. 2049 Mis, Public Works Department, 30 April 1956, TNSA

6

Disasters of Linking Rivers

The widespread water scarcity has led to numerous conflicts in recent years at basins as well as in delta regions among farmers and the states. The issue has got aggravated manifold due to the surging demand from different users like agriculture and industry besides domestic water supply. The problem has now been further exacerbated owing to decline of water quality, caused by pollution. Such disputatious demand for water by different users in addition to the pollution has made the crisis a major focal point.

The options for developing more water resources or augmenting them have been almost exhausted in most of the river basins of India. In other words, the irrigation potential of most of the river basins has been exploited to the maximum possible extent. Hence, it seeks utmost attention on effective management of the scarce resource by the different users seriously. Several strategies and mechanisms have been already adopted in this direction. The Government of India has now come up with a decision to link the different river basins/national rivers in the hope that it would solve the problem once and for all. However, in addition to the existing contentious issues, the decision is likely to give rise to a host of new problems pertaining to international relations, state autonomy, centre-state relations, ecology, environment and displacement. These have to be immediately addressed in order to arrive at a comprehensive understanding of the consequences of the proposed mega-project, the biggest ever to be in the history of Indian Planning.

The project proposal consists of thirty links, with thirty-six dams and canals of the length of 10,800 km to divert 174,000 million cubic meter of water. The rough estimated cost of the project is Rs. 5.6 lakh crore and it may increase in the course of time. It is expected to provide irrigation to about 34 mha of land and

---

The first part of the chapter was published in *Man and Development*, 2004. The second part of the chapter was published in *Mainstream* 2018.

drinking water supply to 101 districts and 5 cities besides generating 34,000 mw electricity. It is generously claimed to be a panacea for water and food scarcity, not only for the current generation but for the posterity as well. The project is also expected to prevent frequent floods, causing extensive damage to crops and property. In addition, it also predicts to create employment opportunities for a large number of workforces.

Since an estimated 80,000 ha of forestland would be submerged, displacing about 4.5 lakh people, the human cost/loss would be colossal. It is an undeniable fact that the mega-project would augment the irrigation potential besides providing water and employment opportunities. But it appears that the most basic issues and the probable collateral damages and other consequences have not been looked at in a broader perspective. Here, an attempt is being made to have a critical appraisal of some of those issues so that enough light is shed on them.

Let us briefly look at the origin and history of linking rivers. The idea of diverting water from one basin to another is not a recent one. Inter-basin water transfer had been under consideration since the early nineteenth century.[1] It was Arthur Thomas Cotton, who had put forth the idea of inter-basin water transfers for the first time. He proposed to divert water from the Bhavani River basin to the Noyyal River basin as early as the nineteenth century. In addition to this, he had also proposed the idea of linking the different river basins for navigational purposes. However, the idea did not materialize due to the development of railways during the second half of the nineteenth century.[2] At home, in the early nineteenth century, the modern Tamil poet and patriot Subramaniya Bharathi has envisaged the similar idea to boost irrigation by removing the barriers and highlighting the concept of national integration in one of his famous verse: *'Vangathil Oodivarum Neerin Migaiyaal Maiyathu Nadukalil Payir Cheykuvom'* (Surplus water of northern rivers should be used in the central regions for cultivation). However, this has never been given serious consideration until independence.

In the post-independence period, politicians from the south, especially Tamil Nadu, have been emphasizing this idea time and again. Even now it is on the agenda of many political parties. Linking the major rivers of the north with those in peninsular India has been under the consideration of the central government also. In spite of the hype surrounding the idea, the proposal of Central Water Commission (CWC) has hardly seen any progress. Based on the commission's earlier work, Kanuru Lakshman Rao, the former union minister for irrigation and electricity, had proposed to link the major rivers in 1972. Subsequently,

Captain Dastur has also come forward with the idea of a 'Garland Canal' in 1977. It was subjected to scrutiny by experts from the Central Water Commission, state governments and professors from the Indian Institute of Technology (IIT) and the University of Roorkee. But, the experts were of the opinion that the proposal was technically unsound and economically prohibitive.[3] Hence, the government gave up this mega-project in the late 1970s.

Later, in the early 1980s, the government reinitiated several measures to study the feasibility of this project. In July 1982, the National Water Development Agency (NWDA) was set up to carry out surveys and prepare feasibility reports. However, the NWDA has not been able to submit the report yet. In September 1987, the National Water Policy has also envisaged interlinking of national rivers. In 1999, the National Commission for Integrated Water Resources Development has also suggested to study several aspects before initiating inter-basin water transfers. In spite of undertaking all these measures, neither has any of the feasibility report been made public nor has interlinking of rivers taken place even in a phased manner.

In 1999, this was included in the National Agenda of Governance of the BJP-led National Democratic Alliance (NDA). The NDA manifesto before the elections said: 'We will examine and take time-bound steps to link Ganga-Cauvery Rivers.'[4] But this has failed to get any attention, with nothing having moved in this direction.

Meanwhile, in 2001, N. Nandhivarman, general secretary, Dravida Peravai, filed a writ petition in the Supreme Court seeking a direction to the authorities to implement the project in a phased manner within a time frame. In 2002, the apex court, disposing of the petition, directed the union government to complete the project within a decade. Accordingly, the government set up a task force to look into the matter.

It was surprising that even after carrying out so many studies to ascertain the feasibility of the project, not a single scheme has ever seen the light of the day in the bygone century. For example, the Sethu Samudram Shipping Channel project in the Palk Strait has seen 22 feasibility studies during the last 150 years but works on the project, started in 2004, have thankfully been halted before it could be completed. On the contrary, inter-basin connectivity, the dream project in the history of Indian planning, has acquired a new dimension following the apex court directive, despite the absence of any authentic and comprehensive study on its feasibility. Given the existing conditions of taking up this ambitious project without studying the consequences, it is natural that doubts arise as to whether the project will bring a lasting solution or turn out to be a nightmare.

First, it is unfortunate that the Supreme Court had given a direction to the government to carry out the project and complete it within a decade. Since irrigation comes under state list, the union government cannot intervene unless there is an inter-state water dispute. As such, how could the centre be expected to complete this project? Further, neither has there been a public debate on the issue nor have the views of the stakeholders of the different basins, farmers, been ascertained.

Failure of judicial intervention in resolving many contentious river water disputes in history bears witness to the prolonged conflicts for decades between states and even within a basin. For example, the persisting conflict between the riparian states over sharing the Cauvery waters has been eluding a practical solution for the last three decades despite the intervention of the Supreme Court. Several steps taken, both by the central and state governments with the help of advisory bodies, have proved to be ineffective. If the failure to implement the Interim Award of the Cauvery Water Dispute Tribunal is one such case, the Supreme Court verdict which brought to a close the legal battle with the setting up of the Cauvery Management Authority is yet to be fully functional. 'Justice delayed is justice denied.' One plausible reason could be that the existing mechanism in dealing the inter-state water conflicts in India is still rudimentary in nature.[5] No state, particularly surplus basin states, has come forward to share the excess water with others. Disagreement on water availability, hydrological data, future requirements, riparian rights, basis and modalities of sharing besides the rigid stand adopted by the states are the major stumbling blocks and prime causes for the conflicts in the different river basins. Unless rivers are nationalized, any attempt at inter-basin connectivity would lead to serious repercussions, impinging on centre-state relations. Under this situation, the deadline set up by the apex court might seem to be a bit unrealistic and impractical.

Second, the waters of the perennial rivers originating from the Himalayan ranges have to be shared with the neighbouring countries as per the existing commitments. Though we have 80 per cent of the basin area, comprising ten Indian states, viz. Uttar Pradesh, Uttarakhand, Himachal Pradesh, Haryana, Rajasthan, Delhi, Madhya Pradesh, Bihar, Chhattisgarh and West Bengal, the river Ganges and some of its tributaries are shared with Tibet, Nepal and Bangladesh. In the Indus River basin, we could claim water from the west-flowing rivers, since we have an agreement with Pakistan. The water rights of Brahmaputra basins are shared by Tibet, Bhutan and Bangladesh. Sharing the waters of fifty-one common rivers, apart from the major rivers, is one of the major bones of contention between India and Bangladesh.[6] India has entered into agreements with these countries with or without the intervention of international agencies.[7] Diverting water without probing into these matters may have international implications. Unfortunately, India does not have cordial relations with most of its neighbouring countries. Hence, diverting the surplus waters cannot be in breach of the existing bilateral or multilateral agreements.

Third, Indian Constitution states water as a 'State Subject'. As such, the union government could not interfere in any water dispute except those pertaining to inter-state rivers. In the Union List (56), it has been pointed out that the centre could only step in to regulate and develop inter-state rivers, through a parliamentary legislation in public interest. 'Parliament may by law provide for the adjudication of any dispute or complaint with respect to the use, distribution or control of the waters of, or in, any inter-state river or river valley' (Art. 262-1). Further, Article 262(2) says: 'Notwithstanding anything in this Constitution, Parliament may by law provide that neither the Supreme Court nor any other Court shall exercise jurisdiction in respect of any such dispute or complaint as is referred to in the clause (1).' The constitution, which has not provided any machinery for adjudication of water disputes, has entrusted the parliament with the responsibility to make appropriate legislations to resolve inter-state water conflicts. The parliament has enacted the River Boards Act, 1956, to deal with the inter-state water conflicts, which, however, is not effective.[8]

The Sarkaria Commission (1988) on centre-state relations also felt that water should not be transferred to the Union List due to the sensitivities and difficulties involved. However, it has observed that though states enjoyed exclusive powers with respect to waters confined to their territories, they could not lay claim to exclusive use of inter-state rivers and deprive others of their just share. Since the jurisdiction of a state by virtue of Article 245 is territorially limited, only the parliament can effectively regulate by law, the beneficial use and distribution of such waters among the states.[9] The National Commission for Integrated Water Resources Development (1999) also ruled out inclusion of water even in the 'Concurrent List' for the same reasons as suggested by the Sarkaria Commission. The commissions and committees had suggested for a constitutional amendment to carry out the task. The problem is that states are already seeking more autonomy. It is inappropriate to imagine that the states would keep silent while the centre takes over a state subject. While the process of decentralization is desirable and needs to be encouraged, it has to be borne in mind that it is not easy for the centre to take over a 'state subject' citing the integrity of the nation. Further, the chance of bringing amendments in the current political scenario also appears bleak.

Fourth, water conflicts are widely prevalent between the tail-end and head-reach farmers in the channels, requiring judicial intervention to resolve the problems in different river basins of the country.[10] Within the river basin, the competing demand among different users, viz. agriculture, industry and domestic, has cropped up since the early twentieth century.[11] Attempts to divert the water from one basin to another had led to several conflicts even in the early twentieth century.[12] Given the historical evidences, conflicts between the basin states have taken a very serious turn in recent years. For example, the dispute between Karnataka and Tamil Nadu in sharing the Cauvery River water had regional, cultural and linguistic overtones. This resulted in riots and violence in which people both in Karnataka and Tamil Nadu were threatened and humiliated and their properties ransacked. Here, it should be underlined that conflicts over riparian rights between Karnataka, Tamil Nadu, Kerala and Puducherry, running for more than three decades, are yet be sorted out. While the Government of India plans to divert the west-flowing river towards the east, the Kerala government is planning to divert the east-flowing Bhavani River to the west. Interestingly, most of the rivers flow through more than one state in peninsular India. The pre-requisite here is to convince the states and consider the modalities to be adopted to seek a congenial remedy.

Fifth, hardly we can forget that we have had experiences of severe water shortages in different channels and distributaries in different dams and river basins of the country.[13] Now, the situation is that no channel or tributary of any dam could comfortably supply the required amount of water at the appropriate time. In fact, even the perennial river Ganga is not exempted from this. Consequently, water conflicts/disputes have become a recurring one throughout the river basins in the country. Well, we have constructed several large, medium and minor dams in the several river basins. An important question to be raised at this juncture is, Have given adequate consideration to the surplus flow in the river basins while constructing new dams? In most of the dams, the surplus has not been taken into account at all. For example, in the Cauvery River basin, many dams were constructed during the post-independence period mostly at the head-reach of the river and across its tributaries by both Karnataka and Tamil Nadu without taking the surplus into account. Karnataka, which irrigated 4.42 lakh acres in the Cauvery basin in 1971, expanded its irrigated areas to 21.38 lakh acres in the 1990s. As against this, in Tamil Nadu, where no new dam was constructed in the Cauvery, small and medium reservoirs have been constructed in its tributaries, enabling increase in the irrigated area in the old canal.[14] Ultimately, the tail-end farmers are not able to get water. Apparently, these diversions providing irrigation facilities to the additional areas have deprived the old irrigated areas of their riparian rights. In other words, many dams were constructed to provide additional irrigation facilities at the cost of the old irrigated areas of the basin. Since some of the dams were constructed to meet political compulsions, the consequences were never studied or neglected. For example, Orathupalayam dam was constructed across the Noyyal River at a cost of Rs.11 crore in the early 1990s to provide irrigation facility. So far, only once water has been distributed from it and the downstream farmers have vehemently opposed it. Now it has been turned out to be a massive storage tank for the toxic effluents discharged by dyeing and bleaching industries in Tirupur. As a result, it is no more a source of water, and even during monsoon, rainwater does not make any remarkable value addition. Hence, it begs the question as to what was the purpose of construction of the dam. Given this scenario, initiation of a project without a detailed and comprehensive study on its impact might lead to its abandonment halfway through or will not help attain the stated benefits.

Sixth, flood control is one of the main objectives of dam construction. But, by and large it has failed. Even now, floods have been occurring almost every year in one or the other region. Though the government has initiated several flood control measures during the plan period, a heavy loss on area of habitation, loss of cropped area, building damages, loss of cattle and human lives have been reported at an alarming frequency in parts of the country. Between 1953 and 1998, 344.258 Mha and 1500.72 million people were affected, 162.49 Mha cropped area and 52,228,654 houses were damaged and 4,320,050 cattle and livestock and 70,353 human lives were lost. The total loss accounted for is Rs.52,659.334 crores.[15] The irrigation dams too have failed miserably in providing irrigation facilities and preventing floods. It clearly shows that mere construction of dams cannot solve the problem since other aspects, like maintenance of water tanks, forests, etc., have to be taken into account. Interestingly, flood damage is not confined to water surplus river basins, but it is true of water scarce basins as well. Hence, inter-basin transfer might not prove to be the ultimate solution to prevent floods in the northern rivers.

Seventh, the question is, whether the surplus water of the basins have catered the maximum irrigation facilities at the present without jeopardizing any future requirement. If yes, then there would not be any problem in diverting water. Indeed, in most of the surplus water basin states, irrigation facilities have not expanded to the maximum extent due to financial constraints and other reasons. For example, some states sharing the Ganga River basin, like Uttar Pradesh and Bihar, are yet to establish sufficient irrigation facilities. In 1998–99, only 66.43 per cent and 47.27 per cent of the gross cropped area was irrigated, respectively, in Uttar Pradesh and Bihar.[16] It indicates that within the basin states, a large extent of the areas has to be provided with irrigation facilities. The Mahanadi and Godavari River basins' states also have a large area to be irrigated within the basin area. Unless the requirements of the particular basin areas are not met, any attempt at diversion to other basins or other states is bound to affect the local subjects and thereby the integrity of the nation itself.

Eighth, in the peninsular south, monsoon starts from May/June, whereas in the northern regions, it starts only from July onwards. Hypothetically speaking, if southern states get enough rainfall during monsoon, water would be sufficient in the peninsular basins for another three more months. In the event of a heavy downfall due to poor monsoon in the months of June and July in the northern states, diversion of water makes little sense. The dreadful impact of climate having its imprint everywhere, monsoon failure would make a mockery of diversion from northern states.

Ninth, before linking the rivers in different parts of the country, the scheduled rivers that have surplus water have to be identified in advance and a study should be carried out to ascertain the future requirements of the basins so as to minimize the problems which might arise. The surplus in a particular river basin has to be preserved to serve the future needs in terms of growing population, industrial development and extension of irrigation facilities among others. According to the National Commission for Integrated Water Resources Development (1999), total water requirement for the country, which was 694 km^3 to 710 km^3 in 2010, is being projected at 973 km^3 to 1180 km^3 in 2050 depending on the low- and high-demand scenarios.[17] The proportion of water requirement for domestic, industries and power, which went up by 4.3 km^3 in 2010 would increase to 111 km^3 in 2050, 37 km^3 to 81 km^3 and 19 km^3 to 70^3 km, respectively, in the next fifty years. Further, the commission indicates that the proposed net water use for all uses in different basins is higher than the utilizable surface water in the subcontinent in 2050.[18] Studies have found that Brahmaputra, Barak and west-flowing rivers from Tadri to Kanyakumari would be only a few among the water-sufficient basins by the middle of this century.[19] Hence, on a pragmatic assessment, water may be invariably scarce in future in most river basins. In such conditions, diverting the surplus without a far-sighted vision is sure to affect future requirements of the basin states.

Tenth, unless the surplus water is diverted to other basins or any attempt is made to reduce the water-intensive strategies, we would have to face in future what we have seen at present in different basins. Owing to the lack of storage sites on the Ganga catchment areas in India, the available flows could not be fully utilized, adding up to the surplus in the river going waste during the monsoons. Again, not only storage sites are limited in the Brahmaputra basin but also the availability of land for irrigation is limited. The west-flowing rivers of Kerala, Karnataka, Maharashtra and Gujarat states too are endowed with a limited land for irrigation and the length of the rivers is also small.[20] Hence, what is of prime importance is storing of water within the basin rather than diverting it into other basins.

Eleventh, most of the river basins in India are polluted[21] primarily due to the industrial effluent discharges. For example, Ganga, Yamuna and Bhavani are highly polluted, and the existing mechanisms have not helped in controlling the pollution. Until and unless water pollution is strictly controlled, further improvement of water resources is a difficult task. According to the commission's (1999) estimate, water requirement for seventeen categories of industries was 15,282.9 mm^3 per year in 1997, with the total wastewater generation remaining at 3,878.3 mm^3 per year.[22] Whereas, in the next fifty years (2050), the required water for these (17) industries will be 102,535.75 mm^3 per year and the wastewater generation would be 66,408.38 mm^3 per year.[23] Of course, this estimate has not taken into account the small and village industries. If included, demand for water would increase manifold. Proportionately, the quantity of wastewater would also increase in future. Hence, the control of water pollution is of paramount importance. If pollution control is not accorded priority, we would allow posterity to stare at water scarcity.

Twelfth, the existing dams have not yet achieved the returns, though each and every one has projected or substantiated through the cost-benefit analysis. Moreover, the irrigation projects also did not receive the revenue due to low water rates and still the lower collections. The recommendations of various committees and commissions to hike the water rates have not successfully implemented due to the lack of political support. Inefficient as well as unreliable water supply by the government could not impose further taxes on the farmers.[24] The water charges are very low and have not been revised for decades together in most of the states.[25] In fact, the water charges are not even sufficient to meet the operations and maintenance costs.[26] Under this situation, it has to be looked on how to get the returns of the huge investment from the beneficiaries. Will it be possible?

Thirteenth: So far, a large number of people have been displaced at different dams without appropriate rehabilitation measures. In this scenario, it is difficult to rehabilitate any more people from different parts of the country who would account for some lakhs. In India, about 16.38 million people have been displaced. The proposed project is going to displace about 4.5 lakhs of people, who have to be rehabilitated. Expecting this to be accomplished appears to be a tall order, given the past experience where those oustees even in the small pockets continue to face official apathy.

Fourteenth: Invariably, those who are affected most because of the dams are, by and large, people belonging to the Scheduled Castes and Tribes. About 62 per cent of the displaced people belong to the Scheduled Castes and Tribes, who constitute about 25 per cent of the total population of the country.[27] Among them, Scheduled Tribes form the major proportion of the displaced. The rate of proportion is very high when compared to their low percentage of population. Thus they account for 40–50 per cent of the oustees, though they are only 8 per cent of the population.[28] In fact, this clearly indicates that they have not benefited from development measures in general. Paradoxically, most of the mega-development projects have only weakened or affected their harmonious conditions of life and livelihood. Under this situation, protection and welfare of these marginal sections of the society cannot be overlooked.

Fifteenth, with existing dams remaining under ecological and environmental threat, their protection has to be the immediate agenda. At the early nineteenth century itself, it was conceptualized with conviction that protection of forests, environment and ecology was vital for sustainable development and bio-harmony. However, efforts in this direction gained some momentum only at the close of the nineteenth century. At the same time, contrary to this avowed goal, the colonial government had encouraged expansion of cultivation in the forest areas. Unfortunately, this even continued under the post-independent governments. This in due course resulted in decline of the forest cover, and at present, dense forest area is less than 14 per cent.[29] It is a fact that huge extent of green cover has been encroached upon by the government and private parties for various purposes. India loses 1.3 million hectares of forests every year. One of the major causes of desertification is the random felling of trees. In this context, the proposed project is certain to submerge vast tracts of forest area, and what makes up for compensation is to be considered seriously.

Lastly, while neglecting the traditional methods of water storage in tanks, lakes and ponds, diverting water from one river to another would not solve the problems. For sustainability of irrigation, we have to revive and sustain recharge mechanism, for which, tanks and watersheds are more appropriately suited. According to official estimates, there were 15.13 lakhs tanks in India in 1986–87, of which 95 per cent are in the states of Andhra Pradesh, Madhya

Pradesh, Karnataka, Kerala, Tamil Nadu, Uttar Pradesh, Maharashtra and West Bengal.[30] Although a large proportion of the tanks were located in the southern peninsular states, it has not received due attention, particularly during the post-independence period. Consequently, the area irrigated by these tanks had declined noticeably, though many new tanks were constructed, during this period. For instance, while 4.78 million hectares of land was irrigated in 1962–63, it has declined to 3.07 million hectares in 1985–86.[31] This is due to the improper utilization and lack of maintenance of many traditional tanks over the period.[32] In other words, the traditionally managed tank system has almost vanished in different parts of the country. In the southern states, watershed schemes have been already initiated in this direction of sustainable water storage methods. In fact, India's National Water Policy clearly suggests that water planning and management needs to be done on a river basin basis.[33] As such, linking canals to tanks is being given serious consideration.[34] Maintaining the traditional tanks acquires greater importance not only in terms of cost but in view of decentralization and environmental sustainability than the superficial linking of the rivers from Himalaya to Kanyakumari. Inter-basin and intra-basin diversions will not be a lasting solution for water problems, as it is bound to create conflicts between counties and states, besides posing a threat to state autonomy, ecology, environment and marginal groups. In other words, instead of solving problems arising out of the competing demand for water, it would only exacerbate them.

Attappadi/Siruvani/Bhavani water diversion

Having seen the macro-picture in the previous section, let us look at the ongoing conflict between the states of Kerala and Tamil Nadu in sharing the east-flowing rivers from the Western Ghats. For Tamil Nadu, the east-flowing rivers from either Kerala or Karnataka are the prime sources of surface water. Invariably, in Tamil Nadu all rivers are flowing towards the east, whereas in neighbouring Kerala, most of the rivers are flowing towards the west. Of the forty-four rivers in Kerala, only three flow towards the east.[35] Even on these three east-flowing rivers, Kerala government has constructed 336 micro watershed projects.[36] In Karnataka, the major east-flowing rivers are Krishna, Cauvery, North Pennar, South Pennar and Palar. Each river has several tributaries. In addition to that, there are nine west-flowing rivers in Karnataka, whose *ayacut* area is limitted.[37] Hence, geologically Tamil Nadu is disadvantaged because of its location.

Therefore, it has to depend on Kerala and Karnataka and to some extent the east-flowing rivers passing through Andhra Pradesh. Hence, whatever is happening at the head of the east-flowing rivers of these neighbouring states becomes a cause of concern for Tamil Nadu, as it curtails the natural flow of those rivers. Consequently, any development initiative upstream is a matter of concern for Tamil Nadu as the state does not have any other option like Kerala or Karnataka, which have far wider options for water resources.

Given the geography and river basins, let us see the history of water conflicts between Tamil Nadu and Kerala in sharing Siruvani River water, a tributary of Bhavani, and the river Bhavani since the early twentieth century. Diverting Bhavani water was contemplated since the early nineteenth century, and the Bavani Sagar dam was constructed finally in 1946. But for the Coimbatore domestic water supply, Siruvani water was diverted only in 1932. Precisely, there was no water conflict in sharing either Siruvani or Bhavani River water until independence, particularly till the reorganization of linguistic states in 1956.

Siruvani River originating in Muthikulam hills of Attappady plateau and the confluence with Kodungarapallam, flows with six other major tributaries, of which five are from Varadimala slopes joining on the right bank and one tributary from Muthikulam hills on the left bank, and finally merging with the Bhavani River. River Bhavani, though originating in the Nilgiris district of Tamil Nadu, flows through Kerala for about fifty kilometre and comes back to Tamil Nadu. These two rivers are very important sources of drinking water for Coimbatore and Tirupur cities besides being the main source for irrigation in Coimbatore, Tirupur, Erode and Karur districts of Tamil Nadu. The sources of Coimbatore water supply scheme are from Siruvani and Bhavani Rivers the tributaries of the Cauvery. The Siruvani-I was started in 1931, Siruvani-II in 1970s and Pillur in 1980s. The Lower Bhavani Project canal was opened to irrigation in 1956.

Kerala-Tamil Nadu Siruvani Agreement

When the project Siruvani-I was proposed in 1912, Palakkad district was the part of Madras Presidency, and hence there was no conflict between the present Kerala and Tamil Nadu region. Indeed, the people of Siruvani's catchment region have not shown any resentment while diverting water for Coimbatore drinking water supply scheme. Even after the reorganization of the linguistic state in 1956, the Kerala government did not raise any issue on Siruvani-I project and Bhavani dam. It has to be emphasized here that the present Kerala region did not object to the diversion of river water either for domestic supply in 1930s or for the irrigation in 1950s.

However, after the reorganization of linguistic states, the Kerala government, while initiating projects on the east-flowing rivers, protested the further diversion towards Tamil Nadu. To meet the increasing demand for water to Coimbatore and Tirupur cities and their neighbouring villages, the Government of Tamil Nadu approached the Kerala government in the 1960s. But then, Kerala government flatly refused to consider the proposal. However, a meeting of the two chief ministers and union minister of irrigation and power was held at Trivandrum on 10 May 1969 to find a working solution for the sharing of river waters between the states. The meeting was presided over by the then union irrigation and power minister Dr K. L. Rao. At the conclusion of the conference, a settlement on Parambikulam-Aliyar Project (PAP), Bhavani project, Pambar basin, Siruvani project supplying drinking water to Coimbatore and Kabini River sharing of waters was finalized.[38] Based on the agreement, a new dam on Siruvani River downstream, in addition to the existing one at Muthikulam, was planned to enable water facilities to Coimbatore city and the neighbouring areas. And, in 1973 an agreement was inked for ninety-nine years between Kerala and Tamil Nadu to divert the Siruvani River water – not more than 1,300 M.cft annually (1 July to 30 June) – to meet the drinking water supply of Coimbatore city.[39] This agreement categorically mentioned that 'drinking water supply includes the supply of water for domestic, community and industrial needs but shall not include for irrigation purposes'.[40] It, further mentioned that Kerala state can divert the regulated flow of five cusecs of water to meet the riparian requirements from the dam.

Attappady Valley Irrigation Project (Kerala)

Since the 1970s, Kerala has proposed for the Attappady Valley Irrigation Project (AVIP), a concrete gravity dam across Siruvani River at Chittur in Agali Village of Mannarkkad taluk in Palakkad district. The proposed reservoir falls within a radius of five kilometres from the interstate boundary of Kerala and Tamil Nadu. It was aimed at impounding 65 Mm^3 (2.29 TMC) of water to facilitate irrigation for a cultivable command area of 4900 ha (gross irrigated area 6150 ha) through water distribution systems of 84 km length including main canals and branch canals.[41] The investigation for location of the dam was carried out during 1975–82 with the assistance of geologists from the Geological Survey of India (GSI). Till 31 March 1983, Rs. 508 lakhs was spent on the project.[42] Due to non-clearance by the Central Water Commission and paucity of funds, the works relating to AVIP were put on hold until 1989. However, this proposal was constantly opposed by the Government of Tamil Nadu from the beginning. Since the 1970s, Kerala has brought the issue to the notice of the Government of India. Various initiatives were taken up by the Government of India, and among the states, viz. Tamil Nadu, Karnataka, Kerala and Puducherry, the differences remained unresolved.

The negotiations between Karnataka and Tamil Nadu pertaining to this and the attempts made by the Government of India since 1970s to amicably resolve the sharing of Cauvery waters have completely failed. Consequently, under the provisions of Inter-State Water Disputes Act, 1956 (33 of 1956), the Government of India constituted the 'Cauvery Water Disputes Tribunal' by a notification dated 2 June 1990. The Kerala government made representation to share the Cauvery water since it has about 2,866 sq. km in the Cauvery basin. The Kerala government stated: 'After the re-organisation of the State, determined efforts have been made for improvement of the basin and diversion of the water in Cauvery basin for utilisation by the State, but their several claims had been objected by the other riparian States.'[43] However, the Kerala government did not get any interim relief under the Cauvery Water Dispute Tribunal's Interim Order in 1991. According to the Tribunal, 'The State of Kerala has not applied for any interim order, therefore, this order is without prejudice to the claims and contentions of the state of Kerala about the equitable distribution.'[44] However, in 2007, in the final order of the tribunal (CWDT),[45] Kerala was awarded 6 TMC from the Bhavani River sub-basin and 2.87 TMC is specifically awarded to the AVIP dam project, giving a fresh lease of life.

Projects of Kerala on Bhavani River

Immediately after the formation of the Kerala State (1958), the Public Works Department (Irrigation Branch) proposed to construct the dam on the Bhavani River at Seramankandi and divert the water south-west through a tunnel to Tenkara and from there towards Ambankadavu Thodu to irrigate around 22,200 acres in Wulluwanad and Palghat taluks of Palghat district.[46] However, this project has not materialized. Though Kerala had not constructed any major dam on the Bhavani River, it has built several micro watershed schemes. At, present, there are ninety-seven micro watershed schemes developed by the Kerala government across the Bhavani River.[47] 'In 2002, the Kerala made an attempt to divert water from Bhavani River at a place called Mukkali, but following strong opposition from Tamil Nadu farmers and Tamil Nadu government, the plan was dropped', recalls K. Kalidas, president of OSAI, an environmental NGO based in Coimbatore.[48]

Based on the Cauvery Water Disputes Tribunal final order, the Kerala government now plans to construct six check-dams across the Bhavani River. In fact, the Minor Irrigation Department of Kerala has begun the construction of two check dams at Thekkuvattai and Padavayal across the Bhavani River in Pudur *panchayats* of Attappadi. It has been proposed to construct three check dams and implement four lift irrigation projects at a cost of Rs. 13 crores. In Padavayal, the Kerala Water Authority (KWA) has proposed to implement drinking water schemes which can also be used for irrigation purposes.

Athikadavu-Avinashi Project

Since the early nineteenth century, utilizing the surplus water of Bhavani River has been contemplated upon. But, it was Arthur Cotton who mooted a concrete proposal in 1834 to put in use the surplus water. Subsequently, several alternative schemes were considered to use the flood waters of Bhavani River but nothing got materialized. Finally, in 1856, it was concluded that without a storage reservoir in the Bhavani River, extension of irrigation would not be feasible.[49] In 1857, a dam site was located at Pulavur, just below the confluence of Siruvani with Bhavani River. Though this proposal was considered, nothing was done to bring it into fruition.[50] After consideration of the proposal in 1857, there was no initiative to take it forward due to the Sepoy Mutiny and reduction of grants.[51] But, again in the 1880s, the importance of constructing a dam across the Bhavani was emphasized, but in a surprise move, there was a suggestion in the official quarters to give it up.[52] Since the early twentieth century, several proposals were made to utilize the surplus water to irrigate Coimbatore district. Of the two important proposals, one was the Lower Bhavani Project (wet) and another Upper Bhavani Project (dry). In 1905, there were three proposals for two sites in Upper Bhavani, and one for the lower reach of the Bhavani River.[53] Subsequently, detailed reports were prepared for all the three proposals. Of the two Upper Bhavani reservoirs, one was proposed at Pulavur and the second one seven miles down the junction of Kundah with the Bhavani River.[54] The Lower Bhavani Project was proposed eighteen miles below Mettupalayam.[55]

Considering the revenue aspects, in 1908, the government decided to construct the Lower Bhavani Project and drop the Upper Bhavani Project.[56] However, there was no further development until 1925 when two alternative estimates were submitted both for Upper and Lower Bhavani Projects. In 1928, the government ordered to drop the Upper Bhavani Project. The Public Works Department prepared the plans and estimates; the government was satisfied with the scheme proposals in 1938, the Coimbatore District Board members and other influential persons made representations to once again take up the Upper Bhavani Project.[57] The government re-examined the Upper Bhavani Project with four alternative proposals and finally dropped it once for all in 1946.[58]

After the construction of the Lower Bhavani Project, there was a constant demand from the people of Avinashi region even before independence onwards. Since Independence, several proposals were also made in different names at different points of time. Claiming that the surplus from Bhavani dam was going waste into the sea, they pressed for the diversion of the surplus water to recharge the tanks and ponds, which will increase the water table in the Avinashi region. The storage capacity of the Bhavani dam is only 53 TMC. For twenty-seven years between 1956 and 1996, there was a surplus waterflow from the Bhavani dam, of which the quantum in fifteen years was 20 TMC and above, four years 10–20 TMC, four years 5–10 TMC and four years less than 5 TMC (see Table 6.1). Hence, the demand for diversion of this surplus towards the Avinashi region to recharge the groundwater table. For this project the required water is only 1.5 TMC.

There was a persistent demand from the people of Avinashi region to revive the Upper Bhavani Project even before independence. Later, they gave it up and stuck to the Athikadavu-Avinashi Project to divert the surplus water of Bhavani dam. But, the demand was not considered by the government since this constituency either elected the Congress representative earlier or All India Anna Dravida Munnetra Kazhagam (AIADMK) later. Hence, Dravida Munnetra Kazhagam (DMK) government did not show any interest in this project. However, the demand got intensified since the last decade of the twentieth century. Finally, in 2012, the Athikadavu-Avinashi Project was implemented to divert the flood water from the Bhavani River at Pillur to 31 tanks maintained by the water resources department, 40 *panchayats* union tanks and 538 ponds combined together in Coimbatore, Tirupur and Erode districts.[59] It has a capacity to irrigate more than 1.5 lakh acres of agricultural lands besides improving the groundwater levels in Coimbatore, Erode

Table 6.1 Surplus water from Bhavani dam: 1956–96 (TMC)

Year	Received water	Surplus water	Year	Received water	Surplus water
1956	58.51	5.51	1975	73.67	20.61
1957	86.98	35.98	1977	66.26	13.26
1958	74.83	21.83	1978	78.77	25.77
1959	115.48	62.48	1979	130.86	77.86
1960	79.86	26.86	1980	86.44	33.44
1961	162.03	109.03	1981	72.27	19.27
1962	98.10	45.10	1982	54.37	1.37
1963	73.58	20.58	1984	63.02	10.02
1964	84.37	41.97	1991	59.99	6.99
1966	54.23	1.23	1992	81.64	28.64
1971	62.60	9.60	1993	53.99	00.99
1972	76.43	23.43	1994	78.54	25.54
1973	63.77	10.77	1996	58.78	5.78
1974	55.99	3.99			

Source: http://avinashiathikadavu.blogspot.in/2013/05/blog-post.html (accessed in January 2017).

and Tirupur districts. 'Athikadavu-Avinashi Flood Canal Project has been conceived to mitigate the effects of flood, by means of excavation of a Flood Carrier Canal from the Pillur Dam water spread area. The Flood Flow Canal includes one Main Canal and two Branch Canals viz., Avinashi Branch Canal and Perundurai Branch Canal to divert flood water to the tanks and ponds in Coimbatore, Tirupur and Erode Districts which act as flood absorbers.'[60] The main purpose of this project is to recharge the groundwater table and to solve the drinking water problem in the towns and villages of Karamadai, Metupalayam, Annur, Avinashi, Puliampatti, Kavilipalayam, Perunduri and Nambiyur in Coimbatore, Erode and Tirupur.

Water Conflict between Kerala and Tamil Nadu

Kerala and Tamil Nadu agreed to share the waters of the east-flowing as well as few west-flowing rivers from the late nineteenth century. For example, the agreement in 1894 between Madras Presidency and the Travancore king was made to divert the west-flowing Periyar River. Even after independence, Kerala government has agreed to divert water from different rivers. In 1973, Siruvani River water was diverted to Coimbatore to meet the drinking water needs. Around the same time, Kerala has agreed to the Parambikulam-Aliyar projects. As long as Kerala acceded to the proposals of Tamil Nadu, there was no problem from the latter. In its final award in 2007, the Cauvery Water Dispute Tribunal granted 6 TMC from the Bhavani sub-basin. As per the Siruvani drinking water project agreement (1973) between Kerala and Tamil Nadu, five cusecs of water has to be diverted to the riparian right holders of Kerala state. But according to the data, the Government of Tamil Nadu never abides by that clause citing scarcity of water in Coimbatore city.

It is an interesting fact that whenever Tamil Nadu wants to divert the river water for irrigation and drinking water supply, they design the project, but oppose the same and make an issue if proposed by Kerala. Tamil Nadu has even gone to the tribunal for redressal of its grievances, forgetting that it is bound by the tribunal's final award. Then, it has approached the Supreme Court. The problem is that the demand for water has always been on the rise. Obviously, every state has to meet these increasing demands. Now, it has reached a level where the available options in the basin and sub-basins have almost been exhausted. In other words, every basin and sub-basin has become a closed basin. For example, in the Bhavani Basin, only four diversions were there until independence, three for irrigation purpose and one for the water supply scheme. One such is the diversion for irrigation from Bhavani River and drinking water supply from its tributary, viz. Siruvani. After independence, through the Lower Bhavani Canal, 2.5 lakh hectares were brought under irrigation through the Bhavani Sagar dam. In addition to that, one more dam from the Siruvani and yet another dam from Bhavani River water was diverted for drinking water purposes. Further, recently Athikadavu-Avinashi project was implemented to divert the 1.5 TMC water for the water recharge programme. In other words, without considering the downstream requirements, we have diverted water right at the head reach of the river and its tributaries, thus turning the basin and sub-basin a closed one. If the diversion of the surplus in the upstream of the river basin is made, maintaining river flow raises a serious challenge. In other words, while diverting the water upstream either for irrigation purposes or for recharging groundwater, it becomes necessary to study and address the concerns arising downstream. The past experience clearly shows how the fertile Thanjavur delta region has slowly become desertified. If best practices are not ensured to keep the natural flow in the river, serious ecological and environmental consequences are inevitable. Further, the demand to divert the water both from Kerala and Tamil Nadu would be on the rise. Hence, there is little relevance to hold empty discussions on the conflict between Kerala and Tamil Nadu. Tamil Nadu state has to think about how to save water and effectively employ water management practices. Picking up conflicts with the neighbouring states will not solve the problems in the long run.

7

Conclusion

Since antiquity, human settlements have come up and flourished around water bodies. Initially, water from streams and rivers was used both for drinking and for cultivation. Later on, water from rivers was diverted to be stored in tanks and ponds for future requirements. These resources, which are common property resources, were managed and maintained by the local communities. This traditional water management system ensured sustainable water supply to the people. In addition to that, village wells and private wells were there to meet the requirements of the village people and other production activities.

Water from different resources was used to cultivate crops, mainly for local consumption. The streams and tanks were channelized through a network of canals and channels. Till recently, water was drawn from wells with the help of animals and by using other traditional methods. This helped maintain the water table. Till the introduction of modern technology, water resources were utilized solely for livelihood purposes. Interestingly, tanks, ponds and community wells were managed by the local communities. In the traditional village administrative system, there were *nirkaties*, who were responsible to manage the water resources. For example, breaches in the bunds, discharging excess water, distribution of water, collection of irrigation tax and so on were carried out by the *nirkaties*, who were rewarded on an annual basis. These traditional water management systems continued until the early nineteenth century or until the early colonial period.

However, this traditional water management system has been undermined or lost its importance ever since the East India Irrigation Company (EIIC) gave priority to establish major irrigation projects. Indeed, the East India Irrigation Company has proposed several irrigation dams in every river basin of the country since the early nineteenth century. Consequently, some large dams were constructed during the mid-nineteenth century.

With an emphasis on the major irrigation dams, the East India Irrigation Company had neglected the maintenance of traditional water sources.

Consequently, several tanks became dysfunctional, with both the supply and distributive channels being encroached upon or rather disappearing. In other words, an option to store water in the traditional forms lost its importance during the colonial period.

Since the early nineteenth century, the East India Company gave priority to increasing land revenue. To that end, several proposals were made in each and every river basin of the Indian subcontinent. However, only some dams were constructed during the late nineteenth century. In the early twentieth century too the number of dams constructed was only limited due to frequent famines and world wars. But, since the late nineteenth century, the demand for water has been increasing due to the emergence of towns. For example, Coimbatore became a municipal town during the third quarter of the nineteenth century. Initially, local tanks were considered a source of drinking water. Later on, nearby sources, especially river basins, were tapped. Interestingly, population was very low in the towns and the demands were met within the basins. However, since the second quarter of the twentieth century, water diversions were made from other basins for domestic water supply.

After independence, population explosion and the attendant mushrooming of unregulated urbanization saw the demand for water increase manifold from domestic water supply to agriculture and industrialization. Apart from surface water, agriculture sector started exploiting groundwater sources since the early nineteenth century. For example, in Coimbatore district, the numbers of wells have tripled from the early nineteenth century to the last quarter of the nineteenth century.[1] With technological advancement like electricity, wells were deepened further for more than 100 feet during the post-independence period. After 1970s, borewells were dug up to 1,000 feet to lift water. As a consequence, water table has gone down drastically. It got further aggravated due to the competitive deepening, leading to desertification of the entire region. Also, well water sources have become defunct in most of the areas. With the river flow getting blocked due to the dams and diversions, the absence of recharge mechanism has led to further depletion of groundwater tables. Adding another dimension to the crisis, the industries let off effluents without any treatment. For example, over 800 dyeing and bleaching industries discharge a huge quantity of effluents, contaminating both groundwater and surface water around a 25-kilometre radius of Tirupur town. Most of the cities and towns continue to discharge untreated sewage water into the river flow. While the demand for water has been increasing, we have failed to manage the used water, particularly domestic water/sewage and industrial effluent discharges.

Now, diversion of water from other river basins has reached its peak. And, most of the river basins have already reached the level of closure. According to the World Bank, except three river basins, all other river basins would become insufficient to meet domestic, agriculture and industrial needs by the mid-twenty-first century. Already, conflicts have emerged within the basin, between the basins, between the states, among the states and between countries. As such, diverting water from other basins is not an option anymore. In other words, almost all river basins and sub-basins have been turned into a closed basin, due to over-exploitation.

Considering the gravity of the problem that stares us in the face, several measures, such as check-dams watershed programmes, water harvesting technology and so on, have been initiated to preserve rainwater. In addition to that, better water management systems, such as drip irrigation and sprinkles, have been introduced since the last decade of the twentieth century. But, the tragedy is the neglect of traditional water storage mechanisms, like tanks, ponds as well as watershed, and other water harvesting options in those regions where water diversion was taken up. It is a sad commentary that tanks were not maintained, leaving the recharge options very defunct. Consequently, the common property character has lost its relevance, resulting in emergence of water as a saleable commodity.

Environmental history of India, with its focus predominantly on colonial and pre-colonial periods, is largely centred on forests and wildlife. The debate on environmental history has by and large neglected agriculture, industry and domestic water supply as well as the consequences on environment and ecology. A comprehensive account of the competing demand for water for both the colonial and post-colonial periods remains either ignored or has not received due attention. Therefore, an attempt has been made to arrive at a comprehensive understanding of competing demand for water, with its various dimensions, in the Noyyal and Bhavani River basins.

This book raises four important questions: (1) Did the policy-makers visualize the future demand while carrying out diversion of water within the basins or from other basins? (2) Was diversion of water from distant places carried out efficiently or has it added to pollution, resulting in serious damage to the entire river basin? (3) While diverting water, have the natural flows been taken care of to preserve the ecology, environment and the recharge mechanism to maintain the water table or not? and (4) What were the factors which aggravated the competing demand for water and its consequences for the future?

In the Bhavani and Noyyal River basins, water was utilized to some extent, primarily for irrigation purposes, through some canals and check-dams. Hence, large quantum of flood water was going as waste and frequently causing distress in Thanjavur and in the Cauvery River basin. Since the early nineteenth century, it has been contemplated to use the surplus water for productive purposes, particularly irrigation. However, only in 1834, Arthur Cotton initiated the proposal for a dam across the Bhavani River. Since then, several proposals were made but shelved till the beginning of the twentieth century.

Since the last quarter of the nineteenth century, demand for domestic water supply has been rising in Coimbatore town. In 1866, Coimbatore became a municipal town, with a population of over 35,000. Till 1880s, water supply for Coimbatore was managed from the wells within the town. But, water scarcity emerged since the last quarter of the nineteenth century, and to meet this demand, several schemes were considered. For example, in 1888, Muthikualam Scheme; in 1892, Noyyal River Scheme; in 1901, Chitrachavadi Channel and Rajavaikkal Scheme; in 1907, Kistnambadi Tank Scheme; and in 1909, Sub-Artesian Springs, Singanallur Scheme were considered. These schemes have not materialized due to prohibitive cost, bad quality of water and protest from the farmers. Hence, options for drinking water supply in the close proximity of the town were given up. Hence, diverting water from a nearby basin was considered since the first decade of twentieth century. In 1912, Siruvani River, a tributary of Bhavani River, was taken up as a viable one for providing water supply to Coimbatore and the scheme was finalized in 1924.

In the meantime, the demand for water for agriculture has also increased simultaneously. Since the early twentieth century, two proposals, namely Upper Bhavani and Lower Bhavani projects, were under active consideration, and finally in 1946, the later one was sanctioned. In the 1950s, Coimbatore's population shot up fivefold with a quantum jump in industrial activities. Further, the number of small towns on the periphery also increased.

Along with the demand for domestic water supply, requirements for industries and irrigation have witnessed a remarkable increase. To meet the bourgeoning domestic water demand of Coimbatore, Tirupur and other cities and villages, more and more water was diverted both from Noyyal and Bhavani River basins. Between 1970 and 1980, Siruvani-II and Pillur dams across the Bhavani were constructed to meet the domestic and industrial water demand of Coimbatore and Tirupur and several other villages. But, pollution of the river course due to domestic discharge as well as industrial effluents continued to be neglected.

Half-hearted and token efforts to regulate these industries have not yielded the desired results.

In the age of consumption, competing demand for water among different sectors has led to the diversion of river waters, resulting in decline of natural flow and adversely affecting recharge options downstream. This poses a grave threat to the ecology and environment as well as other biodiversity resources. Diverted water is used and discharged as a pollutant, compounding the problem in the long run. In such a scenario, any further demand for water would only lead to diversion of upstream sources, eventually resulting in the sub-basins becoming a closed one. Not only will this ultimately lead to desertification but also will fuel conflicts of greater magnitude.

Glossary

anicut A dam made across a stream for maintaining or regulating irrigation.

annas It was the lowest money measurement. Twelve pies equal to one *anna*, 16 *annas* or 172 pies equal to one Company rupee.

ayacut An account of the total landholding to a village and particulars of its distribution and condition, to be kept by an village accountant.

ayacutdars The land owned by the cultivators.

bothies Water courses irrigating an extent of less than 150 acres could be described as field *bothies*.

calingulas A waterway constructed in the bunds of tanks to permit the flow of surplus water, so as to prevent the breach of bunds.

cess A tax or levy.

chain Twenty two yards. One yard is equal to three feet and one foot is equal to twelve inches.

cholam *Sorghum vulgare*.

collector Collector is an Indian Administrative Service (IAS) officer in-charge of revenue collection and administration of a district.

crores Hundred lakhs or 10,000,000.

cumbu Bulrush or spiked millet.

feet It is equal to twelve inches or 30.48 centimetres.

inches A unit of length or equivalent to 2.54 centimetres.

kudimaramattu An institution of customary irrigation management.

lakhs Hundred thousands or 100,000.

mamool A customary collection.

mhote Bucket of a draw well.

mile Eight furlongs or 1.61 kilometres.

Nirkaties The Nirkaties is to take care of the reservoirs or outlet from the tank to the fields.

paisa Equal to one-hundredth of a rupee.

paise One-hundredth part of the rupee of India.

panchayat Local court of arbitration or council of administration.

picotah This is a contrivance for drawing water from the well, channel and lower levels.

ragi Finger millet (*Eleusine Coracana*).

revenue villages It is a small administrative region, a village with defined borders, and it may contain many hamlets.

samei Little millet (*Panicum Miliare*).

ryot A peasant/cultivator.

tahsildar Collector of revenue and sub-magistrate in-charge of a taluk.
thenei Italian millet.
taluk Sub-division of a district.
tirwa Tax on land or land-rent.
traditional bullock mhote A device employed for removal of water from well by bullock power.
varagu Kodo millet (*Panicum Miliaceum*).
vote bank politics It is a practice of creating and maintaining votebanks through divisive policies.
yettam Bucket of a draw well.

Notes

Chapter 1

1. Madhav Gadgil and Ramachandra Guha, *The Fissured Land: An Ecological History of India* (New Delhi: Oxford University Press, 1993), 114.
2. Ibid., 114–115.
3. Ibid., 115.
4. Rohan D'Souza, *Drowned and Dammed: Colonial Capitalism and Flood Control in Eastern India* (New Delhi: Oxford University Press, 2006), 6.
5. Jacques Pouchepadass, 'Colonialism and Environment in India: Comparative Perspective', *Economic and Political Weekly*, 30, no. 33 (1995): 2059; Richard H Grove, Vinita Damodaran and Satpal Sangwan, 'Introduction'. in *Nature and the Orient: Environmental History of South and Southeast Asia*, ed. Richard H. Grove, Satpal Sangwan and Vinita Damodaran (Delhi: Oxford University Press, 1998), 2.
6. Grove, Damodaran and Sangwan 'Introduction', 2; Madhav Gadgil and Ramachandra Guha, 'State Forestry and Social Conflict in British India'. in *Peasant Resistance in India 1858–1914*, ed. David Hardiman (Delhi: Oxford University Press, 1992), 260.
7. Neeladri Bhattacharya, 'Introduction' in *Studies in History*, 14, no. 2 (1998):165; Arun Agrawal and K. Sivaramakrishnan, 'Introduction: Agrarian Environs'. in *Social Nature: Resources, Representations, and Rule in India*, ed. Arun Agrawal and K. Sivaramakrishnan (New Delhi: Oxford University Press, 2001), 4.
8. Ibid.
9. Mahesh Rangarajan, 'Polity, Ecology and Landscape: New Writings on South Asia's Past', *Studies in History*, 18, no. 1, n.s. (2002): 138.
10. Bhattacharya, 'Introduction', 165.
11. For details, see Velayutham Saravanan, *Colonialism, Environment and Tribals in South India, 1792–1947* (London and New York: Routledge, 2017). Velayutham Saravanan, *Environmental History and Tribals in Modern India* (London and New York: Palgrave Macmillan, 2018).
12. Ibid.
13. D'Souza, *Drowned and Dammed*, 12.
14. R. Champakalakshmi, 'Urbanisation in South India: The Role of Ideology and Polity', *Social Scientist*, 15, no. 8/9 (1987): 67.

15 Janine Wilhelm, *Environment and Pollution in Colonial India: Sewerage Technologies Along the Sacred Ganges* (London and New York: Routledge, 2016), 11.
16 Ibid., 12.
17 Ibid., 4.
18 Ibid.
19 Ibid.
20 Ibid.
21 Ibid.
22 Ibid., 5.
23 Brij Narain, *Indian Economic Problems: Part II Source Book for the Study of Indian Economic Problems* (Lahore: The Punjab Printing Works, 1922), 271.
24 Ibid., 282.
25 Ibid.
26 Ibid., 283.
27 Ibid.
28 David Haberman, *River of Love in an Age of Pollution* (California: University of California Press, 2006), 6; M. Mufakharul Islam, *Irrigation, Agriculture and the Raj: Punjab, 1887–1947* (New Delhi: Manohar, 1997), 26.
29 Rohan D'Souza, 'Water in British India: The Making of a "Colonial Hydrology"', *History Compass*, 4, no. 4 (2006): 621.
30 Ibid.
31 Islam, *Irrigation, Agriculture and the Raj*, 41.
32 Ibid., 52.
33 Ibid., 57.
34 David Gilmartin, *Blood and Water: The Indus River Basin in Modern History* (California: University of California Press, 2015).
35 Ibid., 2.
36 Ibid.
37 Elizabeth Whitcombe, *Agrarian Conditions in Northern India, Volume One: The United Province under British Rule, 1860–1900* (Berkeley: University of California Press, 1971).
38 Nirmal Sengupta, 'Indigenous Irrigation Organization in South Bihar', *Indian Economic and Social History Review*, 37, no. 2 (1980): 157–187.
39 David Mosse, *The Rule of Water: Statecraft, Ecology, and Collective Action in South India* (New Delhi: Oxford University Press, 2003), 11–12.
40 Ian Stone, *Canal Irrigation in British India: Perspectives on Technological Change in a Peasant Economy* (Cambridge: Cambridge University Press, 1984), 9.
41 Ibid., 70.
42 Ibid., 4.
43 Ravi Baghel, *River Control in India: Spatial, Governmental and Subjective Dimensions* (Cham: Springer, 2014), 3–8.

44 Haberman, *River of Love in an Age of Pollution*, 6.
45 Islam, *Irrigation, Agriculture and the Raj*, 26.
46 Haberman, *River of Love in an Age of Pollution*, 6–7.
47 Ibid., 7.
48 Ibid., 84.
49 Ibid., 76
50 Ibid.
51 Ibid., 78.
52 Ibid., 83.
53 Ibid.,15.
54 Asit K. Biswas, R. Rangachari and Cecilia Tortajada (ed). *Water Resources of the Indian Subcontinent* (New Delhi: Oxford University Press, 2009), 201.
55 Ibid.
56 Binayak Ray, *Water: The Looming Crisis in India* (Lanham: Lexington Books, 2008), 27.
57 Brian Stoddart, *Land, Water, Language and Politics in Andhra: Regional Evolution in India since 1850* (New Delhi: Routledge, 2011).
58 Amita Baviskar, *In the Belly of the River: Tribal Conflicts over Development in the Narmada Valley* (New Delhi: Oxford University Press, 1995), 241.
59 Ibid., 241.
60 Ibid., 36.
61 Anjal Prakash, Sreoshi Singh, C. G. Goodrich and S. Janakarajan (eds). *Water Resources Policies in South Asia* (New Delhi: Routledge, 2013), 2.
62 Ibid., 5–7.
63 Ibid., 1.
64 Ibid.
65 Ibid., 2.
66 Ray, *Water: The Looming Crisis*, xviii.
67 Ibid.
68 Vandana Asthana, 'Collective Action in the Delhi Water Reform Project: Creating Space for Policy Change', *Indian Journal of Political Science*, 69, no. 4 (2008): 703–717. For details, see Asthana, Vandana, *Water Policy Processes in India: Discourses of Power and Resistance* (London and New York: Routledge, 2009).
69 Vishal Narain and Anjal Prakash (eds), *Water Security in Peri-urban South Asia: Adapting to Climate Change and Urbanisation* (New Delhi: Oxford University Press, 2016).
70 Daniel Klingensmith, *'One Valley and a Thousand': Dams, Nationalism, and Development* (New Delhi: Oxford University Press, 2007).
71 Philippe Cullet and Sujit Kanoon, *Water Law in India: An Introduction to Legal Instruments* (New Delhi: Oxford University Press, 2011), 1.
72 Ibid.
73 Ibid., 2.

74 Ibid., 2 and 199.
75 Ibid., 3.
76 Ibid., 199.
77 Ibid., 200.
78 Peter Mollinga, 'Boundary Concepts for the Interdisciplinary Analysis of Irrigation Water Management in South Asia', in *Controlling the Water: Matching Technology and Institutions in Irrigation and Water Management in India and Nepal*, ed. Dik Roth and Linden Vincent (New Delhi: Oxford University Press, 2013), 342.
79 Ibid.
80 Ibid., 343.
81 Ibid.
82 Sverker Sörlin, 'The Contemporaneity of Environmental History: Negotiating Scholarship, Useful History, and the New Human Condition', *Journal of Contemporary History*, 46, no. 3 (2011): 612.
83 J. R. McNeill 'Population and the Natural Environment: Trends and Challenges', *Population and Development Review*, 32, The Political Economy of Global Population Change, 1950–2050 (2006): 187.
84 David Mosse, 'Ecological Zones and the Culture of Collective Action: The History and Social Organisation of a Tank Irrigation System in Tamil Nadu', *South Indian Studies*, no. 3 (1997): 1.
85 World Water Assessment Programme, *The United Nations World Water Development Report 3: Water in a Changing World* (Paris: UNESCO, and London: Earthscan, 2009), 29.
86 https://esa.un.org/unpd/wup/Downloa48.6d/55.3 (accessed in March 2018).
87 Ibid., 30.
88 Ibid., 128.
89 Ibid., 150.
90 Ibid.
91 Bryan Randolph Bruns and Ruth S. Meinzen-Dick, 'Negotiating Water Rights: Implications for Research and Action', in *Negotiating Water Rights*, ed. B. R. Burns and R. S. Meinzen-Dick (New Delhi: Vistaar Publications, 2000), 23–41; World Bank, *India Irrigation Sector Review*, 2 volumes (Washington, DC: World Bank, 1991), 16; Velayutham Saravanan, *Local Strategies for Water Supply and Conservation Management in the Bhavani and Noyyal River Basins, Part I–Domestic Water Supply and Industrial Sector* (Ottawa: International Development Research Centre, 1998); H. L. Joep Spiertz, 'Water Rights and Legal Pluralism: Some Basics of a Legal Anthropological Approach', in *Negotiating Water Rights*, ed. B. R. Burns and R. S. Meinzen-Dick (New Delhi: Vistaar Publications, 2000), 162–199; Ganjar Kurnia, Teten W. Avianto and B. R. Burns, 'Farmers Factories and the Dynamics of Water Allocation in West Java', in *Negotiating Water Rights*, ed. B. R. Burns and R. S. Meinzen-Dick (New Delhi: Vistaar Publications, 2000), 292–314.

92 Bruns and Meinzen-Dick, 'Negotiating Water Rights', 42–43; Dipak Gyawali and Ajaya Dixit, 'Fractured Institutions and Physical Interdependence: Challenges to Local Water Management in the Tinau River Basin, Nepal', in *Rethinking the Mosaic: Investigations into Local Water Management*, ed. Marcus Moench, Elisabeth Caspari and Ajaya Dixit (Kathmandu: Nepal Water Conservation Foundation and Boulder: Institute for Social and Environmental Transition, 1999), 52–122.

93 Jeffrey D. Brewer, 'Negotiating Seasonal Water Allocation Rules in Krindi Oya, Sri Lanka', in *Negotiating Water Rights*, ed. B. R. Burns and R. S. Meinzen-Dick (New Delhi: Vistaar Publications, 2000), 112–136.

94 Ruth S. Meinzen-Dick, 'Public, Private, and Shared Water: Groundwater Markets and Access in Pakistan', in *Negotiating Water Rights*, ed. B. R. Burns and R. S. Meinzen-Dick (New Delhi: Vistaar Publications, 2000), 245–268; S. Z. Sadeque, 'Nature's Bounty or Scarce Community: Competition and Consensus over Ground Water Use in Rural Bangladesh', in *Negotiating Water Rights*, ed. B. R. Burns and R. S. Meinzen-Dick (New Delhi: Vistaar Publications, 2000), 269–291; Nyoman Sutawan, 'Negotiation of Water Allocation among Irrigators' Associations in Bali, Indonesia', in *Negotiating Water Rights*, ed. B. R. Burns and R. S. Meinzen-Dick (New Delhi: Vistaar Publications, 2000), 315–336.

95 World Bank, *India Irrigation Sector Review*, 16.

96 Ibid., 151.

97 Ibid., xi.

98 Benjamin Cohen, 'Modernising the Urban Environment: The Musi River Flood of 1908 in Hyderabad, India', *Environment and History*, 17, no. 3 (2011): 429.

99 Ruth Meinzen-Dick and P. Appasamy, *Urbanization and Intersectoral Competition for Water, in Finding the Source: The Linkages between Population and Water* (Woodrow Wilson International Centre for Scholars. Washington, DC: ECSP Publication, 2002), 2.

100 Ibid.

101 A. Shiklomanov, *World Water Resources: A New Appraisal and Assessment for the 21st Century* (Paris: United Nations Educational, Scientific and Cultural Organization, 1998), 2.

102 Ibid., 9.

103 Ibid., 26.

104 Ibid., 34.

105 Ibid., 37.

106 Ibid., 37.

107 N. Shantha Mohan, 'Locating Transboundary Water Sharing in India', in *River Water Sharing: Transboundary Conflict and Cooperation in India*, ed. N. Shantha Mohan, Sailen Routray and N. Sashikumar (New Delhi: Routledge, 2010), 3.

108 Ibid., 3.

109 World Bank, *Water Resources Management in Asia*, 9.
110 John R. Wood, *The Politics of Water Resource Development in India: The Narmada Dams Controversy* (New Delhi: Sage Publications, 2007), 59.
111 Moench, 'Allocating the Common Heritage', A-46.
112 Satyajit Singh, *Taming the Waters: The Political Economy of Large Dams in India* (New Delhi: Oxford University Press, 1997), 33.
113 Shantha Mohan, 'Locating Transboundary Water Sharing in India', 11.
114 Ibid.
115 S. Settar, 'Kaveri in Its Historical Setting', in *River Water Sharing: Transboundary Conflict and Cooperation in India*, ed. N. Shantha Mohan, Sailen Routray and N. Sashikumar (New Delhi: Routledge, 2010), 104.
116 A. Vaidyanathan, 'Foreword', in *Water Conflicts in India: A Million Revolts in the Making*, ed. K. J. Joy, Bissham Gujja, Suhas Paranjape, Vinod Goud and Shruti Vispute (New Delhi: Routledge, 2007), xv.
117 World Bank, *Inter-Sectoral Water Allocation, Planning and Management* (Washington, DC: The World Bank and New Delhi: Allied Publishers, 1999), 7–14.
118 Helga Haftendorn, 'Water and International Conflict' *Third World Quarterly*, 21, no. 1 (2000): 52–53.
119 World Bank, *Inter-Sectoral Water Allocation*, 9.
120 Ibid.
121 Government of India, *Report of the National Commission for Integrated Water Resources Development*, Vol. I (New Delhi: Ministry of Water Resources, 1999), 69.
122 Ibid., 422–423.
123 World Bank, *Inter-Sectoral Water Allocation*, 8.
124 K. Sivasubramaniyan, 'Sustainable Development of Small Water Bodies in Tamil Nadu', *Economic and Political Weekly*, 41, no. 26 (2006): 2861.
125 Ibid., 2862.
126 Government of India, *Agricultural Statistics at a Glance, 2015* (New Delhi: Ministry of Agriculture and Farmer Welfare, 2015) http://eands.dacnet.nic.in/Agricultural_Statistics_At_Glance-2015%20E-book/book.swf.
127 Narentar Pani, 'Boundaries of Transboundary Water Sharings', in *River Water Sharing: Transboundary Conflict and Cooperation in India*, ed. N. Shantha Mohan, Sailen Routray and N. Sashikumar (New Delhi: Routledge, 2010), 52.
128 Velayutham Saravanan, 'Chennai Floods and Floods of Politics', *Mainstream*, 54, no. 17 (2016): 17–19.
129 A. Vaidyanathan, *India's Water Resources: Contemporary Issues on Irrigation* (New Delhi: Oxford University Press, 2006), 11.
130 Sailen Routray, 'The Water Sector in India: An Over view', in *River Water Sharing: Transboundary Conflict and Cooperation in India*, ed. N. Shantha Mohan, Sailen Routray and N. Sashikumar (New Delhi: Routledge, 2010), 24.
131 Wood, *The Politics of Water Resource Development in India*, 56.

132 World Bank, *Inter-Sectoral Water Allocation*, 7–14.
133 Government of India, *Report of the National Commission*, 157.
134 Ibid., 454–455.
135 Asian Development Bank, *Asian Water Development Outlook 2007: Achieving Water Security for Asia* (Manila: Asian Development Bank, 2007), 7.
136 Ibid.
137 Central Pollution Control Board, *CPCB ENVIS Newsletter*, Issues 1 (January–April, 2015), 4.
138 Ibid.
139 Asian Development Bank, *Asian Water Development Outlook 2007*, 4.
140 United Nations Development Programme, *Human Development Report 2006: Beyond Scarcity: Power, Poverty and the Global Water Crisis* (New York: Palgrave Macmillan, 2006), 144–145.
141 Velayutham Saravanan, *Urban Drinking Water Options in the Noyyal Basin: Population, Industrial Growth and Water Demand in Coimbatore and Tirupur: 1881–1991*, Submitted to (Ottawa: International Development Research Centre, 1999); Velayutham Saravanan and P. Appasamy, 'Historical Perspectives on Conflicts over Domestic and Industrial Supply in the Bhavani and Noyyal River Basins, Tamil Nadu', in *Rethinking the Mosaic: Investigations into Local Water Management*, eds Marcus Moench, Elisabeth Casperi and Ajaya Dixit (Kathmandu: Nepal Water Conservation Foundation and Boulder: Institute for Social and Environmental Transition, 1999), 161–190.
142 Velayutham Saravanan, 'Inter-Basin Water Transfer: Conflicts in Bhavani-Noyyal River Basins of Tamil Nadu, 1890–1970' (unpublished).
143 S. Janakarajan, 'Conflicts over the Invisible Resource in Tamil Nadu: Is There a Way Out?' in *Rethinking the Mosaic: Investigations into Local Water Management*, ed. Marcus Moench, Elisabeth Caspari and Ajaya Dixit (Kathmandu: Nepal Water Conservation Foundation and Boulder: Institute for Social and Environmental Transition, 1999), 9.
144 United Nations Development Programme, *Human Development Report 2006*, 148–149.
145 Marcus Moench, 'Addressing Constraints in Complex Systems: Meeting Water Management Needs of South Asia in the 21st Century', in *Rethinking the Mosaic: Investigations into Local Water Management*, ed. Marcus Moench, Elisabeth Caspari and Ajaya Dixit (Kathmandu: Nepal Water Conservation Foundation and Boulder: Institute for Social and Environmental Transition, 1999), 2.
146 Philippe Cullet, Water Law, Poverty, and Development: Water sector Reforms in India (New York: Oxford University Press, 2009).
147 Mats Lannerstad, 'Water Realities and Development Trajectories: Global and Local Agricultural Production Dynamics', Linköping Studies in Arts and Science No. 475, Linköping: Department of Water and Environmental Studies, Linköping University (2009), 83.

148 Mats Lannerstad, 'Planned and Unplanned Water Use in a Closed South Indian Basin', *Water Resources Development*, 24, no. 2 (2008): 289.
149 Mats Lannerstad and David Molden, 'Pumped Out: Basin Closure and Farmer Adaptations in the Bhavani Basin in Southern India', in *River Basin Trajectories: Societies, Environments and Development*, ed. Francois Molle and Philippus Wester (UK: CAB International, 1999), 260.
150 Asian Development Bank, *Asian Water Development Outlook 2007*, 2.
151 Ibid., 5.
152 Ibid., 9.
153 Government of Tamil Nadu *State of Environment Report of Tamil Nadu*, p. 52, in www.environment.tn.nic.in/soe.pdf.
154 Government of Tamil Nadu. *Season and Crop Report of Tamil Nadu 1960-61* (Madras: Department of Economics and Statistics, 1960) and Government of Tamil Nadu, *Season and Crop Report of Tamil Nadu 1989-90* (Madras: Department of Economics and Statistics, 1990).
155 Palanisami and Balasubramanian (1993).
156 Janakarajan, 'Conflicts over the Invisible Resource in Tamil Nadu'; Krishna Bharadwaj, *Irrigation in India: Alternative Perspectives* (Monograph) (New Delhi: Indian Council of Social Science Research, 1990); Saravanan and Appasamy, 'Historical Perspectives on Conflicts over Domestic and Industrial Supply'.
157 G. Teekaraman and M. Farooque Ahamed, '*Tanneries vs Agriculture in North Arcot District* (Vellore: Soil Survey and Land Use Organisation, 1990).
158 Janakarajan, 'Conflicts over the Invisible Resource in Tamil Nadu', 126.
159 Saravanan, *Urban Drinking Water Options in the Noyyal Basin*, 20; Janakarajan, 'Conflicts over the Invisible Resource in Tamil Nadu'.
160 C. Thomson Jacob, 'Impact of Industries on the Ground Water Quality of Tirupur and Its Ethical Implications' (PhD thesis, Department of Zoology, University of Madras, Chennai, 1996), 100–101.
161 Saravanan and Appasamy, 'Historical Perspectives on Conflicts over Domestic and Industrial Supply'; Madras Institute of Development Studies, *Stakeholders Meeting on Management of Water Conflicts in the Bhavani and Noyyal River Basins* (Chennai: Madras Institute of Development Studies, 1998); Janakarajan, 'Conflicts over the Invisible Resource in Tamil Nadu'.

Chapter 2

1 F. A. Nicholson, *Manual of the Coimbatore District in the Presidency of Madras* (Madras: The Government Press, 1887), 202.
2 F. A. Nicholson, *Manual of the Coimbatore District in the Presidency of Madras*, Vol. II (Madras: The Government Press, 1898), 190.

3   Nicholson, *Manual of the Coimbatore District*, 1887, 38.
4   Francis Buchanan, *A Journey from Madras, Mysore, Canara, and Malabar*, Vol. II (Madras: The Government Press, 1807), 164.
5   Ibid., 173.
6   A. V. Williamson, 'Indigenous Irrigation Works in Peninsular India', *Geographical Review*, 21, no. 4 (1931): 618.
7   V. Ratna Reddy, 'Irrigation in Colonial India: A Study of Madras Presidency during 1860–1900', *Economic and Political Weekly*, 25, nos. 18/19 (1990): 1047.
8   Ibid.
9   Ibid., 1054.
10 M. Atchi Reddy, 'Travails of an Irrigation Canal Company in South India, 1857–1882', *Economic and Political Weekly*, 25, no. 12 (1990): 619.
11 Ibid., 620.
12 A. R. Cox, *Statistical Appendix and Supplement to the Revised District Manual (1898) for Coimbatore District* (Madras: Government Press, 1933), 171.
13 Nicholson, *Manual of the Coimbatore District*, 1887, 187.
14 C. D. Maclean, *Manual of the Administration of the Madras Presidency*, Vol. II (Madras: Government Press, 1985), 73.
15 Nicholson, *Manual of the Coimbatore District*, 1887, 278–279.
16 Ibid., 384.
17 Ibid., 195.
18 Ibid., 386.
19 Ibid., 460.
20 Ibid., 197.
21 Ibid., 38.
22 Ibid., 381.
23 Buchanan, *A Journey from Madras, Mysore, Canara, and Malabar*, 164.
24 Ibid., 164.
25 Nicholson, *Manual of the Coimbatore District in the Presidency of Madras*, Vol. II, 191.
26 Ibid., 197.
27 Ibid., 377.
28 Ibid., 385.
29 Ibid., 381.
30 Ibid.
31 Ibid., 119.
32 Ibid., 282.
33 Ibid., 192.
34 Ibid., 193–395.
35 Ibid., 194.
36 Williamson, 'Indigenous Irrigation Works in Peninsular India', 624.

37 G. T. Boag, *The Madras Presidency 1881–1931* (Madras: The Government Press, 1933), 8–10.
38 Cox, *Statistical Appendix and supplement to the Revised District*, 29.
39 Census of India 1951, *Census Handbook, Coimbatore District* (Madras: Government Press, 1953), 24.
40 Ibid.
41 Velayutham Saravanan, 'Technological Transformation and Water Conflict in the Bhavani River Basin of Tamil Nadu: 1930–1970', *Environment and History*, VII, no. 3 (2001): 289–334.
42 Government of Tamil Nadu, *Business Plan for Coimbatore Corporation*, Tamil Nadu (Chennai: Urban Development Fund, 2006): 41–43.
43 District Statistical Handbook 2013–14, *Coimbatore District Statistical Handbook 2013–14* (Coimbatore District, Coimbatore: Deputy Director of Statistics, 2014): 169; District Statistical Handbook 2016–17, *Erode District Statistical Handbook 2016–17* (Erode District, Erode: Deputy Director of Statistics, 2017): 161.
44 Government of Tamil Nadu, *Business Plan for Coimbatore Corporation*, 71.

Chapter 3

1 World Commission on Environment and Development, *From One Earth to One World: An Overview* (Oxford: Oxford University Press, 1987), 8.
2 Ibid., 9.
3 Maureen L. Cropper and Wallace E. Oates, 'Environmental Economics: A Survey', *Journal of Economic Literature*, 30, no. 2 (1992): 678.
4 Saravanan, 'Technological Transformation and Water Conflict', 289–334.
5 Ibid.
6 The Kerala state proposed a project to divert the east-flowing Bhavani waters towards west into Bharthapuzha. Conflicts emerged between Tamil Nadu and Kerala state regarding the sharing water in the Bhavani River and its tributaries Siruvani River. Kerala state planned to divert the water from the Bhavani weir to the Bharatpuzha basin, which was opposed by Tamil Nadu. Kerala state argues that Tamil Nadu had been drawing water from Siruvani in excess of its due share of 1.33 TMC feet. Whereas Tamil Nadu state fears that if the diversion is allowed, there would be no water flowing in Bhavani when the river crosses from Kerala to Tamil Nadu and would severely affect irrigation in some 0.2 M Ha and also drinking water schemes in Coimbatore.
7 S. Satish Chandran Nair, 'The Drying Bhavani, Waterless Attappady and the Volatile Cauvery', in *Dams, Rivers and People*, 2002, in http://www.narmada.org/sandrp/dec2002_1.doc.

8   http://www.narmada.org/sandrp/dec2002_1.doc (accessed in May 2005).
9   Saravanan, *Local Strategies for Water Supply and Conservation*.
10   Ibid., Saravanan and Appasamy, 'Historical Perspectives on Conflicts over Domestic and Industrial Supply', 161–190.
11   Saravanan and Appasamy, 'Historical Perspectives on Conflicts', 162.
12   Ibid., 175.
13   See the list of pollution control acts and rules in Tamil Nadu: The Water (Prevention and Control of Pollution) Act, 1974 as amended in 1978 and 1988; The Water (Prevention and Control of Pollution) Cess Act, 1977 as amended in 1991; The Environment (Protection) Act, 1986; The Environment Protection) Rules, 1986; The Hazardous Wastes (Management and Handling) Rules, 1989 as amended in 2000; The Manufacture, Storage and Import of Hazardous Chemical Rules, 1989 as amended in 2000; The Municipal Solid Wastes (Management and Handling) Rules, 2000 (Policy Note on Environment – 2000–2001; Environment and Forest Department Policy Note – 2003–2004, Government of Tamil Nadu).
14   P. Appasamy, *Economic Assessment of Environmental Damage: A Case Study of Industrial Water Pollution in Tirupur*, Project Report (Chennai: Madras School of Economics, 2000), 1.
15   City Corporate Plan – Tirupur (Chennai: Tamil Nadu Urban Development Project-II, 1999), 63.
16   Anna Blomqvist, *Food and Fashion: Water Management and Collective Action Among Irrigation Farmers and Textile Industrialists in South India* (Linkoping: Department of Water and Environmental Studies, Linkoping University, 1996).
17   Saravanan, *Urban Drinking Water Options in the Noyyal Basin*.
18   Velayutham Saravanan, 'Linking the Rivers: Nightmare or Lasting Solutions?', *Man and Development*, 26, no. 3 (2004): 79–88.
19   Meinzen-Dick and Appasamy, *Urbanization and Intersectoral Competition for Water. In Finding the Source*, 15.
20   Tirupur city is the second largest town after Coimbatore, the major textile manufacturing centres of South India.
21   Presidential Address of TEA, 11-8-2003.
22   City Corporate Plan – Tirupur (Chennai: *Tamil Nadu Urban Development Project-II*, 1999), 63.
23   Appasamy, *Economic Assessment of Environmental Damage*, 32.
24   Ibid., 25.
25   http://www.tirupur.com/info.html (accessed in May 2006).
26   'Tirupur Knitwear Exporters Cheer Exim Policy', *Business Line*, http://www.blonnet.com/2003/04/01/stories/2003040101561700.htm (accessed in May 15, 2006).
27   Velayutham Saravanan, 'Export Earning Industries vs Environmental Sustainability: A Case of Tirupur Knitwear Industries in Tamil Nadu, 1980–2000' presented at the

National Seminar on 'National Environmental Policy' (NEP-06) organized by the Department of Economics, Jamia Millia Islamia, New Delhi, February 20–21, 2007.

28 Asha Krishna Kumar, A Pollution Challenge. *Frontline*, 1998, XV (13), June 20–July 3. In http://www.frontlineonnet.com/fl1513/15130660.htm (accessed in May 2006).

29 Different studies estimated that large quantities of industrial effluents were discharged by the industries. But only a low quantity (33.48 MLD) of effluents are planned to treat by the CEPTs. There are: Angeripalayam (0.85 MLD), Andipalayam (4.50 MLD), Chinnakarai (5.00 MLD), Kasipalayam (3.65 MLD), Kunnangapalayam (3.68 MLD), Manickpurampudur (1.60 MLD), Mannarai (4.20 MLD) and Veerapandi (10.00 MLD) (City Corporate Plan – Tirupur, Tamil Nadu Urban development Project-II, 1999), 66.

30 G. Gurumurthy, Effluent Discharge into Noyal River – Erode Farmers Complain against Tirupur Units. *Business Line*, Saturday, 23 March 2002. In http://www.thehindubusinessline.com/bline/2002/03/23/stories/2002032302471700.htm (accessed in May 2006).

31 G. Gurumurthy, 'Pollution in Noyyal River System Being Assessed'. *Business Line*, Wednesday, 29 January 2003.

32 http://www.tirupurghgemissions.com/html/piassesment.htm (accessed in May 2006).

33 J. Harriss, 'Character of an Urban Economy: Small-Scale Production and Labour Markets in Coimbatore', *Economic and Political Weekly*, 7, no. 24 (1982): 993–1002; C. Krishnaswamy, 'Dynamics of the Capitalist Labour Process-Knitting Industry in Tamil Nadu', *Economic and Political Weekly*, 24, no. 24 (1989): 1353–1359; P. Cawthorne, 'The Labour Process under Amoebic Capitalism: A Case Study of the Garment Industry in a South Indian Town', *Development Policy and Practice Working Paper No. 20*. Milton Keynes (UK: The Open University, 1993); P. Cawthorne, 'Of Networks and Markets: The Rise and Rise of a South Indian Town, the Example of Tirupur's Cotton Knitwear Industry', *World Development*, 23, no. 1 (1995): 43–57; Sharad Chari, 'The Agrarian Origins of the Knitwear Industrial Cluster in Tirupur, India', *World Development*, 28, no. 3 (2000): 579–599; N. Neetha, 'Flexible Production, Feminisation and Disorganisation: Evidence from Tirupur Knitwear Industry', *Economic and Political Weekly*, 37, no. 21 (2002): 2045–2052.

34 Urban agglomeration may constitute: (a) A city with continuous outgrowth (the part of outgrowth being outside the statutory limits but falling within the boundaries of the adjoining village or villages); (b) one town with similar outgrowth or two or more adjoining towns with their outgrowth as in (a); or (c) a city and one or more adjoining towns with their outgrowth all of which form a continuous spread. Tirupur urban agglomeration is of the first kind, while the Coimbatore urban agglomeration is of the third kind.

35   Government Order (hereafter G.O.) No. 184 Mis, Local and Municipal [M], 14–2-1889, Tamil Nadu State Archives, Chennai (hereafter TNSA).
36   Saravanan and Appasamy, 'Historical Perspectives on Conflicts over Domestic and Industrial Supply'.
37   Saravanan, *Local Strategies for Water Supply and Conservation Management in the Bhavani and Noyyal River Basins'*.
38   Harriss, 'Character of an Urban Economy', 27:994.
39   Madras Presidency denotes the geographical area prior to the reorganization of the states in 1956, which consist of present Tamil Nadu, Andhra Pradesh except Nizam territory, South Canara district of Karnataka and Kerala. It covered about 140,000 sq miles.
40   http://www.coimbatore-corporation.com/achieve-engineering.asp.
41   Census of India 2001, *Slum Population*.
42   Census of India 1931, 116–253.
43   Tirupur City Corporate Plan 1999, 23.
44   R. Sathiah, 'Water Resources Management of Tirupur: Some Issues', in *Sharing Common Water Resources* (Chennai: Madras Institute of Development Studies, 1994), 2.
45   Cawthorne, 'The Labour Process under Amoebic Capitalism', 23; Neetha, 'Flexible Production, Feminisation and Disorganisation'.
46   Neetha, 'Flexible Production, Feminisation and Disorganisation', 2045–2052.
47   Tirupur Local Planning Area (TLPA) consists of twelve villages in Palladam Taluk, two villages each in Avinashi and Erode Taluks and Tirupur town (City Corporate Plan – Tirupur, Tamil Nadu Urban development Project-II, 1999), 29.
48   Census of India 2001, *Slum Population*, 2001 (http://gisd.tn.in/census-paper2/Statements/stat_81.htm) (accessed in May 2005).
49   City Corporate Plan – Tirupur, *Tamil Nadu Urban development Project-II*, 1999, 31.
50   Judith Heyer, 'The Changing Position of Agricultural Labourers in Villages in Rural Coimbatore, Tamil Nadu, between 1981/2 and 1996', in *Working Paper Number 57* (Oxford: Queen Elizabeth House, 2000), 4.
51   In 1988, 93 cotton cleaning, ginning, spinning and weaving; 36 repair to autos/tyre retreading, etc.; 85 foundry, casting & forging; 79 manufacturing of electric motors & pumps; 92 manufacturing – other engineering products; 164 textile machinery; and 582 miscellaneous industries were existed (Study Report of CIRT, Pune, 1988),7.
52   Structure plan for Coimbatore Local Planning Area 1985, 34.
53   City Corporate Plan – Coimbatore, Tamil Nadu Urban development Project-II, 1999, 29.
54   In 1992, there were 4,763 small-scale industries found in this city. Of which, food industry – 209; textile/clothing and leather – 650; wood and wood products – 453; chemical/coal – 282; non-metallic mineral produce – 197; basic metal industry – 483; fabrication of machines and equipment – 1,291 and other manufacturing industry – 1,198 (M. Kalaimani 'Urban Environment of Coimbatore' in

Proceedings of the Seminar on Urban Environment of Coimbatore (Chennai: Madras Institute of Development Studies, 20 July 1995), 5.
55 C. J. Baker, *The Tamil Countryside: An Indian Rural Economy 1880–1955* (New Delhi: Oxford University Press, 1982), 35.
56 Handbook of Statistics on Cotton Textile Industry (various issues)
57 http://envisjnu.tripod.com/news/nov2k1/nov5.html (accessed in May 2006). http://www1.timesofindia.indiatimes.com/cms.dll/articleshow?art_Id=428661527 (accessed in May 2006).
58 Shanmugam, 'Industrial Growth in Tirupur', in *Sharing of Common Water Resources* (Chennai: Madras Institute of Development Studies, 1994), 3.
59 Neetha, 'Flexible Production, Feminisation and Disorganisation', 2045–2052.
60 Shanmugam, 'Industrial Growth in Tirupur', 2.
61 Appasamy, *Economic Assessment of Environmental Damage*, 22.
62 Chari, 'The Agrarian Origins of the Knitwear Industrial Cluster in Tirupur', 589; Neetha, 'Flexible Production, Feminisation and Disorganisation'.
63 Tirupur city corporate plan.
64 Krishnaswamy, 'Dynamics of the Capitalist Labour Process-Knitting Industry in Tamil Nadu', 1354.
65 Neetha, 'Flexible Production, Feminisation and Disorganisation'.
66 Chari, 'The Agrarian Origins of the Knitwear Industrial Cluster in Tirupur', 582; David Steele, Child Labour in Tamil Nadu: An Initial Survey, 2002.
67 Ibid.
68 Appasamy, *Economic Assessment of Environmental Damage*, 23.
69 Kalaimani and Sathiah, 'Water Resources: Constraints for Urban Growth of the Coimbatore Region', 8.
70 Madras School of Economics, *Economic Analysis of Environment Problems in Bleaching and Dyeing Units and Suggestions for Policy Action* (Chennai: Madras School of Economics, 1998), 33.
71 http://www.indigodev.com/ADBHBApxCases.doc (accessed in May 2006).
72 For more detailed discussion of the water supply schemes for Coimbatore and Tirupur, see Saravanan, *Urban Drinking Water Options in the Noyyal Basin.*
73 Saravanan and Appasamy, 'Historical Perspectives on Conflicts over Domestic and Industrial Supply', 163.
74 Saravanan, *Local Strategies for Water Supply and Conservation Management.*
75 Saravanan, *Local Strategies for Water Supply and Conservation Management*; Saravanan and Appasamy, 'Historical Perspectives on Conflicts over Domestic and Industrial Supply'.
76 N. Murugananthan, collector of Coimbatore district, Presidential Address at the Karl Bubul Foundation in 2002.
77 The entire course of Siruvani is within the state of Kerala. Siruvani has been dammed near its source within Muthikulam forests more than a century ago for

providing drinking water to Coimbatore city. A major dam has replaced this old weir in the late 1970s.
78 http://www.indiaurbaninfo.com/app/wsnsa.dll/niua/citysearch22.r?recno=28 (accessed in May 2005).
79 Structure Plan for Coimbatore Local Planning Area 1985.
80 Coimbatore City Municipal Corporation Administration Report 1991–92, 45.
81 http://www.coimbatore-corporation.com/admin-engg_comm.asp
82 Coimbatore City Municipal Corporation Administration Report 1991–92, 46.
83 Siruvani Water Supply Project Office, Coimbatore, 1985.
84 http://www.tn.nic.in/tnudp/images/infracbe.PDF.
85 Gunilla Bergh, *Water in Expanding Cities – A Case Study of Coimbatore*, Tamil Nadu, India. (Sweden: PLA Nordberg, 1996), 24.
86 Outline Proposal for Providing Infrastructural Facilities to Coimbatore Corporation, 1994, 36.
87 Coimbatore City Municipal Corporation – Engineering, 2001 in http://www.coimbatore-corporation.com/admin-engg_comm.asp (accessed in May 2000).
88 http://www.twadboard.com/cbe.html (accessed in May 2000).
89 http://www.tn.nic.in/tnudp/images/infracbe.PDF (accessed in May 2000).
90 http://www.tn.nic.in/tnudp/images/infracbe.PDF (accessed in May 2000).
91 Tamil Nadu Water Supply and Drainage Board, Demand No. 48, Water Supply, 2001–02.
92 Budget Speech 2002–2003 http://www.tn.gov.in/budget/archives/bp40-54.htm
93 Saravanan and Appasamy, 'Historical Perspectives on Conflicts over Domestic and Industrial Supply', 171.
94 G.O. No. 4965 Mis Local-Self Government (L and M), dated 14 February 1937, TNSA.
95 G.O. No. 3089 Mis, Health, dated 16 November 1954, TNSA.
96 Saravanan and Appasamy, 'Historical Perspectives on Conflicts over Domestic and Industrial Supply', 172.
97 Tirupur City Corporate Plan 1999, 34.
98 http://www.water-technology.net/projects/tirupur/(accessed in May 2000).
99 Municipal Administration and Water Supply Department Policy Note 2001–2002 and 2003–2004.
100 Government of Tamil Nadu, *Tenth Five-Year Plan 2002–2007* (Chennai: Planning Commission, 2003), 222–223.
101 Ann Ninan, Private Water, Public Misery, 2003. in http://www.waterobservatory.org/news/press.cfm?news_id=611 (accessed in May 2000).
102 Policy Note–Municipal Administration and Water Supply 2003–04.
103 T. Ramakrishnan, 'A Much-Awaited Project for Knitwear Town' *The Hindu*, 19 June 2002.

104 City Corporate Plan – Tirupur, Tamil Nadu Urban development Project-II, 1999, 99.
105 Letter No. 2979 Mis, PW & L, 28-11-1931, TNSA.
106 G.O. No. 3010 Mis PW & L (I), 23-10-1929, TNSA.
107 BP. No. 1880 Mis, 24–3-1902, TNSA.
108 G.O. No. 2183 (I) PW & L, 28-9-1927, TNSA.
109 G.O. No. 3010 Mis PW & L (I), 23-10-1929, TNSA.
110 G.O. No.1307, PWD Mis, 16-4-1948, TNSA.
111 G.O. No. 1784 PW & L (I), 19-7-1928, TNSA.
112 G.O. No. 2903 Mis PW & L (I), 19-11-1931, TNSA.
113 G.O. No. 1307 Mis, PWD, 16-4-1948, TNSA.
114 G.O. No. 441 PWD (I), 19-10-1909, TNSA and G.O. No.1200 Mis, PW & L, 1-6-1927, TNSA.
115 G.O. No. 888 Mis, PWD (W), 26-6-1925, TNSA.
116 G.O. No. 1784 PW & L (I), 19-7-1928, TNSA.
117 G.O. No. 2093 Mis PWD, 6-8-1945, TNSA.
118 Ibid.
119 G.O. No. 2538 Mis, Revenue, 19-11-1945, TNSA.
120 G.O. No. 1307 Mis, PWD, 16-4-1948, TNSA.
121 Ibid.
122 G.O. No. 4801 Mis, PWD, 26-11-1951, TNSA.
123 G.O. No. 1797 Mis, PWD, 17-5-1954, TNSA.
124 Appasamy, *Economic Assessment of Environmental Damage*, 38.
125 Ibid., 52.
126 Ibid., 38.
127 City Corporate Plan – Tirupur, Tamil Nadu Urban Development Project-II, 1999, 43.
128 Madras School of Economics, 1998, 66.
129 Ibid., 65 & 111.
130 Jacob, *Impact of Industries on the Ground Water Quality of Tirupur and Its Ethical Implications*, 101–102.
131 Nick Robins and Sarah Roberts, *The Reality of Sustainable Trade* (London: International Institute for Environment and Development, 2000), 88.
132 New Initiative to Protect Garment Workers in South India' Labour behind the Labels' Bulletin 19, July 2003 – India Special, http://www.labourbehindthelabel.org/newsletters/19.htm.
133 Robins and Roberts, *The Reality of Sustainable Trade*, 86.
134 Asha Krishna Kumar, 'A Pollution Challenge', *Frontline*, XV, 13 June 20–July 03, 1998, in http://www.frontlineonnet.com/fl1513/15130660.htm (accessed in May 2000).
135 U. Sankar, *Economic Analysis of Environmental Problems in Tanneries and Textile Bleaching and Dyeing Units and Suggestions for Policy Actions* (Delhi: Allied Publishers Ltd, 2001), 253.

136 Ibid.
137 V. S. Palaniappan, 'Colours of Pollution' *Indian Express*, Sunday, 31 May 1998.
138 Common effluent treatment plants are located in Veerapandi, Chinnakkarai, Kasipalayam, Kunnangalpalayam, Andipalayam, Mannarai, Angeripalayam and Manickampurampudur.
139 Appasamy, *Economic Assessment of Environmental Damage*, 4.
140 Ibid., 49.
141 Ibid., 4 and 54.
142 Ibid., 4.
143 http://www.blonnet.com/2002/04/19/stories/2002041900711700.htm (accessed in May 2000).
144 Appasamy, *Economic Assessment of Environmental Damage*, 37.
145 http://www.blonnet.com/2002/04/19/stories/2002041900711700.htm (accessed in May 2000).
146 http://www.bologi.com/environment/15.htm (accessed in May 2000).
147 G. Gurumurthy, 'Dyers' Failure to Meet Norms – Pollution Notices to Tirupur Units'. *Business Line*, 2002. In http://www.blonnet.com/2002/04/19/stories/2002041900711700.htm; G. Gurumurthy, 'Effluent Discharge into Noyal River – Erode Farmers Complain against Tirupur Units', *Business Line*, Saturday, 23 March 2002. In http://www.thehindubusinessline.com/bline/2002/03/23/stories/2002032302471700.htm (accessed in May 2000).
148 Saravanan, *Local Strategies for Water Supply and Conservation Management*; Saravanan and Appasamy, 'Historical Perspectives on Conflicts over Domestic and Industrial Supply'.
149 Saravanan, 'Linking the Rivers: Nightmare or Lasting Solutions?', 79–88.
150 Saravanan, 'Technological Transformation and Water Conflict', 289–334.

Chapter 4

1 Government Order (hereafter G.O.) No. 184 Mis, L&M [M], 14-2-1889, Tamil Nadu State Archives, Chennai (hereafter TNSA).
2 G.O. No. 9 Mis LSG [L&M], 4-1-1932, TNSA.
3 G.O. No. 1453 W, PWD [B&R-Civil Works], 15-11-1917, TNSA.
4 G.O. No. 556 I PWD, 7-10-1890, TNSA.
5 G.O. No. 53 Mis. L&M [M], 16-1-1893, TNSA.
6 G.O. No. 1490 Mis L&M [M], 10-10-1901, TNSA.
7 G.O. NO. 1664 Mis L&M [M], 9-10-1908, TNSA.
8 Ibid.
9 Ibid.

10 Ibid.
11 Ibid.
12 G.O. No. 1664 Mis L&M [M], 22-7-1909, TNSA.
13 G.O. No. 1151 Mis., L&M [M], 22-7-1909, TNSA.
14 G.O. No. 1 Mis L&M [M], 3-1-1910, TNSA.
15 G.O. No. 1435 M L&M, 5-8-1912, TNSA.
16 G.O. No. 381 W PWD [B&R-Civil works], TNSA.
17 G.O. No. 2158 Mis LSG (PH), 23-10-1925, TNSA.
18 G.O. No. 1453 W PWD [B&R-Civil works], 15-11-1917, TNSA.
19 G.O. No. 381 W PWD, 23-2-1915, TNSA.
20 G.O. No. 4452 Mis LSG [L&M], 14-11-1930, TNSA.
21 G.O. No. 2246 Mis LSG [PH], 5-11-1925, TNSA.
22 G.O. No. 1814 I PWD, 29-11-1926, TNSA.
23 G.O. No. 2094 Mis L&M [PH], 28-8-1930, TNSA.
24 G.O. No. 2320 Mis W PWD, 7-11-1932, TNSA.
25 G.O. No. 2211 Mis Public Health 19-10-1928, TNSA.
26 G.O. No. 2560 W PWD, 9-9-1929, TNSA; G.O.No. 132 Mis PW&L W, 17-3-1931, TNSA.
27 G.O. No. 4452 Mis LSG (L&M), 14-11-1930, TNSA.
28 G.O. No. 1189 I PW&L, 11-4-1930, TNSA.
29 G.O. No. 790 Mis PWD, 2-3-1955, TNSA.
30 G.O. No. 4185 Mis PWD, 7-11-1955, TNSA.
31 G.O. No. 2393 Mis E&PH [H], 21-9-1960, TNSA.
32 Ibid.
33 Ibid.
34 Tamil Nadu State Administrative Report 1983–84, 257.
35 Tamilarasu, October 1970, 35.
36 Tamil Nadu State Administrative Report, 1977–78, 334.
37 Tamil Nadu State Administrative Report, 1984–85, 209.
38 G.O. No. 660 Ms L&M [M], 22-4-1918, TNSA.
39 G.O. No. 4965 Mis LSG [L&M], 14-11-1937, TNSA.
40 G.O. No. 2353 Mis E&PH [PH], 15-8-1936, TNSA.
41 G.O. No. 3089 Mis Health, 16-11-1954, TNSA.
42 G.O. No. 725 Mis PW&L [W], 10-3-1928, TNSA.
43 Ibid.
44 Ibid.
45 Ibid.
46 G.O. No. 809 Mis PW&L [W], 23-3-1931, TNSA.
47 G.O. No. 4068 Mis LA, 30-10-1937, TNSA.
48 G.O. No. 4965 Mis LSG [L&M], 14-11-1934, TNSA.
49 G.O. No. 908 Mis E&PH [PH], 3-3-1941, TNSA.

50. G.O. No. 4203 Mis E&PH [PH], 28-11-1949, TNSA.
51. G.O. No. 844 Mis HELA [H], 3-3-1956, TNSA.
52. G.O. No. 2012 Mis Health, 27-5-1953, TNSA.
53. G.O. No. 4203 Mis E&PH [PH], 28-11-1949, TNSA.
54. G.O. No. 1520 Mis HELA [H], 7-5-1956, TNSA.
55. G.O. No. 844 Mis HELA [H], 3-3-1956, TNSA.
56. G.O. No. 1520 Mis HELA [H], 7-5-1956, TNSA.
57. G.O. No. 844 Mis HELA [H], 3-3-1956, TNSA.
58. G.O. NO. 1520 Mis HELA [H], 7-5-1956, TNSA.
59. Ibid.
60. G.O. No. 496 PWD [I], 9-9-1890, TNSA.
61. G.O. No. 127 PWD [I], 1-3-1890, TNSA.
62. G.O. No. 496 PWD [I], 9-9-1890, TNSA.
63. G.O. No. 2339 I Mis PW&L, 14-10-1927, TNSA.
64. G.O. No. 2112 Mis, LSG [P.H], 26-10-1927, TNSA.
65. G.O. No. 3936 Mis, PWD, 22-10-1949, TNSA.
66. G.O. No. 2544 PWD, 1-10-1945, TNSA.
67. Ibid.
68. G.O. No. 3936 Mis PWD, 22-10-1949, TNSA.
69. Ibid.
70. Ibid.
71. Ibid.
72. Ibid.
73. G.O. No. 3136 Mis, PWD, 4-9-1954, TNSA.
74. G.O. No. 790 Mis, PWD, 2-3-1955, TNSA.
75. G.O. No. 3136 Mis, PWD, 4-9-1954, TNSA.
76. G.O. No. 4182 Mis, PWD, 7-11-1955, TNSA.
77. G.O. No. 1746 Mis PH, 27-11-1924, TNSA.
78. G.O. No. 1787 Mis LSG [PH], 7-10-1926, TNSA.
79. G.O. No. 93 Mis LSG [PH], 19-1-1927, TNSA.
80. G.O. No. 2544 Mis PWD, 1-10-1945, TNSA.
81. G.O. No. 1433 I PW& L, 14-5-1930, TNSA.
82. Ibid.
83. Ibid.
84. Ibid.
85. G.O. No. 1814 I PW&L, 29-11-1926, TNSA.
86. G.O. No. 168 I PW&L, 24-1-1927, TNSA.
87. Ibid.
88. G.O. No. 1297 I PWD, 15-6-1934, TNSA.
89. G.O. No. 1698 Mis I PWD, 30-7-1935, TNSA.
90. G.O. No. 1784 Mis, PWD [I], 31-3-1937, TNSA.

91   G.O. No. 106 Mis, PWD I, 16-1-1946, TNSA.
92   G.O. No. 821 Mis LSG [PH], 28-4-1927, TNSA.
93   G.O. No. 1845 Mis LSG [PH], 23-9-1927, TNSA.
94   G.O. No. 1792 Mis LSG (PH), 26-8-1925, TNSA.
95   G.O. No. 1845 Mis LSG [PH], 23-9-1927, TNSA.
96   G.O. No. 525 Mis PH, 25-3-1927, TNSA.
97   G.O. No. 2269 I PW&L, 25-1-1930, TNSA
98   G.O. No. 1189 I PW&L, 11-4-1930, TNSA.
99   G.O. No. 844 Mis HELA [H], 3-3-1956, TNSA.
100 Ibid.
101 G.O. No. 1520 Mis HELA (H), 7-5-1956, TNSA.
102 G.O. No. 1267 Mis PWD I, 28-5-1936, TNSA.
103 G.O. No. 1297 Mis, PWD (I), 15-6-1934, TNSA.
104 G.O. No. 1267 Mis, PWD (I), 28-5-1936, TNSA.
105 G.O. No. 3066 PWD, 7-1956, TNSA.
106 G.O. No. 1784 Mis, PWD (I), 31-8-1937, TNSA.
107 Ibid.
108 G.O. No. 106 Mis PWD (I), 16-1-1940, TNSA.

Chapter 5

1   M. S. Rathore and R. M. Mathur, 'Local Strategies for Water Management and Conservation: A Study of Shekhawati Basin, Rajasthan', in *Rethinking the Mosaic: Investigations into Local Water Management,* ed. Marcus Moench, Elisabeth Caspari and Ajaya Dixit (Kathmandu: Nepal Water Conservation Foundation and Boulder: Institute for Social and Environmental Transition, 1999), 262; Marcus Moench, 'Addressing Constraints in Complex Systems: Meeting Water Management Needs of South Asia in the 21st Century', in *Rethinking the Mosaic: Investigations into Local Water Management,* ed. Marcus Moench, Elisabeth Caspari and Ajaya Dixit (Kathmandu: Nepal Water Conservation Foundation and Boulder: Institute for Social and Environmental Transition, 1999), 36; S. Mariasusai, *Conflicts over the Use of Surface Water in the Lower Bhavani Basin in Tamil Nadu* (Chennai: Madras Institute of Development Studies, 1999), 1.
2   M.Dinesh Kumar, Shashikant Chopde, Srinivas Mudrakarthas and Anjal Prakash, 'Addressing Water Scarcity: Local Strategy for Water Supply and Conservation Management in the Sabarmathi Basin, Gujarat', in *Rethinking the Mosaic: Investigations into Local Water Management,* ed. Marcus Moench, Elisabeth Caspari and Ajaya Dixit (Kathmandu: Nepal Water Conservation Foundation and Boulder: Institute for Social and Environmental Transition, 1999), 194.

3   Ibid, 192.
4   Meinzen-Dick, 'Public, Private, and Shared Water'.
5   S. Guhan, *The Cauvery River Dispute: Towards Conciliation* (Madras: Frontline Publishers,1993); Steen Folke, 'Conflicts over Water and Land in South Indian Agriculture: A Political Economic Perspective', *Economic and Political Weekly*, 33, no. 7 (1998): 348; Steen Folke, 'Conflicts over Water for Irrigation in the Cauvery delta, South India – Some Institutional Implications', *Journal of Social and Economic Development*, 3, no. 1 (2000): 47; World Bank, *India Irrigation Sector Review*, 128.
6   Guhan, *The Cauvery River Dispute*.
7   Saravanan and Appasamy, 'Historical Perspectives on Conflicts over Domestic and Industrial Supply', 161–190.
8   R. Chambers, *Managing Canal Irrigation: Practical Analysis from South Asia* (Cambridge: Cambridge University Press, 1988), 21–22; Folke, 'Conflicts over Water and Land in South Indian Agriculture, 341; Madras Institute of Development Studies, *National Resource Accounting for Water Resources in the Bhavani Basin – Phase II (Interim Report)* (Chennai: Madras Institute of Development Studies, 1998), 51; A. Vaidyanathan, *Second India Studies Revisited: Water* (Chennai: Madras Institute of Development Studies, 1994), 55; Mariasusai, *Conflicts over the Use of Surface Water*, 20.
9   Robert Wade, 'Access to the Irrigation Department: The Tail-End Problem under South Indian Irrigation Canals', *Indian Journal of Public Administration*, 26, no. 2 (1980), 359.
10 Robert Wade, 'Water to the Fields: India's Changing Strategy', *South Asian Review*, 8, no. 4 (1975): 303.
11 Government of India, *Report on Optimum Utilisation of Irrigation Potential: Lower Bhavani Project (Madras State)* (New Delhi: Committee on Plan Projects, 1964), 8; Wade, 'Water to the Fields', 303; Robert Wade, 'On Substituting Management for Water in Canal Irrigation: A South Indian Case', *Economic and Political Weekly*, 15, no. 51(1980): A–149.
12 Pieter Gorter, 'Canal Irrigation and Agrarian Transformation: The Case of Kesala', *Economic and Political Weekly*, 24, no. 39 (1989): A.101; Wade, 'Access to the Irrigation Department: The Tail-End Problem', 359; Peter P Mollinga, *On the Waterfront: Water Distribution, Technology and Agrarian Change in a South India Canal Irrigation System* (Netherlands: Netherlands Foundation for the Advancement of Tropical Research, 1998), 57.
13 Robert Wade, 'The Social Response to Irrigation: An Indian Case Study', *Journal of Development Studies*, 16, no. 1 (1979): 14–17; Anna Blomqvist, *Food and Fashion: Water Management and Collective Action among Irrigation Farmers and Textile Industrialists in South India* (Linkoping: Department of Water and Environmental Studies, Linkoping University, 1996), 99.

14 Robert Wade, *Village Republics: Economic Conditions for Collective Action in South India* (Cambridge: Cambridge University Press, 1987).
15 Mariasusai, *Conflicts over the Use of Surface Water*, 25–30.
16 David Mosse, 'Ecological Zones and the Culture of Collective Action: The History and Social Organisation of a Tank Irrigation System in Tamil Nadu', *South Indian Studies*, no. 3 (1997): 53.
17 Gorter, 'Canal Irrigation and Agrarian Transformation', A-102.
18 Wade, 'Water to the Fields', 316.
19 Gorter, 'Canal Irrigation and Agrarian Transformation', A-102; Krishna Bharadwaj, *Irrigation in India: Alternative Perspectives* (New Delhi: Indian Council of Social Science Research, 1990), 36.
20 Madras Institute of Development Studies, *Tank Irrigation in Tamil Nadu: Some Macro and Micro Perspectives* (Madras: Madras Institute of Development Studies, 1986), 119; Mosse, 'Ecological Zones and the Culture of Collective Action', 4.
21 Mosse, 'Ecological Zones and the Culture of Collective Action', 9.
22 Folke, 'Conflicts over Water and Land in South Indian Agriculture', 341; Madras Institute of Development Studies, *National Resource Accounting for Water Resources*, 119.
23 Folke, 'Conflicts over Water and Land in South Indian Agriculture', 348.
24 Ibid, 349.
25 Mosse, 'Ecological Zones and the Culture of Collective Action', 58.
26 A. Rajagopal, *Water Management in Agriculture with special Reference to Irrigation Institutions* (unpublished PhD thesis, Centre for Development Studies, Trivandrum, 1991), 245.
27 Bharadwaj, *Irrigation in India: Alternative Perspectives*, 4.
28 Robert Wade, 'Administration and Distribution of Irrigation Benefits', *Economic and Political Weekly*, 10, nos. 44 and 45 (1975): 1743; Robert Wade, 'Collective Responsibility in Construction and Management of Irrigation Canals: Case of Italy', *Economic and Political Weekly*, 14, nos. 51 and 52 (1979):A–155; Wade, 'The Social Response to Irrigation: An Indian Case Study', 14; Wade, 'Access to the Irrigation Department', 359–377; Robert Wade, 'On Substituting Management for Water in Canal Irrigation: A South Indian Case', *Economic and Political Weekly*, 15, no. 51 (1980): A–147–160; Robert Wade and Robert Chambers, 'Managing the Main System: Canal Irrigation's Blind Spot', *Economic and Political Weekly*, 15, no. 39 (1980): A–109; Robert Wade, 'Corruption: Where Does the Money Go?', *Economic and Political Weekly*, 17, no. 40 (1982): 1606; Robert Wade, 'The System of Administrative and Political Corruption: Canal Irrigation in South India', *Journal of Development Studies*, 18, no. 3 (1982): 287–328; Robert Wade, 'The Market for Public Office: Why the Indian State Is Not Better at Development', *World Development*, 13, no. 4 (1985): 467–497.

29 Wade, 'Administration and Distribution of Irrigation Benefits', 1743.
30 Folke, 'Conflicts over Water and Land in South Indian Agriculture', 345.
31 Government of India, *Report on Optimum Utilisation of Irrigation Potential*, 15; Folke, 'Conflicts over Water and Land in South Indian Agriculture', 345–346; Mariasusai, *Conflicts over the Use of Surface Water*, 7.
32 Peter P. Mollinga, 'Constituencies and Commands: The Role of Politicians in Water Control in a South Indian Large Scale Canal Irrigation System', in International Conference on the Political Economy of Water in South Asia: Rural and Urban Action in Interactions (Joint Committee on South Asia Social Science Research Council/American Council of Learned Societies and Madras Institute of Development Studies, 1995), 226.
33 Mollinga, *On the Waterfront: Water Distribution, Technology and Agrarian Change*, 57.
34 Mariasusai, *Conflicts over the Use of Surface Water*, 22.
35 Theodore W. Schultz, *Transforming Traditional Agriculture* (New Haven and London: Yale University Press, 1964), 132–133.
36 Ashok V Desai, 'The Indian Electric Power System', *Economic and Political Weekly*, 22, no. 41 (1989): 1756.
37 Tamil Nadu Electricity Board 1976–77, 5
38 K. S. Sonachalam, *Electricity and Economic Development of Madras State* (Annamalainagar: Annamalai University, 1968), 27–28.
39 C. H. Hanumantha Rao, 'Farm Mechanisation in a Labour-Abundant Economy', *Economic and Political Weekly*, 7, nos. 56 & 57 (1972): 393.
40 Colin Clark, *The Economics of Irrigation* (Oxford: The English Language Book Society and Pergamon Press, 1970), 130; B. D. Dawan, 'Trends of Tubewell Irrigation, 1951–1978', *Economic and Political Weekly*, 14, nos. 51 and 52 (1979): A–152.
41 Michel Vassart, *Technologies for Lifting Irrigation Water* (New Delhi: International Labour Organisation, 1981), 38–40.
42 A. Vaidyanathan, *Water Resource Management Institutions and Irrigation Development in India* (Oxford: Oxford University Press, 1999), 19; G. R. Rao, *Progressive Madras State*, ed. (Madras: The Hindustan Chamber of Commerce, 1967), 151.
43 Madras Institute of Development Studies, *Stakeholders Meeting on Management of Water Conflicts in the Bhavani and Noyyal River Basins* (Chennai: Madras Institute of Development Studies, 1998), 42.
44 Sonachalam, *Electricity and Economic Development*, 92.
45 T. J. Byres, 'The New Technology, Class Formation and Class Action in the Indian Countryside', *The Journal of Peasant Studies*, 8, no. 4 (1981): 420.
46 Tamil Nadu Electricity Board 1976–77, 34.

47 Michel Cartillier, 'Role of Small-Scale Industries in Economic Development: Irrigation Pumpsets Industry in Coimbatore', *Economic and Political Weekly*, 10, nos. 44 & 45 (1975): 1732.
48 Though the cost of irrigation per unit was low, the initial investment is high to install pumpsets. For instance, the total investment per pumpset varied from Rs. 3,100 to Rs. 4,650 per well to Rs. 7,400 to Rs. 14,575. Of this, the major investment on machinery varied from Rs. 2,800 to Rs. 3,800 per pumpset and this variation was mainly due to the model, year of purchase, etc. and the investment on civil structure varied from Rs. 100 to Rs. 1,150 (P. P. Madappa, K. V Patel and N. T. Patel, 'Investment Decisions on Pumpsets: A Case Study of a Saurashtra Village', *Economic and Political Weekly*, 5, no. 1 (1970): 22.
49 Cartillier, 'Role of Small-Scale Industries in Economic Development', 1739.
50 Sonachalam, *Electricity and Economic Development*, 194.
51 Madappa, Patel and Patel, 'Investment Decisions on Pumpsets', 23.
52 Hans Gustafsson, 'Electricity for Development: Problems and Prospects in Equipment Acquisition', *Economic and Political Weekly*, 14, no. 27 (1979): 1117.
53 Desai, 'The Indian Electric Power System', 1753.
54 Cartillier, 'Role of Small Scale Industries in Economic Development', 1741.
55 A. Vaidyanathan, 'Labour Use in Indian Agriculture: An Analysis Based on Farm Management Survey Data', in *Labour Absorption in Indian Agriculture: Some Exploratory Investigations*, ed. P. K. Bardhan, A. Vaidyanathan, Y. Alagh, G. S. Bhalla and A. Bhaduri (Bangkok: ILO-ARTEP publications, 1978), 92.
56 K. Palanisami, *Irrigation Water Management: The Determinants of Canal Water Distribution in India – A Micro Analysis* (New Delhi: Agricole Publishing Academy, 1984), 17.
57 Chhatrapati Singh, 'Research Agenda for Groundwater Law in India', in *Groundwater Law: The Growing Debate*, ed. Marcus Moench (Ahmadabad: VIKSAT-Pacific Institute of Collaborative Groundwater Project, 1995), 174.
58 Ibid, 176.
59 S. Janakarajan, 'Conflicts over the Invisible Resource in Tamil Nadu: Is There a Way Out?', in *Rethinking the Mosaic: Investigations into Local Water Management*, ed. Marcus Moench, Elisabeth Caspari and Ajaya Dixit (Kathmandu: Nepal Water Conservation Foundation and Boulder: Institute for Social and Environmental Transition, 1999), 127; Marcus Moench, *Groundwater Law: The Growing Debate*, ed. Marcus Moench (Ahmadabad: VIKSAT-Pacific Institute Collaborative Groundwater Project, 1995), 1; S. C. Sharma, 'Regulation of Groundwater Development in India: Existing Provisions and Future Options', in *Groundwater Law: The Growing Debate*, ed. Marcus Moench (Ahmadabad: VIKSAT-Pacific Institute of Collaborative Groundwater Project, 1995), 10; Singh, 'Research Agenda for Groundwater Law', 175; C. G. Desai, 'Critical Issues of Groundwater

Development and Management in India-Remedial Measures Thereon', in *Water Management: India's Groundwater Challenge*, ed. Marcus Moench (Ahmadabad: VIKSAT-Pacific Institute Collaborative Groundwater Project, 1993), 8.
60 Marcus Moench, 'Allocating the Common Heritage: Debates over Water Rights and Governance Structure in India', *Economic and Political Weekly*, 33, no. 26 (1998): A-48.
61 Singh 1990, 50.
62 Sharma. 'Regulation of Groundwater Development in India', 10-11.
63 Nirmal Sengupta, 'Irrigation: Traditional and Modern', *Economic and Political Weekly*, 20, nos. 45, 46 and 47 (1985): 1929.
64 Madras Institute of Development Studies. *National Resource Accounting for Water Resources in the Bhavani Basin – Phase II (Interim Report*, 39.
65 Bharadwaj, *Irrigation in India: Alternative Perspectives*, 16.
66 Clark, *The Economics of Irrigation*, 71; Colin Clark, *The Economics of Irrigation in Dry Climates* (Oxford: University of Oxford, 1954), 28; D. S. K. Rao, 'Ground Water Overexploitation through Borehole Technology', *Economic and Political Weekly*, 28, no. 52 (1993): A.129; S. Janakarajan, 'Consequences of Aquifer Over-Exploitation: Prosperity and Deprivation', *Review of Development and Change*, 2, no.1 (1997):56.
67 A. V. Jose, 'Farm Mechanisation in Asian Countries: Some Perspectives', *Economic and Political Weekly*, 19, no. 26 (1984): A-99.
68 Richard B. Reidinger, 'Water Management by Administrative Procedures in an Indian Irrigation System', in *Irrigation and Agricultural Development in Asia: Perspectives from the Social Sciences*, ed. E. Walter Coward, Jr (Ithaca and London: Cornel University Press, 1980), 264-283.
69 Bharadwaj, *Irrigation in India: Alternative Perspectives*, 51.
70 At Kodiveri *anicut*, two irrigation channels take off on either side of the river. The right side channel, known as Tadappalli channel, irrigates about 16,840 acres of wet crops, while the left side channel, called as the Arakkankottai channel, irrigates about 6,895 acres.
71 S. Rasu, *Kalingaroyan Kaalvai* (in Tamil) (Erode: Kongu Research Centre, 1987), 44-49.
72 Government of Madras, *History of the Lower Bhavani Project*, 29.
73 Nirmal Sengupta, *World Commission on Dams India Country Report: Laws, Policies and Institutional Framework for Options Assessment and Decision Making* (Chennai: Madras Institute of Development Studies, 2000), 3.
74 Government Order (hereafter G.O.) No. 4796 Mis, Public Works Department, 29 December 1953 (Chennai: Tamil Nadu State Archives).
75 B. S. Baliga, *Studies in Madras Administration*, Vol. II (Madras: Government of Madras, 1960), 203.
76 Folke, 'Conflicts over Water and Land in South Indian Agriculture', 346; Folke, 'Conflicts over Water for Irrigation in the Cauvery delta, South India', 48; David Mosse, 'Colonial and Contemporary Ideologies of "Community Management":

The Case of Tank Irrigation Development in South India', *Modern Asian Studies*, 33, no. 2 (1999): 309; V. R. Reddy, 'Irrigation in Colonial India: A Study of Madras Presidency during 1860–1900', *Economic and Political Weekly*, 25, no. 17 (1990): 1047; A. T. Arundel, *Irrigation and Communal Labour in the Madras Presidency* (Madras: Lawrence Press, 1879).

77 A waterway constructed in the bunds of tanks to permit the flow of surplus water, so as to prevent the breach of bunds.

78 R. A. Dalyell, *The Standing Orders of the Board of Revenue from 1820 to 1870*, III edition (Madras: Higginbothams and Co., 1871), 41–42.

79 C. D. Maclean, *Glossary of the Madras Presidency* (Madras: Government Press, 1885); David Mosse, 'The Symbolic Making of a Common Property Resources: History, Ecology and Locality in a Tank-Irrigated Landscape in South India', *Development and Change*, 25, no. 3 (1997): 28.

80 Nirmal Sengupta, 'Irrigation: Traditional and Modern', *Economic and Political Weekly*, 20, nos. 45, 46 and 47 (1985): 1923.

81 A. Vaidyanathan, *Strategy for Development of Tank Irrigation* (Madras: Madras Institute of Development Studies, 1992), 8; K. Sivasubramaniyan, *Irrigation Institutions in Two Large Multi-Village Tanks of Tamil Nadu: Structure, Functioning and Impact* (Unpublished PhD thesis, Madras: University of Madras,1995), Appendix 4.1; K. Sivasubramaniyan, 'Maintenance of Irrigation Networks under Major Tanks in Tamil Nadu', *Review of Development and Change*, 3, no. 2 (1998): 267.

82 Vaidyanathan, *Strategy for Development of Tank*, 8–10; Madras Institute of Development Studies, *Tank Irrigation in Tamil Nadu: Some Macro and Micro Perspectives*, 129.

83 Baliga had briefly discussed the history of irrigation management in the Madras Presidency since the colonial government's control over the Kudimaramattu system and how it got disintegrated under the British rule (Baliga, *Studies in Madras Administration*, 199–208; S. Y. Krishnaswami, *Rural Problems in Madras* (Madras: Government of Madras, 1947), 97–102; K. Sivasubramaniyan, Irrigation Institutions in Two Large Multi-Village Tanks, 141; K. Sivasubramaniyan, 'Irrigation Institutions and Two Major System Tanks in Tamil Nadu', *Review of Development and Change*, 2, no. 2 (1997): 358; K. Sivasubramaniyan, 'Water Management under Traditional Tank Irrigation Systems: With Special Reference to Mamulmamas', *Review of Development and Change*, 5, no. 2 (2000); M. S. Vani, *Role of Panchayat Institutions in Irrigation Management: Law and Policy* (New Delhi: The India Law Institute, 1992), 8; Folke, 'Conflicts over Water and Land in South Indian Agriculture', 346; Mosse, 'Colonial and Contemporary Ideologies', Reddy, 'Irrigation in Colonial India, 1047.

84 Mosse, 'Ecological Zones and the Culture of Collective Action', 10.

85 Ibid, 57–58.

86 Jose, 'Farm Mechanisation in Asian Countries', A-99.

87 Sengupta, 'Irrigation: Traditional and Modern', 1925.
88 This is a contrivance for drawing water from the well, channel and lower levels.
89 Letter from the Collector, Coimbatore, to the Secretary to Government through the Board of Revenue, 22 July 1953, TNSA.
90 Letter from the Collector, Coimbatore, to the Secretary to Government through the Board of Revenue, 22 July 1953, TNSA.
91 Turn system means that the branches and sluices supplying water to the fields turn off and on to suit the requirements and the period of supply. All the major distributaries were run continuously while the sluices and branches will work on turns. For instance, water supply allowed in the branches and sluices for five days for irrigating an area would then be stopped for the subsequent five days.
92 G.O. No. 32 I Mis, PW & L, 1936, TNSA.
93 At present about 800 pumpsets exist in this channel (MIDS 1998, 54).
94 Folke, 'Conflicts over Water for Irrigation in the Cauvery Delta', 72.
95 Mariasusai, *Conflicts over the Use of Surface Water*, 21.
96 The tail-end villages are Kodumudi, Chinnasamudram, Nagamanicken Palayam, Vadakkupudupalayam, Pallakattuputhur and Avdayapalayam.
97 The upland head-reach villages are: Pasur, Modakurichi, Kolanalli, Kilambadi, Malayampalayam, Swaminathapalayam, Punjai Kalamangalam, Kolathur Palayam, Pachapalayam, Sanar Palayam, Alunthapalayam, Komaraswamigoundan Palayam, Kuttapalayam, Palanigoundan Palayam, Erode and Mettur.
98 Petition from the Farmers of Chennasamudram, Nagamanicken palayam and Avadayaparai villages in Erode taluk to the Minister of Revenue, Government of Madras, dated 6 July 1953, TNSA.
99 It means that the farmers have to get permission from the local officers to use the water resources for which they have to pay. If they use water without getting permission, they will be penalized by the government.
100 Letter from B. V. Viswanatha Aiyar, Advocate to the Chief Secretary, State of Madras and the Collector of Coimbatore, 30 April 1953, TNSA.
101 Tax on land or land rent.
102 Letter from B. V. Viswanatha Aiyar, Advocate to the Chief Secretary, State of Madras and Collector of Coimbatore, 30 April 1953, TNSA.
103 Dalyell, *The Standing Orders of the Board of Revenue from 1820 to 1870*, III edition, 7.
104 Board of Standing Order (4) Appendix – H.
105 Madras Institute of Development Studies, *Sharing Common Water Resources* (Madras: Madras Institute of Development Studies, 1994), 5.
106 Letter from the Collector, Coimbatore, to the Secretary to the Government through the Board of Revenue, 22 July 1953, TNSA.

107 According to Article 226: 'Notwithstanding anything in article 32, every High Court shall have power, throughout the territories in relation to which it exercises jurisdiction, to issue to any person or authority, including in appropriate cases any Government, within those territories directions, orders or writs, including writs in the nature of habeas corpus, mandumus, prohibition, quo warranto and certiorari, or any of them, [for the enforcement of any of the rights conferred by part III and for any other purpose]'.

108 Writ Petition Numbers 473 and 475 of 1953, Madras High Court, Chennai.

109 Politicians and political parties played a prominent role in resolving the conflicts between the government and peasants. For instance, most of the pumpset-farmers had not paid electricity charges during 1970s and 1980s demanding reduction in power tariff. When the Electricity Board initially imposed surcharges and later disconnected power supply, the peasant organizations and the opposition parties demanded that the government withdrawn the hike. During the elections, all parties invariably assured in their manifestos that, if voted to power, the surcharges would be withdrawn (A. Rajagopal and P. Anbazhagan, 'Problems of Pumpset-Farmers in Tamil Nadu', *Economic and Political Weekly*, 24, no. 7 (1989): 341–342.

110 The backward *goundar* community is the dominant caste, having enormous political clout, in north-west Tamil Nadu. The *goundars*, mostly landed gentry, have huge land holdings.

111 Mariasusai, *Conflicts over the Use of Surface Water*.

112 The names and caste of the petitioners (475 of 1953) are as follows: K. Sengodu Goundar, K. S. Sellakumaraswami Goundar, S. P. Muthusami Goundar, S. P. Subbaraya Goundar, V. L. Ramalinga Goundar, L. K. Kuppusamy Goundar, M. Muthusami Goundar, K. C. Sriranga Goundar, K. C. Rangaswami Goundar, A. V. Muthusami Goundar and K. M. Venugopala Pillai. All the four who filed the other petition (473 of 1953) belonged to the Same Goundar caste: Sengodu Goundar, K. S. Sellakumaraswami Goundar, K. S. Sengappa Goundar, and K. S. Pambana Goundar.

113 Mariasusai, *Conflicts over the Use of Surface Water*, 1999.

114 The upland villages are: Pasur, Modakurichi, Kolanalli, Kilambadi, Malayampalayam, Swaminathapuram, Kolathurpalayam, pachapalayam, Aluthupalayam and Mettur.

115 Petition from K. Periyasamy Gounder, Member of Parliament to the Ministry of Finance & Food, Ministry of Revenue, Ministry of Prohibition, 18 April 1953, TNSA.

116 Erode, Palanigoundanpalayam, Kuttapalayam, Sanarpalayam, Punjai Kolamangalam, Mettur, Kolathupalayam, Komarswamigoundam palayam, Aluthupalayam and Swaminathapuram.

117 It consists of the list of farmers who had customary rights to use the channel water.

118 Letter from B. V. Viswanatha Aiyar, Advocate to the Chief Secretary, State of Madras and the Collector of Coimbatore, 30 April 1953, TNSA.
119 Letter from the Collector, Coimbatore, to the Secretary to Government through the Board of Revenue, 22 July 1953, TNSA.
120 G.O. No. 4796, PWD, 29 December 1953, TNSA.
121 Ibid.
122 Writ Applications Numbers 473 & 475 of 1953, Madras High Court, Chennai.
123 High Court Writ Applications Numbers. 473 and 475 of 1953, Chennai.
124 G.O. No. 56, Mis, PWD, 6 January 1955, TNSA.
125 G.O. No. 3727 Mis PWD, 1 September 1956, TNSA.
126 Rasu, Kalingaroyan Kaalvai, 107.
127 Madras Institute of Development Studies, *Stakeholders Meeting on Management of Water Conflicts in the Bhavani and Noyyal River*, 26.
128 Government of India, *Report on Optimum Utilisation of Irrigation Potential*, 32.
129 G.O. No. 4801 Mis, PWD, 26 November 1951, TNSA.
130 G.O. No. 4801, Mis, PWD, 26 November 1951, TNSA.
131 Government of Madras, *History of the Lower Bhavani Project*, 31.
132 Atchi Reddy, 'Travails of an Irrigation Canal Company in South India', 620.
133 Government of Madras, *Report on the Lower Bhavani Project (1946 scheme)* (Madras: Government Press, 1948), 1–2.
134 Government of India, *Evaluation of Major Irrigation Projects: Some Case Studies Programme Evaluation Organisation* (New Delhi: Planning Commission, 1965), 203.
135 About 44,993 acres unfit for cultivation; 3,764 acres reserved for community purposes; land owners of 15,170 acres were not willing to take up irrigation; 9,029 acres isolated lands and lands required to occupy the distributory system and 12,124 acres excluded due to their elevation, etc. (Government of India. *Evaluation of Major Irrigation Projects*, 204; Government of Madras. Report on the Lower Bhavani Project, 41.
136 Government of India, *Evaluation of Major Irrigation Projects*, 205.
137 For instance, in 1945–46, the total cropped area in Coimbatore district was 2,108,534 acres, of which, paddy accounted for 133,529 acres, cholam 452,870 acres, cumbu 265,738 acres, ragi 162,938 acres, maize 474 acres, bengalgram 2,490 acres, other foodgrains, including pulses 411,368 acres, oilseeds 235,350 acres, condiments and spices 22,330 acres, sugar products 11,906 acres, cotton 299,044 acres, fodder crops 2,497 acres, orchards and garden products 16,771 acres and other miscellaneous non-food crops 90,198 acres. Of the total cropped area, 563,482 acres were irrigated. Of this, 420,434 acres were under wells, 88,613 acres under canal, 19,240 acres under tanks and 35,195 acres from other sources (Census of India 1961, 986).

138 V. Duraisami, K. Meenakshisundram and V. S. Narasimhan, 'Rural Economic Conditions of Coimbatore District', *The Madras Agricultural Journal*, 41, no. 10 (1964): 358.
139 Government of India, *Evaluation of Major Irrigation Projects*, 7.
140 Jose, 'Farm Mechanisation in Asian Countries', 1984,
141 Vaidyanathan, 'Labour use in Indian Agriculture' 97.
142 Ibid., 95–96.
143 Jose, 'Farm Mechanisation in Asian Countries', A-102.
144 Government of Madras, *History of the Lower Bhavani Project, Vol.II-Canals* (Madras: Government Press, 1966), 35.
145 Ibid, 165.
146 Ibid, 14.
147 Ibid, 14 & 35.
148 Ibid, 167.
149 Six miles and two furlongs.
150 Government of Madras, *History of the Lower Bhavani Project*, 51.
151 G.O. No. 53, Mis, PWD, 4-1-1956 TNSA.
152 Government of Madras, *History of the Lower Bhavani Project, Vol.II-Canals*, 16; Government of India, *Report on Optimum Utilisation of Irrigation Potential*, 1.
153 G.O. No. 2367, Mis, Revenue, 21-9-1964, TNSA.
154 Ibid.
155 Ibid.
156 Ibid.
157 Blomqvist, *Food and Fashion: Water Management and Collective Action*, 88.
158 Government of India, *Evaluation of Major Irrigation Projects*, 207.
159 Palanisami, *Irrigation Water Management*' 25.
160 G. O. No. 2843 Mis, Revenue, 21-9-1964, TNSA.
161 Government of India, *Evaluation of Major Irrigation Projects*, 207.
162 It means that 'the ayacut under the sluices situated in the odd miles of the canal were to be irrigated for five days and for the next five days water was to be provided for the ayacut under the sluices in the even miles of the canal' (Government of India 1965).
163 The water from the main canal and distributaries is conveyed to the fields for irrigation purposes through small irrigation channels called field *bothies*. For the purpose of definition, all water courses irrigating an extent of less than 150 acres could be described as field *bothies*. It is also classified as ryot's *bothies* or government *bothies* depending upon the managing agency.
164 G.O. No. 2049, Mis, PWD, 30-4-1956, TNSA.
165 Palanisami, *Irrigation Water Management*, 25.
166 G.O. No. 2049 Mis, PWD, 30-4-1956, TNSA.

167 Government of India, *Evaluation of Major Irrigation Projects,* 215.
168 Madras School of Economics, *Economic Analysis of Environment Problems in Bleaching and Dyeing Units and Suggestions for Policy Action* (Chennai: Madras School of Economics, 1998), 35–36.
169 G.O. No. 3300 Mis, PWD, 27-8-1955, TNSA.
170 Government of India, *Report on Optimum Utilisation of Irrigation Potential,* 39–42; Atos Gordh and Per Kvick, *Study of Design of Small Reservoir (Tank) for Recharging Purposes* (Stockholm: Sweden, 1981), 5; L. P. Swaminathan, 'Ground-Water Development and Its Consequences in Coimbatore District, Tamil Nadu', in *Workshop on Critical Issues in Tamil Nadu Irrigation* (Madras: Madras Institute of Development Studies, 1989), 5–10.
171 GO. No. 1401 Mis, PWD, 29-3-1957, TNSA.
172 G.O. No. 4722, Revenue, 28-12-1954, TNSA.
173 G.O. No. 3559 Mis, PWD, 12-10-1954, TNSA.
174 G.O. No. 486, PWD, 11-2-1955, TNSA.
175 G.O. No. 668 Mis, PWD, 10-2-1956, TNSA.
176 G.O. No. 3015 Revenue, 19-10-1954, TNSA.
177 G.O. No. 1401 Mis, PWD, 29-3-1957, TNSA.
178 Rao, *Progressive Madras State,* 151.
179 Ibid.
180 Cartillier, 'Role of Small-Scale Industries in Economic Development', 1735.
181 G.O. No. 3426 Mis, PWD, 24-10-1957, TNSA.
182 N. Kumaraswami, alias Kumaran, was one of the freedom fighters from Tamil Nadu. He participated in the satyagraha procession with the Congress flag, which was notified as unlawful by the police. When he refused to give up the flag he was targeted and murdered in police action, involving indiscriminate caning. In Tamil Nadu he is popularly known as 'Tirupur Kumaran'.
183 G.O. No. 838 Mis, PWD, 15-3-1963, TNSA.
184 G.O. No. 2552 Mis, PWD, 4-9-1965, TNSA.
185 G.O. No. 2259 Mis, PWD, 3-11-1967, TNSA and G.O. No. 2260 Mis, PWD, 3-11-1967, TNSA.
186 G.O. No. 3365 Mis, PWD, 10-10-1957, TNSA.
187 Letter from Executive Engineer, PWD, Erode Division to the Superintending Engineer, PWD, Coimbatore-Nilgiris Circle, Coimbatore, 20 September 1979, TNSA.
188 Velayutham Saravanan, *Urban Drinking Water Options in the Noyyal Basin: Population, Industrial Growth and Water Demand in Coimbatore and Tirupur: 1881–1991* (Ottawa: International Development Research Centre, 1999), 21.
189 Saravanan, '*Local Strategies for Water Supply and Conservation Management*'; Saravanan, *Urban Drinking Water Options in the Noyyal Basin*'.
190 Saravanan, *Local Strategies for Water Supply,* 1998, 27–33

191 Saravanan and Appasamy, 'Historical Perspectives on Conflicts', 161–190.
192 Appasamy, 'Sharing Common Water Resources: Urban Study-A Review'.

Chapter 6

1. Saravanan, 'Inter-Basin Water Transfer'.
2. Government of India, *Report of the National Commission*, 179.
3. http://wrmin.nic.in/interbasin/transfer.htm (accessed in June 1999).
4. http://www.bjp.org/manifes/manife99.htm#aa (accessed in June 1999).
5. World Bank, *Inter-Sectoral Water Allocation*, 10.
6. Government of India, *Report of the National Commission*, 287.
7. World Bank, *Water Resources Management in Asia*, Vol. I, Main Report (Washington, DC: The World Bank, 1993), 23.
8. Government of India, *Commission on Centre-State Relations Report*, Part I (Delhi: Government Press, 1988), 488.
9. Ibid., 488–489.
10. Saravanan, 'Technological Transformation and Water Conflict', 289–334.
11. Saravanan and Appasamy, 'Historical Perspectives on Conflicts over Domestic and Industrial Supply', 161–190; Saravanan, *Urban Drinking Water Options in the Noyyal Basin*.
12. Saravanan, 'Inter-Basin Water Transfer'.
13. Saravanan, 'Technological Transformation and Water Conflict'.
14. Guhan, *The Cauvery River Dispute*, 19–21.
15. Government of India, *Report of the National Commission*, 429–430.
16. CMIE, *Agriculture* (Mumbai: Centre for Monitoring Indian Economy Pvt. Ltd, 2002), 30–31.
17. Government of India, *Report of the National Commission*, 69.
18. Ibid., 422–423.
19. World Bank, *Inter-Sectoral Water Allocation*, 8.
20. Government of India, *Report of the National Commission*, 38.
21. World Bank, *Inter-Sectoral Water Allocation*, 1.
22. Government of India, *Report of the National Commission*, 157.
23. Ibid., 454–455.
24. Ibid., 18.
25. Government of India, *Report of the National Commission*, 253; World Bank, *Inter-Sectoral Water Allocation*, 26–27; Ashok Gulati, Mark Svendsen and Nandini Roy Choudhury, 'Operation and Maintenance Costs of Canal Irrigation and Their Recovery in India', in *Working paper No.48* (New Delhi: National Council of Applied Economic Research, 1995), 3.

26 Gulati, Svendsen and Choudhury, 'Operation and Maintenance Costs of Canal Irrigation and Their Recovery in India', 23.
27 http://www.narmada.org/archive/tehelka/rightstory.asp%3Fid1=ecology+&+health&id2=features&id3=STORIES&id4=20000623041&fname=eh111400wcd.htm (accessed in April 2003).
28 http://www.corpwatch.org/news/PND.jsp?articleid=1330. http://www.narmada.org/archive/tehelka/rightstory.asp%3Fid1=ecology+&+health&id2=features&id3=STORIES&id4=20000623041&fname=eh111400wcd.htm (accessed in April 2003).
Ravi Hemadri, Harsh Mander and Vijay Nagaraj, *Dams, Displacement, Policy and Law in India* Contributing Paper Independent Experts, India Prepared for Thematic Review I.3, 22 (Referred from: http://www.dams.org/docs/kbase/contrib/soc213.pdf); Shekhar Singh 'The Karma of Dams', in *Indian Express*, 25 October 2000
http://www.indianexpress.com/ie/daily/20001025/ied25033.html) (accessed in April 2003).
29 Government of India, *Report of the National Commission*, 66.
30 Ibid., 170; A. Vaidyanathan (ed.), *Tanks of South India* (New Delhi: Centre for Science and Environment, 2001).
31 Ibid.
32 Government of India, *Report of the National Commission*, 19.
33 World Bank, *Inter-Sectoral Water Allocation*, 10.
34 http://www.worldwaterforum.net/Pressreleases/press3.html (accessed in April 2003).
35 http://www.irrigation.kerala.gov.in/index.php/resources/water-bodies/rivers (accessed in April 2003).
36 http://www.irrigation.kerala.gov.in/index.php/resources/water-bodies/rivers (accessed in April 2003).
37 http://waterresources.kar.nic.in/river_systems.htm (accessed in April 2003).
38 The agreement related between the chief ministers of Kerala and Tamil Nadu and the union minister of irrigation and power during discussions held on 10-5-1969 at Trivandrum regarding the Parambikulam Aliyar Project and other river water questions of Kerala and Tamil Nadu. http://india-wris.nrsc.gov.in/wrpinfo/images/d/d8/120.pdf (accessed in April 2003).
39 Kerala-Tamil Nadu Agreement on Siruvani Drinking Water Supply Agreement, dated 19 August 1973.
40 Ibid.
41 Pre-feasibility Report of Proposed Attappady Valley Irrigation Project (AVIP) in Palakkad District, Kerala, 2016, 6.
42 State Planning Board, *Report of the High Level Committee on Land and Water Resources* (Trivandrum: Government of Kerala, 1984), 117.

43 The Report of the Cauvery Water Disputes Tribunal with the decision, Vol. 1 (New Delhi: Ministry of Water Resources, River Development & Ganga Rejuvination, 2007), 52–53.
44 Ibid., 71.
45 http://wrmin.nic.in/writereaddata/Inter StateWaterDisputes/ FINALDECISIONOFCAUVERYWATERTRIBUNAL4612814121.pdf (accessed in April 2003).
46 Government of Kerala. *Water Resources of Kerala: Advance Report*, Public Works Department (Irrigation Branch), (Trivandrum: Government of Kerala, 1958), 213.
47 http://www.irrigation.kerala.gov.in/index.php/resources/water-bodies/rivers (accessed in April 2003).
48 http://www.thehindu.com/news/national/kerala/Kerala-plans-dam-across-Siruvani-river/article14591071.ece (accessed in April 2003).
49 Government of Madras, *Report on the Lower Bhavani Project*, 1; Government of Madras, *History of the Lower Bhavani Project, Vol.I-Head Works*, 8.
50 Government of Madras, *History of the Lower Bhavani Project, Vol. II-Canals*, 1.
51 Government of Madras, *Report on the Lower Bhavani Project*, 1.
52 Ibid.
53 Government of Madras, *History of the Lower Bhavani Project, Vol.I-Head Works*, 9–10.
54 Ibid., 10.
55 Ibid., 11.
56 Ibid.
57 Ibid., 13.
58 Ibid., 14–18.
59 Government of Tamil Nadu. *Public Works Department, Irrigation, Demand No. 40, Policy Note 2012–13*, 2012, 19.
60 Ibid.

Chapter 7

1 Nicholson, *Manual of the Coimbatore District*, 382.

Bibliography

Agrawal, Arun and Sivaramakrishnan, K. 'Introduction: Agrarian Environs'. In *Social Nature: Resources, Representations, and Rule in India*, edited by Arun Agrawal and K. Sivaramakrishnan, 1–22, New Delhi: Oxford University Press, 2001.

Appasamy, P. Paul. 'Sharing Common Water Resources: Urban Study – A Review'. In *Background Paper for Policy Advisory Committee Meeting*, Chennai: Madras Institute of Development Studies, 1994.

Appasamy, P. Paul. *Economic Assessment of Environmental Damage: A Case Study of Industrial Water Pollution in Tirupur*. Project Report, Chennai: Madras School of Economics, 2000.

Arundel, A. T. *Irrigation and Communal Labour in the Madras Presidency*, Madras: Lawrence Press, 1879.

Asian Development Bank. *Asian Water Development Outlook 2007: Achieving Water Security for Asia*, Manila: Asian Development Bank, 2007.

Asthana, Vandana. 'Collective Action in the Delhi Water Reform Project: Creating Space for Policy Change', *Indian Journal of Political Science*, 69, no. 4 (2008): 703–717.

Asthana, Vandana. *Water Policy Processes in India: Discourses of Power and Resistance*, London and New York: Routledge, 2009.

Atchi Reddy, M. 'Travails of an Irrigation Canal Company in South India: 1857–1882', *Economic and Political Weekly*, 25, no. 12 (1990): 619–628.

Ayres, Robert U. and Allen, V. Kneese. 'Production Consumption and Externalities', *American Economic Review*, 59, no. 3 (1969): 282–297.

Baghel, Ravi. *River Control in India: Spatial, Governmental and Subjective Dimensions*, Cham: Springer, 2014.

Baker, C. J. *The Tamil Countryside: An Indian Rural Economy 1880–1955*, New Delhi: Oxford University Press, 1984.

Baliga, B. S. *Studies in Madras Administration*, Vol. II, Madras: Government of Madras, 1960.

Baviskar, Amita. *In the Belly of the River: Tribal Conflicts over Development in the Narmada Valley*, New Delhi: Oxford University Press, 1995.

Bergh, Gunilla. *Water in Expanding Cities – A Case Study of Coimbatore, Tamil Nadu, India*, Sweden: PLA Nordberg, 1996.

Berkoff, D. J. W. 'Irrigation Management on the Indo-Gangetic Plain'. In *World Bank Technical Paper No. 129*, Washington, DC: The World Bank, 1990.

Bharadwaj, Krishna. *Irrigation in India: Alternative Perspectives* (Monograph), New Delhi: Indian Council of Social Science Research, 1990.

Bhattacharya, Neeladri. 'Introduction', *Studies in History*, 14, no. 2 (1998): 165–171.
Bhattacharya, S. 'Essays in Agrarian History: India 1850 to 1940', *Studies in History* (New Series), 1, no. 2 (1985): 159–167.
Bhattacharya, Sabyasachi, Guha, Sumit, Mahadevan, Raman, Padhi, Sakti, Rajasekhar, D. and Rao, G. N. (eds). *The South Indian Economy: Agrarian Change, Industrial Structure and State Policy, 1914–1947*, Delhi: Oxford University Press, 1991.
Biswas, Asit K., Rangachari, R. and Tortajada, Cecilia (eds). *Water Resources of the Indian Subcontinent*, New Delhi: Oxford University Press, 2009.
Blomqvist, Anna. *Food and Fashion: Water Management and Collective Action among Irrigation Farmers and Textile Industrialists in South India*. Linkoping: Department of Water and Environmental Studies, Linkoping University, 1996.
Boag, G. T. *The Madras Presidency 1881–1931*. Madras: The Government Press, 1933.
Brewer, Jeffrey D. 'Negotiating Seasonal Water Allocation Rules in Krindi Oya, Sri Lanka'. In *Negotiating Water Rights*, edited by B. R. Burns and R. S. Meinzen-Dick, 112–136, New Delhi: Vistaar Publications, 2000.
Bruns, Bryan Randolph and Meinzen-Dick, Ruth S. 'Negotiating Water Rights: Implications for Research and Action'. In *Negotiating Water Rights*, edited by B. R. Burns and R. S. Meinzen-Dick, 353–380, New Delhi: Vistaar Publications, 2000.
Buchanan, Francis. *A Journey from Madras, Mysore, Canara, and Malabar*, Vol. II, Madras: The Government Press, 1807.
Byres, T. J. 'The New Technology, Class Formation and Class Action in the Indian Countryside', *The Journal of Peasant Studies*, 8, no. 4 (1981): 405–454.
Cartillier, Michel. 'Role of Small-Scale Industries in Economic Development: Irrigation Pumpsets Industry in Coimbatore', *Economic and Political Weekly*, 10, nos. 44 & 45 (1975): 1732–1741.
Cawthorne, P. 'The Labour Process under Amoebic Capitalism: A Case Study of the Garment Industry in a South Indian Town'. In *Development Policy and Practice Working Paper No. 20*, Milton Keynes, UK: The Open University, 1993.
Cawthorne, P. 'Of Networks and Markets: The Rise and Rise of a South Indian Town, the Example of Tirupur's Cotton Knitwear Industry', *World Development*, 23, no. 1 (1995): 43–57.
Census of India. 1891. *Imperial and Provincial Tables*, Vol. XIV: British Territory, Madras: Government Press, 1893.
Census of India 1931. *Imperial and Provincial Tables*, Vol. XIV: Part II, Madras: Government Press, 1932.
Census of India 1951. *Census Handbook, Coimbatore District*, Madras: Government Press, 1953.
Census of India 1961. *District Census Handbook, Coimbatore*, Vol. II, Madras: Superintend of Census Operations, 1964.
Census of India 1961. *Migration Tables*, Vol. IX: Part II-C-(II) – ii, Madras: Government Press, 1965.

Census of India 1971. *Tamil Nadu, District Census Handbook, Coimbatore*. Series 19, Part II, Madras: Government Press, 1972.

Census of India 1971. *Migration Tables*, Series 19, Tamil Nadu, Part II-B, DV-DVI, Madras: Government Press, 1978.

Census of India 1981. *India, General Population Tables*. Series I, Part II-A(i), New Delhi: Registrar General and Census Commissioner.

Census of India 1981. *Primary Census Abstract, General Population*. Series I, Part II-B (i).

Census of India 1991. *Primary Census Abstract, General Population*. Part II-B (i), Chennai: Directorate of Census Operations, 1991.

Census of India 1991. Migration Tables, Tamil Nadu, Chennai: Directorate of Census Operations, 1997.

Census of India 2001. *Slum Population, 2001*. In http:/gisd.tn.nic/incensus-paper2/statements/stat_8_1.htm.

Central Pollution Control Board. *CPCB ENVIS* Newsletter, January-April, Issues 1, 2015.

Chambers, R. *Managing Canal Irrigation: Practical Analysis from South Asia*, Cambridge: Cambridge University Press, 1988.

Champakalakshmi, R. 'Urbanisation in South India: The Role of Ideology and Polity', *Social Scientist*, 15, nos. 8/9 (1987): 67–117.

Chari, Sharad. 'The Agrarian Origins of the Knitwear Industrial Cluster in Tirupur, India', *World Development*, 28, no. 3 (2000): 579–599.

Chaudhuri, K. N. *Economic Development of India under the East India Company, 1814–1858: A Selection of Contemporary Writings in Cambridge*, Cambridge: Cambridge University Press, 1971.

Clark, Colin. *The Economics of Irrigation in Dry Climates*, Oxford: University of Oxford, 1960.

Clark, Colin. *The Economics of Irrigation*, Oxford: The English Language Book Society and Pergamon Press, 1970.

CMIE. *Agriculture*, Mumbai: Centre for Monitoring Indian Economy Pvt. Ltd, 2002.

Cohen, Benjamin. 'Modernising the Urban Environment: The Musi River Flood of 1908 in Hyderabad, India', *Environment and History*, 17, no. 3 (2011): 409–432.

Coimbatore City. *Municipal Corporation Administration Report 1991–92*, Coimbatore: Corporation Office, 1992.

Cox, A. R. *Statistical Appendix and Supplement to the Revised District Manual (1898) for Coimbatore District*, Madras: Government Press, 1933.

Cropper, Maureen L. and Oates, Wallace E. 'Environmental Economics: A Survey', *Journal of Economic Literature*, 30, no. 2 (1992): 675–740.

Cullet, Philippe. *Water Law, Poverty, and Development: Water Sector Reforms in India*, New York: Oxford University Press, 2009.

D'Souza, Rohan. *Drowned and Dammed: Colonial Capitalism and Flood Control in Eastern India*, New Delhi: Oxford University Press, 2006.

D'Souza, Rohan. 'Water in British India: The Making of a "Colonial Hydrology"', *History Compass*, 4, no. 4 (2006): 621–628.

Dalyell, R. A. *The Standing Orders of the Board of Revenue from 1820 to 1870*, III edition, Madras: Higginbothams and Co, 1971.

Dandekar, V. M 'Transforming Traditional Agriculture: A Critique of Professor Schultz', *Economic and Political Weekly*, 1, no. 1 (1966): 25–36.

Dasgupta, Subhendu. 'Transnational Corporations in Electric Power Sector, 1947–1967: Continuity of Linkages', *Economic and Political Weekly*, 16, nos. 28–29 (1981): 1189–1204.

Dawan, B. D. 'Trends of Tubewell Irrigation, 1951–1978', *Economic and Political Weekly*, 14, nos. 51 and 52 (1979): A-143-A-154.

Desai, Ashok V. 'The Indian Electric Power System', *Economic and Political Weekly*, 22, no. 41 (1987): 1753–1761.

Desai, C. G. 'Critical Issues of Groundwater Development and Management in India- Remedial Measures Thereon'. In *Water Management: India's Groundwater Challenge*, edited by Marcus Moench, Ahmadabad: VIKSAT-Pacific Institute Collaborative Groundwater Project, 1993.

Dinesh Kumar, M., Chopde, Shashikant, Mudrakarthas, Srinivas and Prakash, Anjal. 'Addressing Water Scarcity: Local Strategy for Water Supply and Conservation Management in the Sabarmathi Basin, Gujarat'. In *Rethinking the Mosaic: Investigations into Local Water Management*, edited by Marcus Moench, Elisabeth Caspari and Ajaya Dixit, 191–246, Kathmandu: Nepal Water Conservation Foundation and Boulder: Institute for Social and Environmental Transition, 1999.

Duraisami, V., Meenakshisundram, K. and Narasimhan, V. S. 'Rural Economic Conditions of Coimbatore District', *The Madras Agricultural Journal*, 41, no. 10 (1964): 357–366.

Fernandes, W. and Paranjpye, V. *Rehabilitation Policy and Law in India: A Right to Livelihood*, New Delhi: ISI and Pune: Econet, 1997.

Folke, Steen. 'Conflicts over Water and Land in South Indian Agriculture: A Political Economic Perspective', *Economic and Political Weekly*, 33, no. 7 (1998): 341–349.

Folke, Steen. 'Conflicts over Water for Irrigation in the Cauvery Delta, South India – Some Institutional Implications', *Journal of Social and Economic Development*, 3, no. 1 (2000): 42–75.

Frederiksen, Harald D., Berkoff, Jeremy and Barber, William. 'Water Resources Management in Asia', Vol. I, Main Report. *World Bank Technical Paper No. 212*. Washington, DC: The World Bank, 1993.

Gadgil, Madhav and Guha, Ramachandra. *The Fissured Land: An Ecological History of India*, New Delhi: Oxford University Press, 1993.

Gilmartin, David. *Blood and Water: The Indus River Basin in Modern History*, California: University of California Press, 2015.

Gordh, Atos and Kvick, Per. *Study of Design of Small Reservoir (Tank) for Recharging Purposes*, Stockholm: Sweden, 1981.

Gorter, Pieter. 'Canal Irrigation and Agrarian Transformation: The Case of Kesala', *Economic and Political Weekly*, 24, no. 39 (1989): A. 94–104.

Government of India. *The First Five Year Plan*, New Delhi: Planning Commission, 1952.

Government of India. *Report on Optimum Utilisation of Irrigation Potential: Lower Bhavani Project (Madras State)*. New Delhi: Committee on Plan Projects, 1964.

Government of India. *Evaluation of Major Irrigation Projects: Some Case Studies Programme Evaluation Organisation*, New Delhi: Planning Commission, 1965.

Government of India. *Commission on Centre-State Relations Report*, Part I, Delhi: Government Press, 1988.

Government of India. *Report of the National Commission for Integrated Water Resources Development*, Vol. I, New Delhi: Ministry of Water Resources, 1999.

Government of India. *National Water Policy 2002*. New Delhi: Ministry of Water Resources, 2002.

Government of Tamil Nadu. *Tamil Nadu Urban development Project – II, City Corporate Plan- Tirupur, in http://www.tn.nic.in/tnudp/Tirupur.htm* (accessed 15 January 2007).

Government of Kerala. *Water Resources of Kerala: Advance Report*, Public Works Department (Irrigation Branch), Trivandrum, 1958.

Government of Madras. *Report on the Lower Bhavani Project (1946 Scheme)*, Madras: Government Press, 1948.

Government of Madras. *Season and Crop Report of the Madras State for the Agricultural Year 1953–54*, Madras: Government of Madras, 1955.

Government of Madras. *History of the Lower Bhavani Project, Vol. I-Head Works*, Madras: Government Press, 1965.

Government of Madras. *History of the Lower Bhavani Project, Vol. II-Canals*, Madras: Government Press, 1966.

Government of Tamil Nadu. *Season and Crop Report of Tamil Nadu 1960–61*, Madras: Department of Economics and Statistics, 1960.

Government of Tamil Nadu. *Tamil Nadu – An Economic Appraisal*, Madras: Government of Tamil Nadu, 1970.

Government of Tamil Nadu. *Season and Crop Report of Tamil Nadu for the Agricultural Year 1970–71*, Madras: Government of Tamil Nadu, 1974.

Government of Tamil Nadu. *Season and Crop Report of Tamil Nadu 1980–81*, Madras: Department of Economics and Statistics, 1980.

Government of Tamil Nadu. *Structure Plan for Coimbatore Local Planning Area*, Madras: Directorate of Town and Country Planning, 1985.

Government of Tamil Nadu. *Ninth Five-Year Plan. Tamil Nadu 1997–2002*, Chennai: State Planning Commission, 1998.

Government of Tamil Nadu. Tamil Nadu Urban Development Project – II. City Corporate Plan- Tirupur, Chennai: Government of Tamil Nadu, 1999.

Government of Tamil Nadu. *Policy Note on Environment – 2000–2001*, Chennai: Government of Tamil Nadu, 2000.

Government of Tamil Nadu. *Municipal Administration and Water Supply Department Policy Note 2001–2002*, Chennai: Government of Tamil Nadu, 2001.

Government of Tamil Nadu. *Water Supply and Drainage Board. Demand No. 48. Water Supply, 2001–2002*, Chennai: Government of Tamil Nadu, 2001.

Government of Tamil Nadu. *Environment and Forest Department Policy Note – 2003–2004*, Chennai: Government of Tamil Nadu, 2003.

Government of Tamil Nadu. *Municipal Administration and Water Supply Department Policy Note 2003–2004*, Chennai: Government of Tamil Nadu, 2003.

Government of Tamil Nadu. *Tenth Five-Year Plan 2002–2007*, Chennai: Planning Commission, 2003.

Government of Tamil Nadu. *Season and Crop Report of Tamil Nadu 2004–05*, Chennai: Department of Economics and Statistics, 2004.

Government of Tamil Nadu. *Public Works Department, Irrigation, Demand No. 40, Policy Note 2012–13*, Chennai: Government of Tamil Nadu, 2012.

Government of Tamil Nadu. *State of Environment Report of Tamil Nadu. Department of Environment*. In http://www.environments.tn.nic.in/soe.pdf.

Government of Tamil Nadu. *Tamil Nadu Urban development Project – II, City Corporate Plan-Tirupur*, in http://www.tn.nic.in/tnudp/Tirupur.htm (accessed 15 January 2007).

Guhan, S. *The Cauvery River Dispute: Towards Conciliation*, Madras: Frontline Publishers, 1993.

Guillet, David. 'Water Property Rights and Resistance to Demand Management in Northwestern Spain'. In *Negotiating Water Rights*, edited by B. R. Burns and R. S. Meinzen-Dick, 222–244, New Delhi: Vistaar Publications, 2000.

Gulati, Ashok, Svendsen, Mark and Choudhury, Nandini Roy. 'Operation and Maintenance Costs of Canal Irrigation and their Recovery in India'. In *Working paper No.48*, New Delhi: National Council of Applied Economic Research, 1995.

Gurumurthy, G. 'Dyers' Failure to Meet Norms – Pollution Notices to Tirupur Units', *Business Line*, 2002. http://www.blonnet.com/2002/04/19/stories/2002041900711700.htm.

Gurumurthy, G., 'Effluent Discharge into Noyal River – Erode Farmers Complain against Tirupur Units', *Business Line*, Saturday, 23 March 2002. In http://www.thehindubusinessline.com/bline/2002/03/23/stories/2002032302471700.htm.

Gurumurthy, G. 'Pollution in Noyyal River System Being Assessed', *Business Line*, Wednesday, 29 January 2003.

Gustafsson, Hans. 'Electricity for Development: Problems and Prospects in Equipment Acquisition', *Economic and Political Weekly*, 14, no. 27 (1979): 1127–1131.

Gyawali, Dipak and Dixit, Ajaya. 'Fractured Institutions and Physical Interdependence: Challenges to Local Water Management in the Tinau River Basin, Nepal'. In *Rethinking the Mosaic: Investigations into Local Water Management*, edited by Marcus Moench, Elisabeth Caspari and Ajaya Dixit, 57–122, Kathmandu: Nepal Water Conservation Foundation and Boulder: Institute for Social and Environmental Transition, 1999.

Haberman, David. *River of Love in an Age of Pollution*, California: University of California Press, 2006.

Haftendorn, Helga. 'Water and International Conflict', *Third World Quarterly*, 21, no. 1 (2000): 51–68.

Hanumantha Rao, C. H. 'Farm Mechanisation in a Labour-Abundant Economy', *Economic and Political Weekly*, 7, nos. 56 & 57 (1972): 393–400.

Harriss, J. 'Character of an Urban Economy: Small-Scale Production and Labour Markets in Coimbatore', *Economic and Political Weekly*, 17, no. 24 (1982): 993–1002.

Hart, Hentry. 'Anarchy, Paternalism, or Collective Responsibility under the Canals?' *Economic and Political Weekly*, 23, nos. 51 and 52 (1978): A.125–A. 134.

Hemadri, Ravi, Mander, Harsh and Nagaraj, Vijay. *Dams, Displacement, Policy and Law in India*, Contributing Paper Independent Experts, India Prepared for Thematic Review I.3 (Referred from:http://www.dams.org/docs/kbase/contrib/soc213.pdf).

Heyer, Judith. 'The Changing Position of Agricultural Labourers in Villages in Rural Coimbatore, Tamil Nadu, between 1981/2 and 1996'. In *Working Paper No. 57*, Oxford: Queen Elizabeth House, 2000.

In http://www.tn.nic.in/tnudp/tirupur.htm.

Irrigation Design and Research Board. *Pre-feasibility Report of Proposed Attappady Valley Irrigation Project (AVIP) in Palakkad district*, Kerala: Irrigation Department, 2016.

Islam, M. Mufakharul. *Irrigation, Agriculture and the Raj: Punjab, 1887–1947*, New Delhi: Manohar, 1997.

Jacob, C. Thomson. *Impact of Industries on the Ground Water Quality of Tirupur and Its Ethical Implications*, PhD thesis, Chennai: Department of Zoology, University of Madras, 1996.

Janakarajan, S. 'Conflicts over the Invisible Resource in Tamil Nadu: Is There a Way Out?' In *Rethinking the Mosaic: Investigations into Local Water Management*, edited by Marcus Moench, Elisabeth Caspari and Ajaya Dixit, 123–159, Kathmandu: Nepal Water Conservation Foundation and Boulder: Institute for Social and Environmental Transition, 1999.

Janakarajan, S. 'Consequences of Aquifer Over-Exploitation: Prosperity and Deprivation', *Review of Development and Change*, 2, no. 1 (1997): 24–51.

Jose, A. V. 'Farm Mechanisation in Asian Countries: Some Perspectives', *Economic and Political Weekly*, 19, no. 26 (1984): 97–103.

Kalaimani, M. and Sathiah, R. 'Water Resources: Constraints for Urban Growth of the Coimbatore Region'. In *Sharing Common Water Resources*, Madras: Madras institute of Development Studies, 1994.

Kalaimani, M. and Sathiah, R. 'Urban Environment of Coimbatore'. In *Proceedings of the Seminar on Urban Environment of Coimbatore*, Madras: Madras Institute of Development Studies, 1995.

Kerala-Tamil Nadu Agreement on Siruvani Drinking Water Supply Agreement, dated 19th August 1973.

Krishna Kumar, Asha. 'Troubled Tirupur', *Frontline*, 7 April 1995.

Krishna Kumar, Asha. 'A Pollution Challenge', *Frontline*, 15 no. 13 (20 June–03 July 1998), in http://www.frontlineonnet.com/fl1513/15130660.htm.

Krishnaswami, S. Y. *Rural Problems in Madras (Monograph)*, Madras: Government of Madras, 1947.

Krishnaswamy, C. 'Dynamics of the Capitalist Labour Process-Knitting Industry in Tamil Nadu', *Economic and Political Weekly*, 24, no. 24 (1989): 1353–1359.

Kumar, Dharma. *Land and Caste in South India: Agricultural Labour in Madras Presidency in the Nineteenth Century*, Cambridge: Cambridge University Press, 1965.

Kumar, Dharma. *The Cambridge Economic History of India*, Vol. 2: c. 1750 c.1970 (ed.), New Delhi: Cambridge University Press, 1983.

Kurnia, Ganjar, Avianto, Teten W. and Burns, B. R. 'Farmers Factories and the Dynamics of Water Allocation in West Java'. In *Negotiating Water Rights*, edited by B. R. Burns and R. S. Meinzen-Dick, 292–314, New Delhi: Vistaar Publications, 2000.

Lannerstad, Mats. 'Planned and Unplanned Water Use in a Closed South Indian Basin', *Water Resources Development*, 24, no. 2 (2008): 289–304.

Lannerstad, Mats. 'Water Realities and Development Trajectories: Global and Local Agricultural Production Dynamics', PhD thesis, Linköping Studies in Arts and Science No. 475, Linköping University, Department of Water and Environmental Studies, Linköping, 2009.

Lannerstad, Mats and Molden, David. 'Pumped Out: Basin Closure and Farmer Adaptations in the Bhavani Basin in Southern India'. In *River Basin Trajectories: Societies, Environments and Development*, edited by Francois Molle and Philippus Wester, 38–262, UK: CAB International, 2, 1999.

Maclean, C. D. *Glossary of the Madras Presidency*, Madras: Government Press, 1985.

Maclean, C. D. *Manual of the Administration of the Madras Presidency*, Vol. I, Madras: Government Press, 1985.

Maclean, C. D. *Manual of the Administration of the Madras Presidency*, Vol. II, Madras: Government Press, 1985.

Madappa, P.P, Patel, K.V and Patel, N.T. 'Investment Decisions on Pumpsets: A Case Study of a Saurashtra Village', *Economic and Political Weekly*, 5, no.1 (1970):21–25.

Madras Institute of Development Studies. *Tank Irrigation in Tamil Nadu: Some Macro and Micro Perspectives*, Madras: Madras Institute of Development Studies, 1986.

Madras Institute of Development Studies. *Sharing Common Water Resources*, Madras: Madras Institute of Development Studies, 1994.

Madras Institute of Development Studies. *Capacity 21 Programmes – I Phase*, Chennai: Madras Institute of Development Studies, 1997.

Madras Institute of Development Studies. *National Resource Accounting for Water Resources in the Bhavani Basin – Phase II (Interim Report)*, Chennai: Madras Institute of Development Studies, 1998.

Madras Institute of Development Studies. *Stakeholders Meeting on Management of Water Conflicts in the Bhavani and Noyyal River Basins*, Chennai: Madras Institute of Development Studies, 1998.

Madras School of Economics. *Economic Analysis of Environment Problems in Bleaching and Dyeing Units and Suggestions for Policy Action*, Chennai: Madras School of Economics, 1998.

Mariasusai, S. *Conflicts over the Use of Surface Water in the Lower Bhavani Basin in Tamil Nadu*, Chennai: Madras Institute of Development Studies, 1999.

McNeill, J. R. 'Population and the Natural Environment: Trends and Challenges', *Population and Development Review*, 32, The Political Economy of Global Population Change, 1950–2050 (2006): 183–201.

Meinzen-Dick, Ruth S. 'Public, Private, and Shared Water: Groundwater Markets and Access in Pakistan'. In *Negotiating Water Rights*, edited by B. R. Burns and R. S. Meinzen-Dick, 245–268, New Delhi: Vistaar Publications, 2000.

Meinzen-Dick, Ruth and Appasamy, Paul P. *Urbanization and Intersectoral Competition for Water in Finding the Source: The Linkages between Population and Water*, Woodrow Wilson International Centre for Scholars, Washington DC: ECSP Publication, 2002.

Meinzen-Dick, Ruth S. and Bruns, Bryan Randolph. 'Negotiating Water Rights: Introduction'. In *Negotiating Water Rights*, edited by B. R. Burns and R. S. Meinzen-Dick, 23–55, New Delhi: Vistaar Publications, 2000.

Menon, A. et al. *Tamil Nadu Urban Environmental Challenge – A Study of Eight Secondary Cities/Towns*, Chennai: Madras Institute of Development Studies, 1997.

Moench, Marcus. (ed) *Groundwater Law: The Growing Debate*, Ahmedabad: VIKSAT-Pacific Institute Collaborative Groundwater Project, 1995.

Moench, Marcus. 'Allocating the Common Heritage: Debates over Water Rights and Governance Structure in India', *Economic and Political Weekly*, 33, no. 26 (1998): A-46–53.

Moench, Marcus. 'Addressing Constraints in Complex Systems: Meeting Water Management Needs of South Asia in the 21st Century'. In *Rethinking the Mosaic: Investigations into Local Water Management*, edited by Marcus Moench, Elisabeth Caspari and Ajaya Dixit, 1–56, Kathmandu: Nepal Water Conservation Foundation and Boulder: Institute for Social and Environmental Transition, 1999.

Moench, Marcus et.al. (ed) *Water Management: India's Groundwater Challenge*, Ahmadabad: VIKSAT-Pacific Institute Collaborative Groundwater Project, 1993.

Mollinga, Peter P. 'Constituencies and Commands: The Role of Politicians in Water Control in a South Indian Large Scale Canal Irrigation System', presented in International Conference on *The Political Economy of Water in South Asia: Rural and Urban Action in Interactions* organised by Joint Committee on South Asia Social Science Research Council/American Council of Learned Societies and Madras Institute of Development Studies, 1995, 226–240.

Mollinga, Peter P. *On the Waterfront: Water Distribution, Technology and Agrarian Change in a South India Canal Irrigation System*, Netherlands: Netherlands Foundation for the Advancement of Tropical Research, 1998.

Mollinga, Peter. 'Boundary Concepts for the Interdisciplinary Analysis of Irrigation Water Management in South Asia'. In *Controlling the Water: Matching Technology and Institutions in Irrigation and Water Management in India and Nepal*, edited by Dik Roth and Linden Vincent, 342–365, New Delhi: Oxford University Press, 2013.

Morris, Sebastian. 'Political Economy of Electric Power in India', *Economic and Political Weekly*, 31, no. 20 (1996): 1201–1210.

Mosse, David. 'Ecological Zones and the Culture of Collective Action: The History and Social Organisation of a Tank Irrigation System in Tamil Nadu', *South Indian Studies*, 3 (1997): 1–88.

Mosse, David. 'The Symbolic Making of a Common Property Resources: History, Ecology and Locality in a Tank-Irrigated Landscape in South India', *Development and Change*, 25, no. 3 (1997): 467–504.

Mosse, David. 'Colonial and Contemporary Ideologies of "Community Management": The Case of Tank Irrigation Development in South India', *Modern Asian Studies*, 33, no. 2 (1999): 303–338.

Mosse, David. *The Rule of Water: Statecraft, Ecology, and Collective Action in South India*, New Delhi: Oxford University Press, 2003.

Narain, Brij. *Indian Economic Problems: Part II Source Book for the Study of Indian Economic Problems*, Lahore: The Punjab Printing Works, 1922.

Narain, Vishal. 'Urbanization, Climate Change, and Peri-urban Water Security in South Asia-A Framework for Analysis'. In *Water Security in Peri-urban South Asia: Adapting to Climate Change and Urbanisation*, edited by Vishal Narain and Anjal Prakash, 1–31, New Delhi: Oxford University Press, 2016.

Narain, Vishal and Prakash, Anjal. (eds) *Water Security in Peri-urban South Asia: Adapting to Climate Change and Urbanisation*, New Delhi: Oxford University Press, 2016.

Neetha, N. 'Flexible Production, Feminisation and Disorganisation: Evidence from Tirupur Knitwear Industry', *Economic and Political Weekly*, 37, 21 (2002): 2045–2052.

Nicholson, F. A. *Manual of the Coimbatore District in the Presidency of Madras*, Vol. I, Madras: The Government Press, 1887.

Nicholson, F. A. *Manual of the Coimbatore District in the Presidency of Madras*, Vol. II, Madras: The Government Press, 1898.

Ninan, Ann. 'Private Water, Public Misery', 2003, In http://www.waterobservatory.org/news/press.cfm?news_id=611.

Outline Proposal for Providing Infrastructural Facilities to Coimbatore Corporation, Coimbatore: Corporation Office, 1994.

Palaniappan, V. S. 'Colours of Pollution', *Indian Express*, Sunday, 31 May 1998.

Palanisami, K. *Irrigation Water Management: The Determinants of Canal Water Distribution in India – A Micro Analysis*, New Delhi: Agricole Publishing Academy, 1984.

Palanisami, K. 'River Pumping in Bhavani Basin – Economics and Constraints'. In *Sharing Common Water Resources*, 46–56, Madras: Madras Institute of Development Studies, 1994.

Pani, Narentar. 'Boundaries of Transboundry Water Sharings'. In *River Water Sharing: Transboundary Conflict and Cooperation in India*, edited by N.Shantha Mohan, Sailen Routray and N. Sashikumar, 47–65, New Delhi: Routledge, 2010.

Pouchepadass, Jacques. 'Colonialism and Environment in India: Comparative Perspective', *Economic and Political Weekly*, 30, no. 33 (1995): 2059–2067.

Pradhan, Rajendra and Pradhan, Ujjwal. 'Negotiating Access and Rights: Disputes over Rights to an Irrigation Water Source in Nepal'. In *Negotiating Water Rights*, edited by B. R. Burns and R. S. Meinzen-Dick, 200–221, New Delhi: Vistaar Publications, 2000.

Prakash, Anjal, Singh, Sreoshi, Goodrich, C. G, Janakarajan, S (eds). *Water Resources Policies in South Asia*, New Delhi: Routledge, 2013.

Rajagopal, A. *Water Management in Agriculture with Special Reference to Irrigation Institutions*, PhD thesis, Trivandrum: Centre for Development Studies, 1991.

Rajagopal, A. and Anbazhagan, P. 'Problems of Pumpset-Farmers in Tamil Nadu', *Economic and Political Weekly*, 24, no. 7 (1989): 341–342.

Ramakrishnan, T. 'A Much-Awaited Project for Knitwear Town', *The Hindu*, 19 June 2002.

Rangarajan, Mahesh. 'Polity, Ecology and Lanscape: New Writings on South Asia's Past', *Studies in History*, 18, no. 1 (2002): 135–147.

Rao, D. S. K. 'Ground Water Overexploitation through Borehole Technology', *Economic and Political Weekly*, 28, no. 52 (1993): A.129–134.

Rao, G. R. (ed.) *Progressive Madras State*, Madras: The Hindustan Chamber of Commerce, 1967.

Rao, K. L. *India's Water Wealth: Its Assessment, Uses and Projections*, New Delhi: Orient Longman, 1975.

Rasu, S. *Kalingaroyan Kaalvai, (in Tamil)*, Erode: Kongu Research Centre, 1987.

Rathore, M. S. and Mathur, R. M. 'Local Strategies for Water Management and Conservation: A Study of Shekhawati Basin, Rajasthan'. In *Rethinking the Mosaic: Investigations into Local Water Management*, edited by Marcus Moench, Elisabeth Caspari and Ajaya Dixit, 261–300, Kathmandu: Nepal Water Conservation Foundation and Boulder: Institute for Social and Environmental Transition, 1999.

Ratna Reddy, V. 'Irrigation in Colonial India: A Study of Madras Presidency during 1860–1900', *Economic and Political Weekly*, 25, nos. 18/19 (1990): 1047–1054.

Ratnagar, Shereen. 'Traditional Technologies in Indian Agriculture', *Economic and Political Weekly*, 24, no. 42 (1989): 2359–2361.

Ray, Binayak. *Water: The Looming Crisis in India*, Lanham: Lexington Books, 2008.

Reidinger, Richard B. 'Water Management by Administrative Procedures in an Indian Irrigation System'. In *Irrigation and Agricultural Development in Asia: Perspectives from the Social Sciences*, edited by E. Walter Coward Jr., 262–288, Ithaca and London: Cornel University Press, 1980.

Robins, Nick and Roberts, Sarah. *The Reality of Sustainable Trade*, London: International Institute for Environment and Development, 2000.

Roth, Dik and Linden Vincent (eds). *Controlling Water: Matching Technology and Institutions in Irrigation Management in India and Nepal*, New Delhi: Oxford University Press, 2013.

Routrary, Sailen. 'The Water Sector in India: An Overview'. In *River Water Sharing: Transboundary Conflict and Cooperation in India*, edited by N. Shantha Mohan, Sailen Routray and N. Sashikumar, 23–44, New Delhi: Routledge, 2010.

Sadeque, S. Z. 'Nature's Bounty or Scarce Community: Competition and Consensus over Ground Water use in Rural Bangladesh'. In *Negotiating Water Rights*, edited by B. R. Burns and R. S. Meinzen-Dick, 269–291, New Delhi: Vistaar Publications, 2000.

Sampath, Anitha, Balakrishnan Kedarnath, Chandrika Ramanujam, Hozefa Haidery, Rajesh Rao, Ravishankar Arunachalam, Sandhya Govindaraju, Vennila Thirumalavan, Vishv Jeet, 'Water Privatization and Implications in India', 2003. In http://studentorgs.utexas.edu/aidaustin/water/water_privatization.pdf.

Sankar, U. *Economic Analysis of Environmental Problems in Tanneries and Textile Bleaching and Dyeing Units and Suggestions for Policy Actions*, Delhi: Allied Publishers Ltd, 2001.

Saravanan, Velayutham (a). 'Inter-Basin Water Transfer: Conflicts in Bhavani-Noyyal River Basins of Tamil Nadu, 1890–1970' (unpublished).

Saravanan, Velayutham. *Local Strategies for Water Supply and Conservation Management in the Bhavani and Noyyal River Basins. Part I–Domestic Water Supply and Industrial Sector*. Project Report, International Development Research Centre (IDRC), Ottawa, Canada, in August, 1998a.

Saravanan, Velayutham. *Local Strategies for Water Supply and Conservation Management in the Bhavani and Noyyal River Basins. Part II–Agriculture Sector*. Project Report, Ottawa: International Development Research Centre, 1998b.

Saravanan, Velayutham. *Urban Drinking Water Options in the Noyyal Basin: Population, Industrial Growth and Water Demand in Coimbatore and Tirupur: 1881–1991*, Project Report, Ottawa, Canada: International Development Research Centre (IDRC), 1999.

Saravanan, Velayutham. 'Technological Transformation and Water Conflict in the Bhavani River Basin of Tamil Nadu: 1930–1970', *Environment and History*, 7, no. 3 (2001): 289–334.

Saravanan, Velayutham. 'Linking the Rivers: Nightmare or Lasting Solutions?' *Man and Development*, 26, no. 3 (2004): 79–88.

Saravanan, Velayutham. 'Competing Demand and Management Practices', *The Book Review*, 30, no. 4 (2006): 25–26.

Saravanan, Velayutham. 'Competing Demand for Water in Tamil Nadu: Urbanisation, Industrialisation and Environmental Damages in the Bhavani and Noyyal Basins, 1880s–2000s', *Journal of Social and Economic Development*, 9, no. 2 (2007): 199–238.

Saravanan, Velayutham. 'Export Earning Industries vs Environmental Sustainability: A Case of Tirupur Knitwear Industries in Tamil Nadu, 1980–2005', Presented at the National Seminar on 'National Environmental Policy (NEP-06)' Organised by the Department of Economics, Jamia Millia Islamia, New Delhi, 20–21 February 2007.

Saravanan, Velayutham 'Chennai Floods and Floods of Politics', *Mainstream*, 54, no. 17 (2016): 17–19.

Saravanan, Velayutham. *Colonialism, Environment and Tribals in South India, 1792-1947*, London and New York: Routledge, 2017.

Saravanan,Velayutham. *Environmental History and Tribals in Modern India*, London and New York: Palgrave Macmillan, 2018.

Saravanan, Velayutham. 'Tamil Nadu-Kerala Water Conflicts: A Pragmatic Picture', *Mainstream*, 56, no. 16 (2018): 15–20.

Saravanan, Velayutham and Paul P. Appasamy. 'Historical Perspectives on Conflicts over Domestic and Industrial Supply in the Bhavani and Noyyal River Basins, Tamil Nadu'. In *Rethinking the Mosaic: Investigations into Local Water Management*, edited by Marcus Moench, Elisabeth Casperi and Ajaya Dixit, 161–190, Kathmandu: Nepal Water Conservation Foundation and Boulder: Institute for Social and Environmental Transition, 1999.

Sathiah, R. 'Water Resources Management of Tirupur: Some Issues'. In Sharing Common Water Resources, Chennai: Madras Institute of Development Studies, 1994.

Satish Chandran Nair, S. 'The Drying Bhavani, "Waterless Attappady and the Volatile Cauvery" in Dams, Rivers and People', 2002, in http://www.narmada.org/sandrp/dec2002_1.doc.

Schultz, Theodore W. *Transforming Traditional Agriculture*, New Haven and London: Yale University Press, 1964.

Sengodu, K. P. 'Lower Bhavani Project – Irrigation – Water – Resources Development – Environmental Protection – A View'. In *Natural Resources Accounting of Water Resources of the Bhavani Basin*, Chennai: Madras Institute of Development Studies, 1997.

Sengupta, Nirmal. 'Indigenous Irrigation Organisation in South Bihar', *Indian Economic and Social History Review*, 37, no. 2 (1980): 157–187.

Sengupta, Nirmal. 'Irrigation: Traditional and Modern', *Economic and Political Weekly*, 20, nos. 45, 46 and 47 (1985): 1919–1938.

Sengupta, Nirmal. *Managing Common Property: Irrigation in India and Phillipines*, New Delhi: Sage Publications, 1991.

Sengupta, Nirmal. *World Commission on Dams India Country Report: Laws, Policies and Institutional Framework for Options Assessment and Decision Making*, Chennai: Madras Institute of Development Studies, 2000.

Shanmugam, 'Industrial Growth in Tirupur'. In *Sharing of Common Water Resources*, Chennai: Madras Institute of Development Studies, 1994.

Shantha Mohan, N. 'Locating Transboundary Water Sharing in India'. In *River Water Sharing: Transboundary Conflict and Cooperation in India*, edited by N. Shantha Mohan, Sailen Routray and N. Sashikumar, 3–22, New Delhi: Routledge, 2010.

Sharma, S. C. 'Regulation of Groundwater Development in India: Existing Provisions and Future Options'. In *Groundwater Law: The Growing Debate*, edited by Marcus

Moench, 6–17, Ahmadabad: VIKSAT-Pacific Institute of Collaborative Groundwater Project, 1995.

Shiklomanov, A. *World Water Resources: A New Appraisal and Assessment for the 21st Century*, Paris: United Nations Educational, Scientific and Cultural Organization, 1998.

Singh, Chharapati. 'Research Agenda for Groundwater Law in India'. In *Groundwater Law: The Growing Debate*, edited by Marcus Moench, 174–180, Ahmedabad: VIKSAT-Pacific Institute of Collaborative Groundwater Project, 1995.

Singh, Satyajit. *Taming the Waters: The Political Economy of Large Dams in India*, Delhi: Oxford University Press, 1997.

Singh, Shekhar. 'The Karma of Dams', *Indian Express*, Wednesday, 25 October 2000.

Sivasubramaniyan, K. *Irrigation Institutions in Two Large Multi-Village Tanks of Tamil Nadu: Structure, Functioning and Impact*, PhD thesis, Madras: University of Madras, 1995.

Sivasubramaniyan, K. 'Irrigation Institutions and Two Major System Tanks in Tamil Nadu', *Review of Development and Change*, 2, no. 2 (1997): 355–377.

Sivasubramaniyan, K. 'Maintenance of Irrigation Networks under Major Tanks in Tamil Nadu', *Review of Development and Change*, 3, no. 2 (1998): 264–296.

Sivasubramaniyan, K. 'Water Management under Traditional Tank Irrigation Systems: With Special Reference to Mamulmamas', *Review of Development and Change*, 5, no. 2 (2000): 268–308.

Sivasubramaniyan, K. 'Sustainable Development of Small Water Bodies in Tamil Nadu', *Economic and Political Weekly*, 41, no. 26 (2006): 2854–2863.

Soll, David, *Empire of Water: An Environmental and Political History of the New York City Water Supply*, Ithaca & London: Cornell University Press, 2013.

Sonachalam, K. S. *Electricity and Economic Development of Madras State*, Annamalainagar: Annamalai University, 1968.

Sörlin, Sverker. 'The Contemporaneity of Environmental History: Negotiating Scholarship, Useful History, and the New Human Condition', *Journal of Contemporary History*, 46, no. 3 (2011): 610–630.

South Indian Hosiery Manufactures Association (SIHMA). *Bulletin*, 1998.

Spiertz, H. L. Joep. 'Water Rights and Legal Pluralism: Some Basics of a Legal Anthropological Approach'. In *Negotiating Water Rights*, edited by B. R.Burns and R. S. Meinzen-Dick, 162–199, New Delhi: Vistaar Publications, 2000.

State Planning Board. *Report of the High Level Committee on Land and Water Resources*, Trivandrum: Government of Kerala, 1984.

Steele, David. 'Child Labour in Tamil Nadu: An Initial Survey', 2002, In http://www.eti.org.uk/pub/publications/2002/05-chlab-lit/index.shtml#note3 (accessed in January 2007).

Stoddart, Brian. *Land, Water, Language and Politics in Andhra: Regional Evolution in India since 1850*, New Delhi: Routledge, 2011.

Stone, Ian. *Canal Irrigation in British India: Perspectives on Technological Change in a Peasant Economy*, Cambridge: Cambridge University Press, 1984.

Structure Plan for Coimbatore Local Planning Area. Directorate of Town and Country Planning, 1985.

Study Report of CIRT, Pune, 1988.

Sutawan, Nyoman. 'Negotiation of Water Allocation among Irrigators' Associations in Bali, Indonesia'. In *Negotiating Water Rights*, edited by B. R. Burns and R. S. Meinzen-Dick, 315–336, New Delhi: Vistaar Publications, 2000.

Swaminathan, L. P. 'Ground-Water Development and Its Consequences in Coimbatore District, Tamil Nadu'. In *Workshop on Critical Issues in Tamil Nadu Irrigation*, held at Madras: Madras Institute of Development Studies, 1989.

Swaminathan, L. P. and Sivanappan, R. K. *A Study on the Cost of Irrigation Water in Coimbatore District*, Water Technology Centre, Coimbatore: Tamil Nadu Agricultural University, 1986.

Tamil Nadu Electricity Board. *Administration Report of the Tamil Nadu Electricity Board for 1976-77*, Madras: Government of Tamil Nadu.

Teekaraman, G. and Ahamed, M. Farooque. *Tanneries vs Agriculture in North Arcot District*, Vellore: Soil Survey and Land Use Organisation, 1990.

The agreement related between the chief ministers of Kerala and Tamil Nadu and the union minister of irrigation and power during discussions held on 10.5.1969 at Trivandrum regarding the Parambikulam Aliyar Project and other river water questions of Kerala and Tamil Nadu, In *Legal Instruments on Rivers in India* (Vol.III) *Agreements on Inter State Rivers*, part two, 128–131, New Delhi: Inter State Matters Directorate, Central Water Commission, 2015.

The Report of the Cauvery Water Disputes Tribunal with the Decision, Vol. 1, New Delhi: Government of India, 2007.

United Nations Development Programme. *Human Development Report 2006: Beyond Scarcity: Power, Poverty and the Global Water Crisis*, New York: Palgrave Macmillan, 2006.

Vaidyanathan, A. 'Labour Use in Indian Agriculture: An Analysis Based on Farm Management Survey Data'. In *Labour Absorption in Indian Agriculture: Some Exploratory Investigations*, edited by P. K.Bardhan, A. Vaidyanathan, Y. Alagh, G. S. Bhalla and A. Bhaduri, 33–118, Bangkok: ILO-ARTEP publications, 1978.

Vaidyanathan, A. 'The Indian Economy since Independence (1947–70)'. In *Cambridge Economic History of India*, Vol. II: C.1757-C.1970, edited by Dharma Kumar, 947–994, Cambridge: Cambridge University Press, 1983.

Vaidyanathan, A. *Strategy for Development of Tank Irrigation*, Madras: Madras Institute of Development Studies, 1992.

Vaidyanathan, A. *Second India Studies Revisited: Water*, Chennai: Madras Institute of Development Studies, 1994.

Vaidyanathan, A. *Water Resource Management Institutions and Irrigation Development in India*, New Delhi: Oxford University Press, 1999.

Vaidyanathan, A. (ed). *Tanks of South India*, New Delhi: Centre for Science and Environment, 2001.

Vaidyanathan, A. *India's Water Resources: Contemporary Issues on Irrigation*, New Delhi: Oxford University Press, 2006.

Vaidyanathan, A. 'Foreword'. In *Water Conflicts in India: A Million Revolts in the Making*, edited by Joy, K. J., Gujja, Bissham, Paranjape, Suhas, Goud, Vinod and Vispute, Shruti, New Delhi: Routledge, 2007.

Vander Velde, Edward J. 'Local Consequences of a Large-Scale Irrigation System in India'. In *Irrigation and Agricultural Development in Asia: Perspectives from the Social Sciences*, edited by Walter Coward Jr., Ithaka and London: Cornel University Press, 1980.

Vani, M. S. *Role of Panchayat Institutions in Irrigation Management: Law and Policy*, New Delhi: The India Law Institute, 1992.

Vassart, Michel. *Technologies for Lifting Irrigation Water*, New Delhi: International Labour Organisation, 1981.

Venkatachalam, L. 'National Resources Accounting for Water Resource: A Case Study of the Bhavani Basin'. In *Natural Resources Accounting of Water Resources of the Bhavani Basin*, Chennai: Madras Institute of Development Studies, 1997.

Verma, Samar. 'Export Competitiveness of Indian Textile and Garment Industry'. In *Working Paper No. 94*, New Delhi: Indian Council for Research on International Economic Relations, 2000.

Wade, Robert. 'Administration and Distribution of Irrigation Benefits', *Economic and Political Weekly*, 10, nos. 44 and 45 (1975): 1743–1747.

Wade, Robert. 'Water to the Fields: India's Changing Strategy', *South Asian Review*, 8, no. 4 (1975): 301–321.

Wade, Robert. 'Water Supply an Instrument of Agricultural Policy: A Case Study', *Economic and Political Weekly*, 8, 12 (1978): A.9–13.

Wade, Robert. 'Collective Responsibility in Construction and Management of Irrigation Canals: Case of Italy', *Economic and Political Weekly*, 14, nos. 51 and 52 (1979): A-155–160.

Wade, Robert. 'The Social Response to Irrigation: An Indian Case Study', *Journal of Development Studies*, 16, no. 1 (1979): 3–26.

Wade, Robert. 'Access to the Irrigation Department: The Tail-End Problem under South Indian Irrigation Canals'. *Indian Journal of Public Administration*, 26, no. 2 (1980): 359–378.

Wade, Robert. 'On Substituting Management for Water in Canal Irrigation: A South Indian Case', *Economic and Political Weekly*, 15, no. 51 (1980): A-147–160.

Wade, Robert. 'Corruption: Where Does the Money Go?' *Economic and Political Weekly*, 17, no. 40 (1982): 1606.

Wade, Robert. 'Group Action for Irrigation', *Economic and Political Weekly*, 17, no. 39 (1982): A.103–107.

Wade, Robert. 'The System of Administrative and Political Corruption: Canal Irrigation in South India', *Journal of Development Studies*, 18, no. 3 (1982): 287–328.

Wade, Robert. 'The Market for Public Office: Why the Indian State Is not Better at Development', *World Development*, 13, no. 4 (1985): 467–497.

Wade, Robert. *Village Republics: Economic Conditions for Collective Action in South India*, Cambridge: Cambridge University Press, 1987.

Wade, Robert and Chambers, Robert. 'Managing the Main System: Canal Irrigation's Blind Spot', *Economic and Political Weekly*, 15, no. 39 (1980): A-107–112.

Whitcombe, Elizabeth. *Agrarian Conditions in Northern India, Volume One The United Province under British Rule, 1860–1900*, Berkeley: University of California Press, 1971.

Wilhelm, Janine. *Environment and Pollution in Colonial India: Sewerage Technologies along the Sacred Ganges*, London and New York: Routledge, 2016.

Williamson, A. V. 'Indigenous Irrigation Works in Peninsular India', *Geographical Review*, 21, no. 4 (1931): 613–626.

Wood, John R. *The Politics of Water Resource Development in India: The Narmada Dams Controversy*, New Delhi: Sage Publications, 2007.

World Bank. *India Irrigation Sector Review*, 2 volumes, Washington, DC: World Bank, 1991.

World Bank. *Water Resources Management in Asia*, Vol. I, Main Report. Washington, DC: The World Bank, 1993.

World Bank. *Inter-Sectoral Water Allocation, Planning and Management*, Washington, DC: The World Bank and New Delhi: Allied Publishers, 1999.

World Commission on Environment and Development. *From One Earth to One World: An Overview*. Oxford: Oxford University Press, 1987.

World Water Assessment Programme. *The United Nations World Water Development Report 3: Water in a Changing World*, Paris: UNESCO and London: Earthscan, 2009. www.eti.org.uk/pub/publications/2002/05-chlab-lit/index.shtml#note3.

Index

agrarian history
    irrigation sources 2, 11, 18, 33–45, 89, 90, 120, 123, 153
    land revenue 2, 6, 27, 37, 65, 68
    mode of production 2
    productivity 2, 5, 12, 21, 28, 29, 66, 93, 96, 146, 156
    wage rate 2
Arakankottai 34, 40
Athikadavu-Avinashi Project 177, 178, 180
Avinasi-Athikadavu scheme 85

Bhavani Sagar dam
    droughts 38, 39, 114, 148
    famines 6, 30, 39, 148, 184
    floods 4, 6, 10, 14, 15, 18, 24, 34, 61, 164, 169
    low rainfall 82, 101

canals
    Arakankottai 34, 40
    customary rights 129, 134
    Kalingarayan canal 34, 40
    Lower Bhavani Project 21, 32, 52, 115–17, 133, 135, 147, 174–8, 186
    precipitation 6
    pre-colonial period 4, 34, 40
    sedimentation 6
    Tadapalli 34, 35, 40
    waterlogging 5, 6
Cauvery Water Disputes Tribunal 176, 177
centre-state relations 163, 166, 167
    Cauvery Water Disputes Tribunal 176, 177
    Central Water Commission 164, 165, 176
    national water policy 9, 165, 173
    Sarkaria Commission 167
    state subject 167
colonialism 3, 137
    commercialization 2, 5, 12, 33
    commodification 1, 2

de-industrialization 2
    irrigation projects 37, 171, 183
    land revenue 2
    modernization 4, 6, 16, 33
    traditional tanks 41, 173
commercialization 2, 5, 12, 33
commodification 1, 2
competing demand for water
    agriculture sector 25, 97, 184
    domestic water supply 2, 3, 7, 12, 13, 17, 18, 25–31, 46, 48, 53, 84, 87, 97, 100, 116, 119–26, 163, 174, 184–6
    industrial effluents 8, 25, 28, 29, 59, 66, 87, 90, 126, 171, 184, 186
    industrial pollution 30, 46, 125
    industrial sector 15, 48, 62, 72, 77, 97, 125, 126, 146, 157
    population growth 3, 12, 15–18, 46, 53, 67–74
    spinning mill 99, 134
    truck-tankers 157
    water market 29, 31, 65

displacement 6, 32, 163
domestic water supply scheme
    Kistnambadi tank 103, 106, 107, 186
    Koilveli Springs 114
    Muthannankulam tank 105
    Muthikulam scheme 103, 104
    Pillur scheme 83, 84, 104, 112
    Siruvani water supply scheme 24, 40, 53, 54, 65, 82–4, 97, 100, 104, 108–22, 157, 173–7, 180, 186
    sub-artesian springs 108
dyeing and bleaching industries 59, 63, 74, 77, 81, 86, 169, 184

economic history 2. *See also* agrarian history
    arable lands 2
    commercialization 2

de-industrialization 2
modernization 4, 6, 16, 33
railways 2, 87–9, 98, 109, 125, 157, 164
trade and commerce 2
economic transformation 67, 73, 76, 126, 186
environmental degradation 4, 16, 28
industrialization 1–3, 7, 9, 12–19, 30, 46, 48, 67–78, 82, 97, 102, 184
urbanization 3, 7–18, 29, 30, 46–53, 67–9, 77, 82, 84, 97, 98, 102, 184
effluent treatment plants 66, 95
environmental history 2–4, 11, 185
commercialization 2, 5, 12, 33
commodification 1, 2
displacement 6, 32, 163
forests 2, 8, 12, 41, 42, 66, 169, 172, 185
neglected agrarian history 2
pastoral lands 2, 5
tribals 2, 8
urbanization 3, 7–18, 29, 30, 46–53, 67–9, 77, 82, 84, 97, 98, 102, 184
water diversion 3, 7, 11, 12, 27–32, 54, 62, 65, 88, 89, 97–100, 116–25, 173, 184, 185
water pollution 2, 12, 15, 19–21, 28–30, 93, 96, 171
wildlife 2, 185

green revolution 19, 21, 27, 49, 53, 65, 129
cropping pattern 12, 21, 28, 45, 59, 62, 126, 135–9, 155–8
electric pump-sets 51, 53, 62, 133, 154–7
groundwater table 10, 53, 134, 179, 184
mechanization 27, 53, 126, 129, 157
pumpset industries 133
tractor 133

hydrology 2, 24, 29, 33, 50, 62

industrial growth
Coimbatore 78
Tirupur 80
water-consuming industries 18, 67, 78, 81, 93
industrial pollution
dyeing and bleaching industries 59, 63, 74, 77, 81, 86, 169, 184
industrial effluents 8, 25, 28, 59, 66, 87, 90, 186

industrial waste 7, 19, 93
Orathupalayam 52, 59, 93, 169
river pollution 3, 4
water market 29, 31, 65
water pollution 2, 12, 15, 19–21, 28–30, 93, 96, 171
water quality 7, 17, 19, 32, 87, 91, 92, 163
interdisciplinary approach 11, 30
inter-state water conflicts 166, 167

judiciary
high court 82, 95, 96, 141, 144, 145
Indian Easement Act 21
Indian Penal Code Act 21
supreme court 95, 129, 165–7, 180
tribunals 129
writ petition 95, 141, 145, 165

Kalingarayan canal 34, 40
Karnataka 24, 168, 173–6
Kerala 32, 48, 64, 70, 111, 112, 129, 168–81
Kodiveri *anicut* 27, 34, 136
kudimaramattu 27, 38, 136, 137

linking rivers 32, 164
Bharathi, Subramaniya 164
Cotton, Arthur Thomas 147, 164
Dastur, Captain 165
displacement 6, 32, 163
feasibility studies 165
mega-project 163–5
Nandhivarman, N 165
national democratic alliance 165
Rao, K.L 164, 175
Lower Bhavani Project 21, 32, 52, 115–17, 133, 135, 147, 174–8, 186

Madras High Court 82, 95, 96, 145
Mysore 17, 37, 40, 48

Nilgiris 39, 109, 132, 174
non-arable lands
common property resources 2, 6, 12, 49, 183
domestic water supply 2, 3, 7, 12, 13, 17–18, 25–31, 46–53, 83–7, 97, 100, 116–26, 163, 174, 184–6
forests 2, 8, 12, 41, 42, 66, 169, 172, 185

pastoral lands 2, 5
water pollution 2, 12, 15, 19–21, 28–30, 93, 96, 171

Parambikulam-Aliyar Project 175
pumpset industries 133
rain-fed tanks 34, 36, 41
river water pollution
   agricultural waste 3
   industrial effluents 8, 25, 28, 59, 66, 87, 90, 186
   industrial waste 7, 19, 93
   industrialization 1–3, 7, 9, 12–19, 30, 46, 48, 67–78, 82, 97, 102, 184
   religious practices 9
   solid waste 8
   urbanization 3, 7–18, 29, 30, 46–53, 67–9, 77, 82, 84, 97, 98, 102, 184

Sepoy Mutiny 177
Siruvani dam 111, 117, 118
Siruvani river 65, 82, 104, 108–11, 121, 174, 175, 186
stream-fed tanks 41, 42
Supreme Court Order 95, 129, 165–7, 180
sustainable development 63, 172

Tadapalli 34, 35, 40
Tamil Nadu Pollution Control Board 95
traditional water management
   calingulas 137
   kudimaramattu 27, 38, 136, 137
   mamool
   nirkaties 183
   riparian rights 16, 136–9, 146, 158, 166–9
   yettam 42

Upper Bhavani Project 147, 177, 178
urban agglomeration 53, 67–73, 84

vote bank politics 20, 48
   All India Anna Dravida Munnetra Kazhagam 178
   caste groups 131
   Dravida Munnetra Kazhagam 178
   electricity subsidies 21
   member of legislative assembly 135, 141
   member of parliament 135, 141

water charges 88–92, 123, 124, 171
water conflicts
   chargesheet 140
   between countries 185
   farmers and the state 123
   head-reach farmers 130, 138–41, 151–3
   inter-basin 31, 32, 65, 115, 118, 119, 125, 164–6, 169, 173
   inter-department 119
   inter-state 166, 167, 176
   Karnataka 168, 173–6
   Kerala 32, 48, 64, 111, 112, 129, 168, 171–81
   local bodies and state 119, 124
   Mysore 17, 37, 40, 48
   petition 95, 107, 122, 130, 138–45, 152, 153, 165
   Pondicherry 129
   tail-end farmers 32, 130, 138–46, 152–8, 168
   water charges 88–92, 123, 124, 171
water diversion
   inter-basin transfer 164
   linking rivers 32, 164
   mega-project 163–5
water market 29, 31, 65
water pollution 2, 12, 15, 19–21, 28–30, 93, 96, 171
wildlife 2, 185
World Bank 21, 25, 185

www.ingramcontent.com/pod-product-compliance
Lightning Source LLC
Chambersburg PA
CBHW070029010526
44117CB00011B/1755